I0091830

"Milner has historically been constructed as a subsidiary figure to D.W. Winnicott within the British Independent Group. She is however a very important figure within early- to mid-twentieth century psychoanalysis. This book provides a concerted, careful and theoretically-engaged analysis of Milner. It is an original work that stands to make a substantial contribution to the field of psychoanalytic studies, literary studies, and twentieth-century cultural history."
—**Jo Winning**, *Professor, Birkbeck, University of London, UK*

The Marion Milner Method

This book traces the development of British psychoanalyst Marion Milner's (1900–98) autobiographical acts throughout her lifetime, proposing that Milner is a thinker to whom we can turn to explore the therapeutic potentialities of autobiographical and creative self-expression.

Milner's experimentation with aesthetic, self-expressive techniques are a means to therapeutic ends, forming what Emilia Halton-Hernandez calls her "autobiographical cure." This book considers whether Milner's work champions this site for therapeutic work over that of the relationship between patient and analyst in the psychoanalytic setting. This book brings to light a theory and practice which is latent and sometimes hidden, but which is central to understanding what drives Milner's autobiographical work. It is by doing this work of elucidation and organisation that Halton-Hernandez finds Milner to be a thinker with a unique take on psychoanalysis, object relations theory, creativity, and autobiography, working at the interstices of each.

Divided into two fascinating sections exploring Milner's distinctive method and the legacy and influence of her work, this book will appeal to psychoanalysts, art therapists, philosophers, and art and literary researchers alike.

Emilia Halton-Hernandez is Lecturer in the Department of Psychosocial and Psychoanalytic Studies at the University of Essex. She has written on psychoanalysis, the infant mind, visual art, and literature. She lives in Brighton and London, UK.

The Marion Milner Method

Psychoanalysis, Autobiography, Creativity

Emilia Halton-Hernandez

Routledge
Taylor & Francis Group

LONDON AND NEW YORK

Designed cover image: "Self-Portrait" by Marion Milner. By permission of The Marsh Agency Ltd., on behalf of The Estate of Marion Milner.

First published 2023
by Routledge
4 Park Square, Milton Park, Abingdon, Oxon OX14 4RN

and by Routledge
605 Third Avenue, New York, NY 10158

Routledge is an imprint of the Taylor & Francis Group, an informa business

© 2023 Emilia Halton-Hernandez

The right of Emilia Halton-Hernandez to be identified as author of this work has been asserted in accordance with sections 77 and 78 of the Copyright, Designs and Patents Act 1988.

All rights reserved. No part of this book may be reprinted or reproduced or utilised in any form or by any electronic, mechanical, or other means, now known or hereafter invented, including photocopying and recording, or in any information storage or retrieval system, without permission in writing from the publishers.

Trademark notice: Product or corporate names may be trademarks or registered trademarks, and are used only for identification and explanation without intent to infringe.

British Library Cataloguing-in-Publication Data
A catalogue record for this book is available from the British Library

ISBN: 978-1-032-28407-1 (hbk)
ISBN: 978-1-032-28295-4 (pbk)
ISBN: 978-1-003-29672-0 (ebk)

DOI: 10.4324/9781003296720

Typeset in Times New Roman
by Apex CoVantage, LLC

Contents

List of illustrations   viii
Acknowledgements   ix

Introduction   1

PART 1
The Milner method   23

1   *A Life of One's Own* and the birth of a diary keeping
    method to rival psychoanalysis   25

2   *On Not Being Able to Paint* and drawing and painting
    for psychoanalysis   57

3   *Bothered by Alligators* and compensating for the failures
    of a "couch analysis"   93

PART 2
The Milner tradition   121

4   Tracing Milner's influence in the twentieth century   123

5   Milner in the comic frame: Lynda Barry and Alison
    Bechdel's autobiographical cures   151

    Conclusion: in search of legibility?   174

Index   179

Illustrations

0.1   "The Hens" by Marion Milner.   5

0.2   Linocut by Marion Milner, 1960.   7

2.1   "Horrified Tadpole" by Marion Milner.   63

2.2   "Two Jugs" by Marion Milner.   67

2.3   Ruth's drawing in "The Communication of Primary Sensual Experience" (1955).   77

2.4   Susan's "The Post-E.C.T. drawing."   82

2.5   "Bursting Seed-pod" by Marion Milner.   89

3.1   "The Green Baby" by Marion Milner.   100

3.2   Photo of a selection of Marion Milner's clay heads in Giles Milner's personal collection. Titles and dates unknown.   101

3.3   Page from John Milner's story-book.   103

3.4   "At Royal Free July 95" by Marion Milner.   114

3.5   "Chaos" by Marion Milner.   115

4.1   Marion Milner's copy of "Christ Blessing Job and his wife."   129

4.2   Marion Milner's copy of the "The God of Eliphaz."   130

5.1   Lynda Barry's *What It Is*.   152

5.2   Alison Bechdel.   171

6.1   Document by Marion Milner.   176

Acknowledgements

Firstly, I am grateful to Giles Milner for graciously allowing me access to his family's collection of Milner's art, and for sharing with me his personal recollections of his grandmother. My thanks to Ewan O'Neill at The British Psychoanalytical Society Archive and the archivists at the Wellcome Collection for their assistance with archival research. I would like to extend my gratitude to The Marsh Agency on behalf of The Marion Milner Estate, Lynda Barry, and Riva Lehrer for generously allowing me to reproduce a number of their images and quotes in this book.

I owe a special thanks to Vicky Lebeau for her support and assiduous and thoughtful feedback on the many drafts of this book. My thanks also to Jo Winning, Hope Wolf, and Helen Tyson and the anonymous reviewers whose insights, suggestions, and perceptive comments have helped develop this project. Thank you to my colleagues at the University of Sussex for their unwavering support throughout the various stages of researching and writing: Laura Gallon, Di Yang, Aanchal Vij, Yuri Enjo, Elle J Whitcroft, Shalini Sengupta, and Hannah Davita Ludikhuijze.

I am grateful to the editorial and production staff at Routledge, especially Zoe Meyer and Jana Craddock for their expertise and guidance throughout the publication process.

Lastly, my deepest thanks to my parents, my sister, and Angus. Thank you for being there for me, and with me, in so many ways, and for making this book a possibility.

Introduction

This book's cover image is a self-portrait painted by the British psychoanalyst and author Marion Milner. Dressed in the painter's archetypal blue smock, at easel and with palette and brush at hand, Milner rests her gaze intently on the canvas as the viewer catches her in the act of creation. The painting is undated but, given the subject's youthful appearance, was likely created during Milner's younger years—just one iteration of the many acts of self-representation Milner produced over her lifetime across different media. This self-portrait, however, is a rare instance of a figurative, naturalistic self-portrayal. Milner's autobiographical books, published throughout her lifetime, involve a sustained dedication to representing the vistas and contours of the inner world, rather than those of the external. And if in this self-portrait Milner's brush strokes on her canvas are obscured from our view, visible only to the painter herself, Milner's autobiographical books reveal to her readers in careful detail the marks she makes in order to capture an inner life. In continuity with the rest of her work, however, this self-portrait is a representation of a subject immersed in the throes of creativity and self-depiction. Here is a portrait of the artist as a young woman, and as this study will examine, it is also the portrait of a psychoanalytic thinker exploring the site of creative expression for therapeutic self-transformation.

This book traces the development of Marion Milner's autobiographical acts throughout her lifetime, as expressed in her published work and in work now contained in her archives. It proposes that Milner is a thinker to whom we can turn to explore the therapeutic potentialities of autobiographical and creative self-expression. Specifically, this book draws out the ideas of a psychoanalytic thinker whose work proposes that autobiographical acts can provide an equivalent nurturing and attuning function to what object relations theorists understand the mother and analyst as providing infant and analysand. Milner's autobiographical books: *A Life of One's Own* (1934), *An Experiment in Leisure* (1937), *On Not Being Able to Paint* (1950), *Eternity's Sunrise: A Way of Keeping a Diary* (1987), and the posthumously published *Bothered by Alligators* (2013) are read as constituting a life-long engagement with the development of a therapeutic practice located at the site of creative self-reflection.[1] One of the questions this study asks is whether

DOI: 10.4324/9781003296720-1

Milner's work champions this site for therapeutic work over that of the relationship between patient and analyst in the psychoanalytic setting.

Milner's work does not present itself as a unified metapsychology, cohesive theory, or methodology. Unlike Sigmund Freud's deliberate efforts to present psychoanalysis as a distinctive science, with foundational axioms, metapsychological theories, and clinical data, Milner's autobiographical books present a loose set of terms and methods that emerge out of the work recorded in them, and which occasionally, though not always, make the crossover into her published theoretical and clinical psychoanalytic papers and books. It is the aim of this study, however, to bring to light a theory and practice which is latent and sometimes hidden, but which is central to understanding what drives her autobiographical work. It is by doing this work of elucidation and organisation that this study finds Milner to be a thinker with a unique take on psychoanalysis, object relations theory, and autobiography, working at the interstices of each. Her experimentation with aesthetic, self-expressive techniques are a means to therapeutic ends, forming what I am calling her "autobiographical cure."

Milner's autobiographical books are difficult to define generically, since they are not autobiographies in the traditional sense of the term. In general, they provide very little factual detail about a life lived out in the world, and the events that form it. I understand these books as commonly defined by an experimentation with different forms of autobiographical acts for the purpose of gaining self-insight and promoting self-development. They explore various mark-making techniques that might make the inner world better known, visible for observation, and ripe for analysis. They are all written with a reader in mind, who is invited to witness Milner's own methods for transformation, and in doing so, might want to follow her lead and engage in a similar undertaking of their own. Characterising her books as self-help handbooks with a prescriptive method for the reader to follow, would, however, be misleading. Milner serves instead as a kind of example to those like herself who might learn from her strategies for self-transformation.

Broadly speaking, *A Life of One's Own* (1934), *An Experiment in Leisure* (1937), and *Eternity's Sunrise: A Way of Keeping a Diary* (1987) engage with written autobiographical acts in the form of free associative writing experiments and diary keeping. *On Not Being Able to Paint* (1950), as its title suggests, dedicates itself to forms of visual mark-making—painting, drawing, and doodling. Milner's final book, written up until the last days of her life in 1998, *Bothered by Alligators* (2013), engages with all of these aesthetic acts and more, including the making of collages out of her old paintings. These books are written and published before, during, and after Milner's long career as a full-time practicing psychoanalyst and active member of the British Psychoanalytical Society.

Milner's work has enjoyed something of a resurgence in the last decade, thanks in particular to Emma Letley's biography *Marion Milner: The Life* (2014) and her work commissioning new editions of Milner's books with Routledge (2011–13). Milner's books have experienced a somewhat chequered publication history: *An Experiment in Leisure* was blitzed out of print during the Second World War, and for some time *A Life of One's Own* and *An Experiment in Leisure* were published under the penname of Joanna Field, driving at times a disconnect between Milner and her works.[2] Routledge's new editions offer the reader a renewed examination of Milner's work, with introductions by cultural, literary, and psychoanalytic critics including Rachel Bowlby, Maud Ellmann, Janet Sayers, Adam Phillips, Hugh Haughton, and Margaret Walters. More recently, *Critical Quarterly* published a special issue "Marion Milner: Modernism, Politics, Psychoanalysis" in 2021 which includes an interview with Adam Phillips and my article on Milner's engagement with the work of artist and poet William Blake: "'A poet of human nature': Marion Milner's William Blake." At the time of writing, *The Marion Milner Tradition* (part of the Lines of Development Series published by Routledge) edited by Margaret Boyle Spelman and Joan Raphael-Leff is forthcoming (November 2022) and promises discussion of Milner's work from a range of clinicians and thinkers.

Milner has historically been constructed as a subsidiary figure to Winnicott within the British Independent Group, and critical engagement with both her psychoanalytic practice and theory, as well as her autobiographical practice as an author and a painter, has been limited. The emergence of new scholarly writing on Milner's work has gone some way towards cementing her legacy as an important contributor to psychoanalytic thought in her own right, granting her attention in the twenty-first century by scholars in psychoanalysis, but also such fields as literature, modernist studies, art history, life writing, and autobiography studies. The variety and range of scholarly attention Milner's work has inspired has I think much to do with the unusual heterogeneity of her work and thinking.

This book seeks to make its own contribution by engaging with Milner's distinctive search for a therapeutic cure that takes place in the relationships between pen and paper, paint and canvas. In so doing, we are introduced to a thinker dedicated to a distinctive version of object relations theory, one that attends to the relational inner world of the writer and artist.

The life

Marion Milner, née Nina Marion Blackett, was born in London on 1 February, 1900, to a middle-class English family. Her father, Arthur Blackett, worked for some time on the London Stock Exchange as a stock jobber, though as a "dreamy Victorian Romantic" with a love for nature and poetry, he was suitably unsuited for a city job (Patrick Blackett qtd. in Letley 2). Milner's mother, Caroline Maynard, was also interested in the arts and descended from a pioneer in the field of education—her mother Constance Maynard was one of the first female undergraduates admitted to Girton College, Cambridge, and became the head of Westfield College, University of London from 1881–1913. Milner had two siblings, an older sister Winifred with whom she was not particularly close, and a preferred older brother, Patrick Blackett who went on to win a Nobel Prize in Physics in 1948. Illustrious achievements were also accompanied, however, by a difficult home life. Arthur and Caroline's marriage was not a particularly happy one, and in 1911 when Milner was eleven years old, her father, to whom Milner was greatly attached, suffered a mental breakdown.

Milner's earliest form of autobiographical writing was a nature diary, which at the age of eleven, was likely influenced by her father's naturalist bent and their frequent excursions into the English countryside. Her diary entitled "Mollie Blackett's Nature Diary" after her family nickname, records the sights and sounds of the natural world in careful detail, an early display of Milner's powers of observation that she would later turn to good account in chronicling observations on herself and her inner life.[3] At seventeen Milner was forced to leave the Godolphin boarding school in Wiltshire due to lack of family funds to pay for a sixth form education. She turned to tutoring a seven-year-old boy in reading, an experience that introduced her to the ideas of Montessori and the importance of play in learning. Following this she began training at a Montessori nursery school training college, but this experience was short lived; a year later she enrolled in an undergraduate degree in psychology and physiology at University College, London. It is here that Milner first encountered the ideas of Sigmund Freud in lectures comparing the physiologist Charles Scott Sherrington's descriptions of the functions of the nervous system with Freud's principles of unconscious functioning. At this time, her brother Patrick also gave her a copy of Freud's *Introductory Lectures on Psychoanalysis*, though at this point in her education Milner admits to having been more taken by physiology than with psychoanalysis (*HOLG* xli). Following her studies, for which she received a first-class degree in 1923, Milner went on to work with the educational psychologist Cyril Burt, followed by a Laura Spelman Rockefeller Scholarship from 1927–28 studying under the Australian psychologist, Elton Mayo in Boston, USA. It is in Boston that Milner also had her first, albeit short, experience as a patient of talking therapy with the American analyst Dr Ira Putnam.

When Milner decided to undertake a psychoanalytic training in 1939, she already had a successful career as an industrial psychologist, had married playwright Dennis Milner, and was mother to a son, John. She had also undergone a period of analysis with a Jungian analyst back in England, had published two autobiographical books—*A Life of One's Own* (1934), and *An Experiment in Leisure* (1937), and written a book about research on the education system in a girl's school, *The Human Problem in Schools* (1938) for the Girls Public Day School Trust (GPDST). Milner describes in detail her journey to eventually training to become a psychoanalyst at the Institute of Psychoanalysis in London in 1939, and qualification four years later in 1943, in the Preface to *The Hands of the Living God: An Account of a Psycho-analytic Treatment* (1969).[4] She attributes her decision to "begin a Freudian analysis with Sylvia Payne, and in 1939 to apply for and be accepted by the British Psycho-Analytical Society" to hearing "a public lecture, in 1938, by D.W. Winnicott" (Milner, *HOLG* xlvi). Winnicott would later become a close colleague of Milner's and her analyst for a period of around four years. Milner also undertook her training analysis with Sylvia Payne, and after the analysis with Winnicott, was a patient of the Kleinian Canadian analyst, Clifford Scott. In the course of her training and post qualification work she received clinical supervision for her work with patients from Melanie Klein, Joan Riviere, and Ella Sharpe, all significant figures in the British Psychoanalytic Society at the time.

Milner's thinking and her professional alliances were, and still are, most associated with the British Independent Group, or the Middle Group, that emerged out of the wartime Controversial Discussions. These heated disputes arose within the society between Melanie Klein and Anna Freud about early infantile mentation, clinical technique, child development, and Freudian apostasy. The Independent Group, as its name implies, saw itself as non-aligned, taking on the role of ad hoc moderators for the two factions. Along with Milner, its members would come to include figures such as Sylvia Payne, Ella Sharpe, Donald Winnicott, and Michael Balint.

After Milner's death in 1998, close friend and cultural critic Margaret Walters describes the impression made on her by one of Milner's paintings hung in her house in Provost Road (Figure 0.1), and how well it symbolised

Figure 0.1 "The Hens" by Marion Milner. Giles Milner's personal collection.

Source: By permission of The Marsh Agency Ltd., on behalf of The Estate of Marion Milner.

Milner's place within the analytic community. Walters describes the large painting as a:

> rather sumptuous canvas in varying shades of deep, dark, rich reds; in a way, it was a trick painting—at a second glance, it arranged itself into farmyard scene: two hens aggressively confronting each other over a tiny egg. Marion would take any new visitor to look at the painting and announce that it was about Melanie Klein and Anna Freud squabbling over who'd given birth to the British Psycho-Analytical Society.
>
> (131)

Milner as a painter seems to situate herself as an outside observer of these squabbling subjects, removed from the political factions they spearheaded. With Klein as a supervisor, and Anna Freud providing a foreword to her book *On Not Being Able to Paint*, she seems, however, to have managed a productive working relationship with analysts from both camps. Milner was also a regular member of the Imago Group founded by the art critic Adrian Stokes, a group broadly revolving around the thinking of Melanie Klein that met regularly to discuss psychoanalysis and its relations with art (members also included post-Kleinian thinkers, such as Wilfred R. Bion, Donald Meltzer, and Roger Money-Kyrle). As a visual counterpoint to the squabbling hens, a linocut of Milner's from 1960 depicts a lone chicken in starlight, a vision more representative perhaps of Milner's independent, intermediary, and non-partisan position within the psychoanalytic world (Figure 0.2).

Milner published several psychoanalytic papers that found their way into the journals and annals of psychoanalysis; most of these papers were published in the collection *The Supressed Madness of Sane Men: Forty-Four Years of Exploring Psychoanalysis* (1987). This book shows, however, that despite Milner's wide-ranging psychoanalytic influences, her analytic preoccupations were closest to those of Winnicott. Milner was in "continuing dialogue" with Winnicott throughout much of her career, and her 1972 paper "Winnicott and the Two-way Journey" provides an example of their shared interests around thinking about creativity and psychic health (Caldwell and Joyce 249). Like Winnicott, Milner disagreed with Klein's notion that the infant had an innate, or at the very least an early awareness of a rudimentary self and a fleeting awareness of object separateness, and agreed that the illusion of oneness with the mother better described the earliest stages of infantile psychic life.[5] Contemporary scholarship suggests this disagreement is more a matter of emphasis than clear difference of view, but in Milner's day it was a hotly disputed issue upon which a theory of technique and therapeutic efficacy depended, for example, in whether narcissistic states of withdrawal were considered pathological or of developmental necessity.

Autobiography and psychoanalysis

In the introduction to *The Suppressed Madness of Sane Men: Forty-Four Years of Exploring Psychoanalysis* and the Preface to her earlier case study *The Hands of the Living God*, Milner provides the reader with an autobiographical account of her

Figure 0.2 Linocut by Marion Milner, 1960. Marion Milner's own art. P01-H-A. Marion Milner collection, Archives of the British Psychoanalytical Society.

Source: By permission of The Marsh Agency Ltd., on behalf of The Estate of Marion Milner.[6]

professional analytic life not unlike the one I have sketched here (more similar perhaps to Freud's "periautobiography," his account of his professional life in *An Autobiographical Study* (1927) than what he came to see as his "true autobiography," *The Interpretation of Dreams* (1899) and its account of his inner life (Marcus, *Sigmund Freud's The Interpretation of Dreams: New Interdisciplinary Essays* 55)). Milner's self-portraits of the psychoanalyst as a young woman, however, do hint at the development of a different therapeutic endeavour taking place alongside, as well as influencing, her analytic career. In *The Hands of the Living God* she tells the reader how:

> in 1926 I had tried to experiment with 'free association' writing, putting down whatever came into my head. . . . The results, both of this and the diary, were

an immense surprise to me, as I have described in that first book. There was now no escaping from the fact that Freud was right, that there was a part of my mind the working of which I was totally unaware of.

(xlii)

From here she "developed a belief in the value of diaries" (xliii). It is free associative writing and diary keeping that is ultimately attributed with providing the first real proof of the unconscious at work inside of her, and that proves Freud right. Here then, Milner introduces another route to psychological insight, one that takes place at the site of diary keeping, the self in dialogue with the self. It gestures to another, parallel, but distinctive career trajectory that follows her through her life and that this book is committed to tracing: the development of her autobiographical cure. The publication of *Eternity's Sunrise: A Way of Keeping a Diary* in 1987, the same year as Milner published *The Suppressed Madness of Sane Men*, offers a particularly striking picture of a thinker engaged in both a psychoanalytic and autobiographical enterprise—enterprises that are at the same time congruent, but also separate projects.

Milner's autobiographical cure therefore takes place at the crossroads between psychoanalysis and autobiographical mark-making. The relationship between psychoanalysis and autobiography has long gripped critics in the fields of psychoanalysis, life-writing, and beyond, with the genesis of each understood as intimately intertwined. Augustine's *Confessions*, written between AD 397 and 400 is widely considered as the first (known) Western autobiography ever written, and the first form of proto-psychoanalytic thinking, a "manifesto for the unexpected, hidden qualities of the inner world—the conscientia" (Brown 205). And what is considered Freud's "true autobiography," *The Interpretation of Dreams*, has now been understood as an autobiographical endeavour that set into motion the psychoanalytic movement. Derrida's well-known question: "How can an autobiographical writing, in the abyss of an unterminated self-analysis, give to a world-wide institution its birth?" ascribes Freud's autobiographical writing with the utmost significance and impact (qtd. in Forrester 43). In this view, psychoanalysis seems to have needed autobiography in order to give birth to itself.

Like Milner, Freud was a prolific life writer—a writer of autobiography and self-analysis (*An Interpretation of Dreams*), a writer and reader of letters, and in later life at the age of 73 also a diary keeper, recording in what is now known as *The Diary of Sigmund Freud, 1929–1939: A Record of the Final Decade* (1992) the major personal and world events of this period. Ultimately, however, Freud was dedicated to the development, theory, and practice of psychoanalysis, his "talking cure" for the exploration of self and psyche and for the treatment of neurosis. Fundamentally, the insights made by the autobiographical "writing cure" of his dream-book were used in the service of developing a therapeutic technique that takes place in the encounter between analyst and patient.

As both autobiography and psychoanalysis involve a practice of self-telling, critics from the fields of literature and psychoanalysis have closely explored how the aims of psychoanalysis as theory and practice, and autobiography as literary genre, might overlap and interconnect (Marcus "Autobiography and Psychoanalysis" 257). Adam Philips in his piece "The Telling of Selves: Notes on Psychoanalysis and Autobiography" (1994) observes how "psychoanalysis is clearly akin to autobiography in the sense that it involves a self-telling, and the belief that there is nowhere else to go for the story of our lives" (Phillips 69). The psychoanalyst Charles Rycroft in his 1983 essay "On Autobiography" draws out their similarities further, suggesting the analyst might be called the "assistant autobiographer" to his patient, the work of finding and constructing the patient's life story a joint narrative enterprise produced from the psychoanalytic relationship (Rycroft qtd. in Marcus, "Autobiography and Psychoanalysis" 259).

Nevertheless, both Phillips and Rycroft recognise the ultimate irreconcilability of autobiography and psychoanalysis. These break points include Phillips' sense that psychoanalysis is more appropriately considered a precursor to autobiography since the aim of analysis "is not to recover the past, but to make recovery of the past possible, the past that is frozen in repetition; and in this sense psychoanalysis might be more of a prelude to autobiography" (Phillips 69). Laura Marcus finds that despite their affinities, there is "not enough to create a symmetry between the two practices, and from the early twentieth century onwards there has been a sense of missed opportunities and failed relationships" (*Auto/biographical Discourses* 214). Ultimately, the "projects of psychoanalysis and autobiography, while having some important connections, miss each other at a number of crucial junctures" (Marcus, "Autobiography and Psychoanalysis" 261). Milner's autobiographical cure, with its searching for how autobiographical acts can do something psychoanalytic, does, I think, open new ways for thinking about the connections between psychoanalysis and autobiography.

The links between psychoanalysis and autobiography have also been considered in relation to the proliferation of psychoanalysts' autobiographical writing and patients' autobiographical accounts of their experiences on the couch. These are the "two broad genres" that Maud Ellmann suggests "psychoanalytic autobiographies may be grouped into" ("Psychoanalysis and Autobiography" 314). Those by analysts include Ernest Jones's *Free Associations: Memories of a Psychoanalyst* (1958), Wilfred Bion's *The Long Week-End 1897–1919: Part of a Life* (1982), a reminiscence of the first twenty-one years of Bion's life, and later *All My Sins Remembered: Another Part of a Life and the Other Side of Genius* (1985). In the second group we might include Joseph Wortis's record of his analysis with Freud beginning in 1934, *Fragments of an Analysis with Freud* (1954) and H.D.'s (Hilda Doolittle) *Tribute to Freud* (1956). Milner's autobiographical books, particularly *Bothered by Alligators*, straddle both camps in their providing autobiographical explorations from the perspective of the psychoanalyst as well as the psychoanalytic patient. But Milner's work I think also opens a third category of psychoanalytic autobiography for consideration: one in which autobiographical writing is used to do something specifically and explicitly psychoanalytic.

Discussion around psychoanalysis and autobiography has also tackled how psychoanalysis and its conception of the self as containing multiple selves and objects in a dynamic relation to one another profoundly disrupted the autobiographical subject's sense of possessing a unified "I" in the twentieth century and beyond. This has inspired autobiographies where the self is conceived at the very outset as fragmented and multiple. Lyndsey Stonebridge's "Taking care of ourselves and looking after the subject: Marion Milner's autobiographical acts" (1994) explicitly questions what a psychoanalytically informed autobiography involves in relation to Milner's self-analytic work. Stonebridge asks:

> If, as psychoanalysis tells us, the subject is motivated by the unconscious, by another scene unmasterable by self-reflection, then immediately the autobiographical imperative to represent a unified self would be called into question by such an exercise. It follows that an autobiography written with psychoanalytic hindsight would not attempt to speak in the voice of an authentic self but rather, surrendering to the unconscious determinants of writing, would reveal the manifest fictions of a "subject in process."
>
> (120)

Meg Harris Williams's approach to the connections between psychoanalysis and autobiography in "On psychoanalytic autobiography" (2012) focuses on the shared emotional effects provided by autobiography and psychoanalysis, an approach closer to the focus of this study. Specifically, autobiography and psychoanalysis are understood as providing the writer or patient with a way of finding out their identity. Harris Williams understands "autobiography as a particular mode of writing which, like psychoanalysis, attempts to answer the question posed so simply and eloquently by King Lear: 'Who is it that can tell me who I am?'" (398). Moreover, Harris Williams proposes that Bion's definition of psychoanalysis as a means of introducing the patient to himself might also be used as a definition for autobiography (Harris Williams 398). Harris's understanding here resonates with autobiography scholar Phillipe Lejeune's estimation that "Identity is the real starting point of autobiography" ("*Le pacte autobiographique*" 24) and that "Autobiography is a discourse on the self in which the question, 'who am I?' is answered by a narrative that tells 'how I became who I am'" (124). The notion that autobiography might help constitute a sense of self and identity in the same way the psychoanalytic relationship does is at the heart of Milner's autobiographical project.

Building upon this existing work on psychoanalysis and its links with autobiography, this book hopes to introduce Milner and her method as providing a new approach to the relationship between psychoanalysis and autobiography: one that we shall see sometimes positions the therapeutic work of autobiography as a rival to psychoanalysis, as an influence and accompaniment to psychoanalytic practice, and at other times as a corrective for the failed experience of being a patient of psychoanalysis.

Legacies

Milner's legacy within the psychoanalytic world reflects her interest in these two therapeutic endeavours. The psychoanalyst and past president of the British Psychoanalytical Society, Donald Campbell, when asked by Milner's autobiographer Emma Letley in 2008 to comment upon her place in the history of psychoanalysis stated plainly that "Milner was more artist than analyst and thus difficult to fit in psychoanalytically" (Campbell qtd. in Letley 152). "The psychoanalytic establishment," Letley concurs, "does not really know what to make of her, what to do with her" (166). The analyst Simon Grolnick considers her status as a "misfit" or maverick more favourably, suggesting that her "artistic inclinations" ultimately meant she "could not accept any rigidities within a fixed psychoanalytic movement" (295). Grolnick adds that the fact that "she rode out the next 44 years within psychoanalysis is a tribute both to Milner and to the psychoanalytic movement" (293). Milner herself seems to have enjoyed this insider-outsider status, resisting categorisation and total inclusion. Margaret Walters writes how "though she committed her life to it, Marion could take a healthily sceptical—indeed, very mischievous—attitude towards psychoanalytic orthodoxy" (131). Milner's unusual legacy as an analyst is, I think, well captured in a review by Rosemary Dinnage of *The Suppressed Madness of Sane Men* for the *Times Literary Supplement*, where she writes how "Milner was an original writer before she became an analyst and she has integrated her self-explorations into her psychoanalytic work. Among analysts that is rare if not unique" (Dinnage qtd. in Fielding 65). Milner's work cannot, it seems, be easily contained within a purely psychoanalytic framework. It is her self-explorations at the site of autobiography before but also during her career as a psychoanalyst, and its influence on her psychoanalytic work, that we shall see resists the conventions of the psychoanalytic canon, or, indeed, of any other canon.[7]

Increasing attention to Milner's work from scholars outside of psychoanalysis has begun to open up new ways of approaching her work. Vanessa Smith and Helen Tyson have placed Milner's work within the context of modernist experimentation. In her article "Transferred debts: Marion Milner's *A Life of One's Own* and the limits of analysis" (2018), Smith emphasises the connections between a young Milner and the Bloomsbury Group, describing *A Life of One's Own* as "an elusive critical object" which "sidles up to and then shies away from the two dominant discourses through which selfhood was rethought between the wars— psychoanalysis and Modernism" (Smith 96). Helen Tyson's article " 'Catching butterflies': Marion Milner and stream of consciousness writing" (2020) presents new findings from Milner's unpublished diaries and notebooks that sheds further light on the influence of modernist authors' experiments with stream of consciousness writing and Milner's own writing experiments. Mary Jacobus's *The Poetics of Psychoanalysis: In the Wake of Klein* (2005) also provides a literary critic's view of object relations theory, with Jacobus attending to the literary and aesthetic dimensions of Milner's clinical work recorded in *The Hands of the Living God*. Jo Winning's chapter "Love and the Art Object" in *Modernism and Affect* (2015) considers Milner's theories about creativity in relation to the "*affect* of production" of the lesbian modernist art object (112).

In his introduction to the 2013 edition of *Eternity's Sunrise*, Hugh Haughton places the book within a twentieth-century literary tradition influenced by psychoanalysis that, like H.D.'s *Memoir of Freud* and D.H. Lawrence's *Fantasia of the Unconscious*, offers a "fundamentally poetic take on the new Freudian unconscious" (xx). For Haughton, Milner's work is a "maverick take on psychoanalytic theory and her interest in art as it is created by or seen by people who are not 'artists,' art historians or psychoanalysts" (xxi). This book continues the work of these scholars, exploring Milner's distinctive project for its investments in the domains of the psychoanalytic, literary, and aesthetic. It seeks to draw out the methods and theories Milner develops to procure for herself something like a psychoanalytic cure at the site of autobiographical and aesthetic experimentation.

Seeking the maternal provision

As Freud's *The Interpretation of Dreams* is seen to "embody 'the person' of Freud" in contrast to "the 'impersonality'" of *An Autobiographical Study*, Milner's autobiographical books provide us with insight into her emotional life and self-development (Marcus, *Sigmund Freud's The Interpretation of Dreams: New Interdisciplinary Essays*, 44). Her final book, *Bothered by Alligators*, expands the parameters of autobiographical reflection to include that of her early life, and she comes to consider a Winnicottian perspective on her own formation. In her eighties, Milner learns an important biographical detail about her experience of being breastfed that prompts a deeper understanding of her early life. She states in an interview how "in the 80s, my mother told something I had never known: that she had weaned me at four months because she had a breast abscess. So I had to think about everything in my past in a totally new way, starting again from the beginning. But one always has to do that" (Milner qtd. in Hopkins 242). In *Bothered by Alligators* she wonders about the implications of this experience for her adult emotional life:

> if it is true, as they say it is, that most babies gaze into their mother's eyes while sucking at her breast, could it then be that I had seen in her eyes the pain I was causing? But was not yet separated out enough for it to be known as a "not-me" pain? . . . Here I had to ask myself, was it that I had always been trying not to see my mother's pain and woes because of my not yet having properly separated out hers from mine?
>
> (183–220)

Her mother's suffering was likely to have been not only physical but also emotional, given the difficulties of her marriage with Arthur Blackett. "Very slowly," Milner writes "I began to face the possibility that my mother had been secretly unhappy, in her marriage, perhaps from the very beginning of my life" (218).

"Although my mother was a most predictable person both in character and devotedness," Milner finds that knowledge about "her breast abscess changed things" (238). This growing understanding leads her to ask the Winnicottian question about herself: "did this mean that I would never have any 'continuity of being'?" (238).

Winnicott's term "continuity of being" relates to the understanding that the infant's sense of self is dependent on the quality of care from its caregivers, namely its mother. In his paper "The Theory of the Parent-Infant Relationship" (1960) Winnicott explains this term, writing how that with good enough maternal care the infant

> begins to build up what might be called a continuity of being . . . the inherited potential gradually develops into an individual infant. If maternal care is not good enough then the infant does not really come into existence . . . instead the personality becomes built on the basis of reactions to environmental impingement.
>
> (594)

The good enough mother's providing the baby with a sense of continuity of being belongs to the earliest stage in the infant's development, when baby is not yet capable of considering itself a viable separate unit from its mother. Winnicott himself understood Milner's early experiences within the framework of his object relations thinking. In his role as her analyst for four years during the 1940s, Milner believes Winnicott wrote about her and the difficulties of her early life disguised in one of his clinical cases. She claims her colleague "Masud [Khan] told me that I was one of the cases in Winnicott's book *Playing and Reality*. I was described as 'someone with an unpredictable mother'" (Milner qtd. in Hopkins 242). Milner's first autobiographical book after her psychoanalytic training, *On Not Being Able to Paint* (1950), also speculates on the lack of maternal attunement she experienced in infancy.

To put into context Milner's attentions to the importance of the maternal provision, we must take a brief detour through the development of psychoanalytic thinking and the emergence object relations theory. By the time Milner comes to train as a psychoanalyst in 1939, the Freudian instinctual model of the mind (with exceptions like his paper "Mourning and Melancholia" (1917) which is now considered proto-relational) which understood attachment to objects as driven by instinctual needs had been progressively accompanied by Melanie Klein, Ronald Fairbairn, and Winnicott's object relations approach. Rather than postulating as Freud had, that the infant's instincts lead to the seeking of links to objects that can satisfy instinctual desires, these later thinkers understood the mind as existing from the very beginning in a relationship, with instincts and desires taking on meaning and unfolding as a result of relationship. Hence, the term object relations theory—the theory of how the human mind and personality can only be understood, and studied, in its natural environment and setting, which is a human relationship. Winnicott's famous maxim, that there is no such thing as a baby, pithily encapsulates this: that without a mother or primary caregiver, one cannot speak meaningfully about the baby. These thinkers therefore came to privilege the mother-infant relationship as the main way of understanding the structuring of the human psyche and its early beginnings.

Winnicott along with Wilfred Bion would go on to deepen our understanding of the particular qualities of care required by the mother to ensure the infant's healthy development. Their thinking would come to explore the murky terrains of preverbal life and how interactions between mother and baby facilitate, or disrupt, emotional growth. Winnicott's concepts of holding (1960) and mirroring (1967), and Bion's theory of containment (1962), in particular, describe the qualities of psychic care that ideally the mother is able to provide her baby. The maternal provision of these caring and containing functions supports the baby's fragile needs, and give rise to a sense of "going on being" or "continuity of being," which in turn facilitates the infant's growing awareness of object separateness.[8] In Winnicott's model, if the facilitating environment is good enough and supports the baby's need for a sense of omnipotence, manageable differentiation can proceed in small steps and the infant's omnipotent control can be progressively relinquished. The rudimentary self can then develop further into a lively engagement with external objects.

A shared principle of both Winnicott and Bion's thinking is that the analyst can also provide these attuning functions for the patient within the analytic relationship. The analytic relationship can provide the patient with an experience of receptive attention, an experience of being held and contained. If this had not been provided for in the original dyadic relationship of mother and baby, then in the transference, early experiences will be unconsciously re-enacted and can be made manifest and available for conscious thought and reflection by analyst and patient.

Freud's model of psychoanalysis emphasised the analyst's role in facilitating the excavation and reclamation of repressed memories and affects through interpretation. Object relations thinkers, by contrast, although not eschewing interpretation altogether, emphasise the analyst's assigned roles in the transference brought about by the patient's projections. The transference and countertransference relationship thus enables the rediscovery of not just repressed memories, but unconscious affects and ideas embedded in early nonverbal communications and interactions. In his work "Mirror-role of Mother and Family in Child Development," Winnicott defines the work of the analyst in the following way:

> This glimpse of the baby's and child's seeing the self in the mother's face, and afterwards in a mirror, gives a way of looking at analysis and at the psychotherapeutic task. Psychotherapy is not making clever and apt interpretations; by and large it is a long-term giving the patient back what the patient brings. It is a complex derivative of the face that reflects what is there to be seen. I like to think of my work this way, and to think that if I do this well enough the patient will find his or her own self, and will be able to exist and

to feel real. Feeling real is more than existing; it is finding a way to exist as oneself, and to relate to objects as oneself, and to have a self into which to retreat for relaxation.

(Playing and Reality 5)

This passage, along with my brief sketch of Winnicott and Bion's thinking, provides a condensed summary of British object relations theory which Milner's psychoanalytic career emerged alongside. Her intuitive sense of lacking a continuity of being in herself found a home and conceptual articulation in particular with Winnicott's work. Milner is in many ways then both a product of, and contributor to, object relations theory in the Independent tradition. Yet despite being deeply immersed within this theoretical framework, we shall see how her autobiographical acts propose a different site for the provision of maternal attunement, one that dispenses with an intersubjective relationship. Milner is instead invested in developing ways of writing and drawing about herself as a method for self-cure.

This study will attempt to draw out from Milner's autobiographical books the methods, terminology, and neologisms that collectively I argue make up her "autobiographical cure." Her terms include "Answering Activity," "bead memories," "pliable medium," and the "frame." Understood as terms that describe different curative functions of autobiographical mark-making, this book excavates and elaborates these concepts. Some are described and developed prior to or in tandem with Winnicott and Bion's thinking, her work presenting us with something of a parallel set of theories to object relations theory—informed by it, informing it, but also fundamentally different from it. In its essence, Milner's is a therapeutic method that moves away from the locale of the consulting room and the "talking cure" to the page and canvas, for a "writing and drawing cure." It is a project that we shall come to see is also taken up by some of her readers in the twentieth and twenty-first centuries.

To what extent Milner's methods are successful in doing this work of self-discovery and self-constitution this study does not seek to directly answer. I have not intended this book to be an assessment of Milner's methods, to recommend or dissuade their usage, or to evaluate clinical outcomes. Instead, I aim to contextualise and present my understanding of Milner's singular ideas, techniques, and orientation for what it means to "get better," and to leave the reader to make up their own minds.

Psychoanalysis, creativity, cure

Through an analysis of Milner's work, this book is concerned with how creative and autobiographical acts are understood as one of the means by which an individual may engage in the pursuit of self-knowledge, self-development, and self-cure. In this respect, Milner, without necessarily negating other psychoanalytic theories about creativity, differs from them. Freud's primary interest in creativity was how it functioned as a defence mechanism, a way for libido, conflict, and sexual energy to be sublimated through creativity. Art-making and creativity, in Freud's model, is a way of giving expression to and dealing with various psychic pressures. Freud's term "pathography," which he coined in his essay on Leonardo Da Vinci (1910), is summarised by Nicky Glover as "the viewing of art as a privileged form of neurosis where the analyst-critic explores the artwork in order to understand and unearth the vicissitudes of the creator's psychological motivations" (36). As a result, Freud's approach considers the artistic process as another site for the expression of neurotic symptoms. Milner's approach may not essentially disagree with this, but her work considers how creative acts, whilst expressions of personal, often unconscious conflicts, are also themselves capable of bringing therapeutic assistance to these same problems.

Milner's approach is also different from that of Kleinian thinking on the psychic aims and motivations behind creative activity. For Klein, creativity is considered crucial in relation to the function of reparation, and integral to her theory of the depressive position (e.g., her paper "Mourning and Its Relation to Manic Depressive States" (1939)). The guilt arising from the damage done to one's objects provides the impetus behind the creative impulse to make amends, restore, and repair these objects. We find an illustration of this approach in Klein's paper from 1929, "Infantile Anxiety-Situations Reflected in a Work of Art and in the Creative Impulse." Klein uses a literary description by the writer Karin Michaelis of the painter Ruth Kjär's flattering portrait of her mother as an example of a daughter's act of reparation towards her mother. A Milnerian reading of Kjär's creative act might instead emphasise how her relationship to the mediums of paint and canvas provided her with an ideal maternal attunement that in her real life she failed to receive.

Winnicott's thinking provides perhaps the fullest engagement with creativity and psychic health after Freud and Klein. For Winnicott, the capacity for creativity, for living creatively, is a universal marker of emotional wellbeing. "The creative impulse," wrote Winnicott in 1971, "is present as much in the moment-by-moment living of a . . . child who is enjoying breathing as it is in the inspiration of an architect who suddenly knows what it is that he wishes to construct" (*Playing and Reality* 69). The idea of creativity to which Winnicott refers here is the individual's capacity for a creative sensorial relationship to external reality, whether it be an inhalation of air or the sudden discovery of the solution to a complex architectural problem. Successful maternal mirroring forges a sense of creative apperception, described as the following: "When I look I am seen, so I exist. I can now afford to look and see. I now look creatively and what I apperceive I also perceive" (3). Looking creatively, or creative apperception, is the name Winnicott gives to what "more than anything else . . . makes the individual feel that life is worth living" (*Playing and Reality* 65). It is out of this sense of existing that the child can be creative. In "Living Creatively" (1970) he asserts, "I come back to the maxim: Be before Do. Be has to develop behind Do. Then eventually the child rides even the instincts without loss of sense of self" (215). The child must feel it exists before it can live creatively, before it can be creative, before it can make use of the potential space where self and other, inner, and outer intermingle. In Milner's thinking and psychoanalytic technique, however, we shall see how she understands the capacity of doing as developing being; in other words, the doing of creative activity helping to forge a sense of being.

Recent work in the Winnicottian tradition includes Kenneth Wright's *Mirroring and Attunement: Self-Realization in Psychoanalysis and Art* (2009) which proposes "a new approach to psychoanalysis" whereby artistic creation and religion, like psychoanalysis, "can be seen as cultural attempts to provide the self with resonant containment," thus providing "renewed opportunities for holding and emotional growth" (Wright 7). Wright turns to the work of Winnicott, Daniel Stern, and Susanne Langer and applies their ideas to propose that these other practices can provide a sense of attunement that was originally found in those moments of togetherness and repose that were facilitated by the understanding sensitivity of the mother. Wright's study, however, does not refer to Milner's work or her ideas. It is also the aim of this study to bring awareness to a thinker for whom such studies might find a likeminded theorist.

Lesley Caldwell's *Art, Creativity, Living* (2000) does take on Milner's ideas and applies them to the work of the artist. The book is described as a "volume in the Winnicott Studies series . . . dedicated to the life and work of Marion Milner and reflects, in varying ways, her unique use of Winnicott's work to shape her own thinking about art and creativity" (Caldwell 63). Caldwell considers the following about the motivations of the artist and what their art-making might mean for them emotionally:

> If artists are those who dedicate their life, in an almost compulsive way, to the creation of emotionally resonating forms, what is it that leads them to do this? . . . [are artists] those who know what they want—they have had a taste of attuning experience, but not enough—and now feel that their lives depend on creating it for themselves? Are they, in short, those who have had a relatively depriving experience in the area of attunement—a crisis of confidence in the mother, perhaps—which has made them feel that the only security would lie in creating the forms they need for themselves?
>
> (3)

Milner's project, however, invites us not to just analyse the professional artist but to be the layperson, like herself, and to join her in the therapeutic search for attunement with techniques available to anyone—diary keeping, doodling, the making of collages and clay figures—to name but a few.

Milner's use of these techniques to enact psychic change also brings to the fore psychoanalysis's long and stormy relationship in identifying itself as undertaking an activity oriented in the direction of science or something more poetically inclined. Freud's allegiance with science for his method for studying and coming to knowledge about the unconscious is perhaps less straightforward than he claimed. Sabine Prokhoris's *The Witch's Kitchen: Freud, Faust and the*

Transference (1995), for example, examines the influence of Goethe's *Faust* on Freud's development of psychoanalysis, and particularly his theory of the transference. Prokhoris looks at how "Freud's text is haunted, possessed, carried along" by the story of Faust, with numerous citations of Goethe's mushrooming up in Freud's psychoanalytic writings (vii–viii). In contradiction to Freud's own proclaimed allegiance with the scientist, she writes how this "interference of a poet in Freud's affairs certainly qualifies as an act of violence directed against science" (15). It is rather this penetration of the poetic into Freud's writing and thinking that defines his project of psychoanalysis:

> Freud is of legitimate, respectable scientific descent, even if he seems in many ways to be the *enfant terrible* of the Meynerts, Breuers, and Bruckes. I am much more interested in another genealogy. It is a bastard line, springing, in some sense, from an unhallowed union—one, moreover, that Freud partially disavows. Its existence is betrayed by the relations he maintains with the poets.
>
> (6)

If Freud partly denies the extent of the influence of the poets on his thinking and methods, this book contends that Milner is an out and proud inheritor of this bastard line, championing her dealings with the creative and curative methods of the writers and artists.

Book outline

This book is divided into two parts. Part 1, "The Milner Method," is made up of three chapters which explore the theories and methods I argue make up Milner's autobiographical cure. Part 2, "The Milner Tradition," consists of two final chapters that examine the influence of the autobiographical cure on Milner's readers in the twentieth and twenty-first centuries.

Chapter 1 starts where Milner begins: with her first published autobiographical book *A Life of One's Own* (1934). Written almost ten years prior to Milner's becoming a psychoanalyst, this book marks the beginning of Milner's developing her own therapeutic methods of diary keeping. In this early book Milner deliberately carves out a space for herself and her method, positioning it as a rival to the psychoanalytic talking cure. A term that she coins three years later in 1937, "the Answering Activity" describes an emotional receptivity provided by certain ways of writing and is considered in relation to Milner's therapeutic efforts in *A Life*. This term, along with Milner's notion of "bead memories" are analysed for how they might deepen our understanding of diary keeping and the autobiographical subject.

Chapter 2 explores *On Not Being Able to Paint* (1950), Milner's study of painting, drawing, creativity, and its impediments. Written and published some years after Milner first started practicing as a psychoanalyst, this chapter considers Milner's autobiographical cure at the site of visual expression. In her experiments with painting and free associative drawing, Milner attends to the relational world of the painter for what it can tell her about her earliest relationships and its subsequent shaping of her adult psyche. Through drawing and painting experiments, Milner develops the concepts of the "pliable medium" and the "frame," terms that describe the attuning capabilities of visual mark-making. We shall see how these self-explorations at the site of drawing go on to influence Milner's clinical work with her patients and how her analytic technique extends to encouraging her patients' own acts of drawing both inside and outside the consulting room.

Chapter 3 turns to the autobiographical works of Milner's later years, with the main focus on her final book, *Bothered by Alligators* (2013) and its description of the failures of what she calls her "couch analysis," primarily relating to her experience as Winnicott's patient. This chapter traces the deliberate drive at the end of Milner's life to compensate for past failed experiences as a psychoanalytic patient with her own creative and autobiographical methods for self-cure.

Part 2 begins with Chapter 4, which reviews Milner's legacy and the influence of her autobiographical cure on her readers in the twentieth century. It explores Milner's own relationship to influence and goes on to assess what kind of influence Milner has on her readers through an examination of her fan letters and the work of other authors. Milner, I demonstrate, has quietly though evidently inspired a shared idiom of therapeutic work at the site of autobiographical mark-making.

Lastly, Chapter 5 explores the recent work of two graphic memoirists, Lynda Barry and Alison Bechdel, working in the twenty-first century. I examine how these authors take up the autobiographical cure in their visual-verbal narratives and how directly and indirectly they are in dialogue with Milner through their creative and autobiographical projects.

Notes

1   Throughout the book in-text citations will use the following shorthand to refer to her books: LOO (*A Life of One's Own*), EIL (*An Experiment in Leisure*), ONBAP (*On Not Being Able to Paint*), HOLG (*The Hands of the Living God: An Account of a Psychoanalytic Treatment*), ES (*Eternity's Sunrise: A Way of Keeping a Diary*), SMSM (*The Supressed Madness of Sane Men: Forty-Four Years of Exploring Psychoanalysis*) and BBA (*Bothered by Alligators*).

2   Milner used the penname Joanna Field in the first editions of *A Life of One's Own, An Experiment in Leisure,* and *On Not Being Able to Paint* because she felt it was appropriate to have an alias when undertaking psychological research work in schools. She also liked the associations to the word "field" (Letley 29). The psychoanalyst Alexander Newman, who read *A Life* in his younger years, said that in his case it took him a long time to realise that Field was actually Milner (29).

3   Some excerpts of the nature diary are included in *An Experiment in Leisure*. The full document resides in the John Milner Papers collection.

4   Milner qualified as an adult psychoanalyst in the summer of 1943 and as a child analyst some months later in the autumn of the same year.

5 See also Milner's clinical psychoanalytic papers, such as "The communication of primary sensual experience" (1955) which considers her patients' early life and their ambivalence around the desire for differentiation or an oceanic togetherness with the mother.
6 The back of the card reads: "With love and best wishes for Christmas and 1960 from Marion (My first linocut!)."
7 It is perhaps not surprising then that, as Emma Letley has noted, "Milner has been seen as a mystic" by some critics (133). For further discussion, see Janet Sayers article in *The International Journal of Psychoanalysis*, "Marion Milner, Mysticism and Psychoanalysis" and Kelley A. Raab's "Creativity and Transcendence in the Work of Marion Milner" in *American Imago*.
8 Similarly, Bion and Winnicott have their own respective terms for describing the infant's experience of when holding and containment fail or are insufficient—see Winnicott's description of "archaic anxiety" in "A clinical study of the effect of a failure of the average expectable environment on a child's mental functioning" (1965) and Bion's "nameless dread" in "A Theory of Thinking" in *Second Thoughts* (1967) for further discussion.

References

Brown, Peter. *Augustine of Hippo: A Biography*. Faber, 2000.
Caldwell, Lesley, editor. *Art, Creativity, Living*. Karnac Books, 2000. http://dx.doi.org/10.4324/9780429471971
Caldwell, Lesley, and Angela Joyce, editors. *Reading Winnicott*. Routledge, 2011. http://dx.doi.org/10.4324/9780203813591
Ellmann, Maud. "Psychoanalysis and Autobiography." *A History of English Autobiography*, edited by Adam Smyth. Cambridge University Press, 2016, pp. 313–328.
Fielding, John. "Telling the Beads: A Review of Eternity's Sunrise by John Fielding." *A Celebration of the Life and Work of Marion Milner*, Special Issue of Winnicott Studies: The Journal of the Squiggle Foundation, vol. 3, 1988, pp. 64–68.
Forrester, John. "Dream Readers." *Sigmund Freud's the Interpretation of Dreams: New Interdisciplinary Essays*, edited by Laura Marcus. Manchester University Press, 1999, pp. 83–122.
Grolnick, Simon. Review of *"The Suppressed Madness of Sane: Forty-Four Years of Exploring Psychoanalysis"* by Marion Milner. *Journal of the American Psychoanalytic Association*, no. 39, 1991, pp. 292–296.
Harris Williams, Meg. "On psychoanalytic autobiography." *Psychodynamic Practice*, vol. 18, no. 4, 2012, pp. 397–412. http://dx.doi.org/10.1080/14753634.2012.719737
Haughton, Hugh. "New Introduction." *Eternity's Sunrise: A Way of Keeping a Diary*, edited by Marion Milner. Routledge, 2011. http://dx.doi.org/10.4324/9780203720677
Hopkins, Linda. "Red Shoes, Untapped Madness, and Winnicott on the Cross: An Interview with Marion Milner." *Annual of Psychoanalysis*, vol. 32, 2004, pp. 233–243.
Lejeune, Philippe. "Le pacte autobiographique." *Poétique*, vol. 14, 1973, pp. 137–162.
Letley, Emma. *Marion Milner: The Life*. Routledge, 2014. http://dx.doi.org/10.4324/9780203767122
Marcus, Laura. *Auto/Biographical Discourses: Theory, Criticism, Practice*. Manchester University Press, 1994.
Marcus, Laura. "Autobiography and Psychoanalysis." *On Life-writing*, edited by Zachary Leader. Oxford University Press, 2015, pp. 257–283.

Marcus, Laura, editor. *Sigmund Freud's the Interpretation of Dreams: New Interdisciplinary Essays*. Manchester University Press, 1999.

Milner, Marion. *Bothered by Alligators*. Routledge, 2013. http://dx.doi.org/10.4324/9780203140147

Milner, Marion. *The Hands of the Living God: An Account of a Psycho-analytic Treatment*. 1969. Routledge, 2010. http://dx.doi.org/10.4324/9780203833643

Phillips, Adam. *On Flirtation*. Harvard University Press, 1994.

Prokhoris, Sabine. *The Witch's Kitchen: Freud, Faust and the Transference*. Cornell University Press, 1995.

Smith, Vanessa. "Transferred Debts: Marion Milner's A Life of One's Own and the Limits of Analysis." *Feminist Modernist Studies*, vol. 1, no. 1–2, 2018, pp. 96–111. http://dx.doi.org/10.1080/24692921.2017.1371929

Stonebridge, Lyndsey. "Taking Care of Ourselves and Looking after the Subject: Marion Milner's Autobiographical Acts." *Paragraph*, vol. 17, no. 2, 1994, pp. 120–133.

Walters, Margaret. "New Introduction." *Bothered by Alligators*, edited by Marion Milner. Routledge, 2013. http://dx.doi.org/10.4324/9780203140147

Winnicott, D.W. "Living Creatively." *Home is Where We Start from: Essays by a Psychoanalyst*, edited by D.W. Winnicott, and Clare Winnicott. Penguin, 1986/1970.

Winnicott, D.W. "Mirror-Role of Mother and Family in Child Development." *The Predicament of the Family: A Psycho-Analytical Symposium*, edited by Peter Lomas. International University Press, 1967, pp. 26–31.

Winnicott, D.W. *Playing and Reality*. Tavistock Publications, 1971. http://dx.doi.org/10.4324/9780203441022

Winnicott, D.W. "The Theory of the Parent-Infant Relationship." *International Journal of Psycho-Analysis*, vol. 41, 1960, pp. 585–595.

Winning, Joanne. "Love and the Art Object." *Modernism and Affect*, edited by Julie Taylor. Edinburgh University Press, 2015, pp. 111–130. http://dx.doi.org/10.1515/9780748693269

Wright, Kenneth. *Mirroring and Attunement: Self-Realization in Psychoanalysis and Art*. Routledge, 2009.

Part 1

The Milner method

A Life of One's Own and the birth of a diary keeping method to rival psychoanalysis

The voice of Robinson Crusoe weaves itself in and out of Milner's first autobiographical book *A Life of One's Own* (1934). In one of the many epigraphs quoting Defoe's work, the passage that introduces her chapter "Discovering that thought can be blind" captures the spirit of Milner's project in this book. Here Crusoe describes his doubts about making a boat that could launch his voyages across the sea: "I pleased myself with the design without determining whether I was ever able to undertake it; not but that the difficulty of launching my boat came often into my head" (Defoe qtd. in Milner, *LOO* 83). But, he recounts,

> I put a stop to my own inquiries into it by this foolish answer which I gave myself—'Let me first make it, I'll warrant that I'll find some way or other to get it along when it is done.' This was a most preposterous method; but the eagerness of my fancy prevailed, and to work I went and felled a cedar-tree.
>
> (83)

Although the epigraph does not continue to include the eventual failure of the boat to launch, Crusoe's determination in following his "preposterous method" seem to strike a chord with Milner. For *A Life* similarly tells a story of a lone explorer whose methods and tools for exploration are built in the inventor's spirit of hopeful determination.

Like Defoe's protagonist, Milner engages with various acts of diary keeping in her journeys of exploration. But whereas Crusoe's journals are day-to-day records of his survival on the Island of Despair, Milner's discoveries take place in the unchartered and unmapped regions of her inner world. And for Milner, as we shall see, diary keeping is the main tool wielded in her expedition of self-discovery. Integral to her enterprise is her independent creation of the methods and techniques for self-discovery. Whereas Crusoe found himself shipwrecked onto his island of solitude through no choice of his own, Milner's acts of writing and diary keeping involve a volitional isolation from the influence of others. Indeed, we shall see how Milner presents her therapeutic writing techniques as a rival to the psychoanalytic talking cure, whereby self-discovery requires only the resources of self, pen, and paper.

DOI: 10.4324/9781003296720-3

This chapter will primarily focus on Milner's first book, *A Life of One's Own*, which, along with its successor, *An Experiment in Leisure* (1937), have been called Milner's "pre-Freudian writings" (Watsky 457). Both were written and published prior to Milner's training to become a psychoanalyst in 1939. And yet, this first book, as this chapter will explore, propels into motion a therapeutic method at the site of diary writing that starts well before Milner's psychoanalytic training, and continues long after it. In the final years of her life, Milner considered *A Life of One's Own* to have "initiated change in my inner world that has been going on continuously ever since" (Milner, *BBA* 238). This book marks the beginning of a lifelong search for aesthetic techniques that come to be recorded in her later autobiographical books, *An Experiment in Leisure* (1937), *On Not Being Able to Paint* (1950), *Eternity's Sunrise: A Way of Keeping a Diary* (1987), and *Bothered by Alligators* (2012). Particularly in *A Life* and *An Experiment*, Milner situates herself as an outsider to psychoanalysis, presenting her therapeutic work at the site of autobiography as a rival and substitute for psychoanalysis.

Accordingly, this chapter follows the twists and turns at the beginning of a journey of a thinker invested in developing a method for coming to know herself and establish a clearer sense of her identity, away from the psychoanalytic couch. I will then go on to explore Milner's term "the answering activity," which she first coins in *An Experiment in Leisure*. From Milner's own descriptions and my reading of the term, I consider the answering activity an important concept for describing an emotional receptivity that, in Milner's view, particular forms of writing can provide. It is a term that describes an attuning function that might be compared to Winnicott's later notion of mirroring and Bion's function of containing. Milner's answering activity, however, is a function provided by the act of writing rather than in the dynamic of interpersonal relations. In *A Life* we witness how diary writing is felt to give access to the otherwise hidden terrains of her subjectivity and unconscious, by reflecting and mirroring a deeper, fuller, sense of self back to her. Finally, Milner's concept of "bead memories," developed in her later book *Eternity's Sunrise: A Way of Keeping a Diary* (1987) which revives her earlier experimentation with diaries, will also be explored as another term to describe the therapeutic function of diary keeping. These terms, the answering activity and bead memories, form part of the theoretical framework of Milner's autobiographical cure.

The search for the self

A Life of One's Own is not an autobiographical book in the conventional sense. The usual events and milestones of a life lived out in the world that most autobiographies describe are conspicuously missing from Milner's account. Rather, *A Life* records something anterior to this form of autobiographical expression: the search for a life, for a sense of self, through various autobiographical writing acts. This book, we are told, "grew out of the fact that when I was 26 (in

December 1926), I began to keep a diary. This was because it had slowly become clear that my life was not as it ought to be" (Milner *LOO* 173). *A Life* is the culmination of this eight-year practice of keeping a diary, and a study of the emotional transformation it sets into motion.

As the title of *A Life of One's Own* indicates, having a sense of possession of one's life, and by extension oneself, is central to the aims of the book. As Rachel Bowlby notes, Milner's *A Life of One's Own* likely alludes to Virginia Woolf's *A Room of One's Own* published in 1929. Milner's title, however, expands the parameters of possession beyond the spatial and material to one's own subjectivity and psyche (xxxi). Montaigne's essays are directly referenced as an influence for embarking on her project. Milner writes how she had been "stimulated by reading Montaigne's essays and his insistence that what he calls the soul is totally different from all that one expects it to be, often being the very opposite" (*LOO* 173).

This is a book, therefore, about a need to find out who one is, to tighten one's grip on a sense of self and identity that can be felt to easily slip out of one's grasp. As we have seen, Milner's last book, *Bothered by Alligators,* considers whether these kinds of feelings might stem from early failures of care in infancy, where the development of a sense of self, the feeling of having a "continuity in being" are first established (238). *A Life of One's Own*, however, does not present us with an object relations understanding of the self as formed in infancy. Milner later recounts how during the period of writing *A Life* she "had some knowledge of early Freud, particularly what he had called the Oedipus complex, but had never heard of D. W. Winnicott or Melanie Klein, and Bowlby's work on the intensity of an infant's attachment to the mother was still far in the future" (13). This first book instead expresses unconsciously the manifestations in adult life of these early failures in establishing a sense of continuity of being. Milner's desire in this book to find "a method for discovering one's true likes and dislikes," we shall see, stems from these original problems around selfhood (*LOO* xxxiv).

Specifically, the motivations for developing a therapeutic method come from a fear of losing her own identity. She tells us how in *A Life*, through the course of her self-explorations "[c]ertain fears began to take form, shadowy and elusive as yet, but intense as a missed heart-beat. Chiefly there seemed to be a fear of losing myself or being overtaken by something" (54). One evening, upon getting into bed, a dread of what she describes as being engulfed by "the jaws of death" is understood as "a fear that my personal identity would be swallowed up" (115). She has a recurring dream in which she experiences being swept over by a tidal wave. This, she thinks, "stood for the panic dread of being overwhelmed by the boundless sea of what was not myself" (128). These fears, in which something other threatens to engulf one's sense of self, are further fleshed out in Milner's subsequent book, *An Experiment in Leisure*, published three years after *A Life* and a continuation of her work in this first book. If in *A Life* these problems around identity are first explored through the prism of finding out what she likes or dislikes, in *An Experiment* they are presented as a problem around how to know how she wants to spend her spare time. We are told that:

> This book began with an attempt to solve certain aspects of the everyday problem of what to do with one's spare time. Obviously, for a large number of people this is not a problem at all, it is not a problem for those people who are quite sure who they are, and who have definite clear-cut opinions about everything. But there are others who are less certain in their attitudes, who are often more aware of other people's identity than their own, and for them I think the problem is real.
>
> (Milner, *EIL* xliii)

Milner identifies herself as one of these people for whom a workable day-to-day awareness of oneself cannot be taken for granted, and for whom a clear sense of purpose is not a given. Her method is for those people who easily feel themselves taken over by people Milner characterises as being so sure of who they are.

Despite the general paucity of biographical information in *An Experiment*, Milner does on two occasions connect her difficulties around her sense of identity to her relationships in childhood. She recounts feeling that "as a child, I had come to feel that not to be what those I loved expected of me was a matter of eternal damnation—disapproval, a 'row' from them was something that I had felt utterly destroyed my being, and I had lived in continual dread of it" (69). Later in the book she tells us how:

> I remembered all the people from my childhood upwards, mostly women, since I had been educated by women, who by sheer force of a loud voice or a show of anger or sarcasm, had had the power to make me "lose my head," to wipe out from me all sense of my own identity, not only to thwart me in what I wanted, but to produce such a state that I no longer knew what I wanted at all, I was aware only of them, utterly possessed by them.
>
> (148)

To lose one's head here is not only to lose one's composure and self-control in the conventional meaning of the word; in this scenario, it is a terrifying loss of self and being to the domineering power of another. Milner describes how in adulthood this feeling of her identity being wiped out comes to haunt her, for "you can become obsessed by memories and forebodings, 'the dark backward and abyss of time', can become a looming presence overshadowing and threatening your own existence. It can make you feel you are as nothing, nothing to say, nothing to feel, nothing to be" (145). To feel this loss of identity is to feel an emotional devastation that Milner painfully describes as feeling like being taken over by a "sense of blankness that would . . . catch me unawares and sweep me to despair" (146).

In *An Experiment*, the burning desire to combat this existential threat of feeling oneself to have no bearing manifests itself in various ways. In a diary note transcribed in the book, the desire for what Milner calls "crystallization" evocatively describes this emotional need:

> revolt against nature, it's so unformed—in the small, yes, there's form there, in the shape of flowers, cells under the microscope, the pattern on a butterfly's wing, crystals, living bodies—but it's so inchoate in the large. Just roaming the country is not now what I want, I want form, crystallization, that timelessness of fine paintings. . . . I don't want to wander abroad seeing things, I want quiet and a rhythm of routine, so that I can bring form out of this chaos of nature, raise the fire within till something crystallizes into shape.
>
> (129)

In a later note meditating on what this passage might mean, Milner concludes that "[t]his idea of crystallization had developed through the months till I had become full of this thought of shaping one's life into a whole, in order somehow to possess it" (129). The desire for a life with form and a sense of wholeness that can be possessed—a life of one's own—speaks of a need to establish an internal sense of organisation before she can set off to freely engage with the outside world that awaits her. In the final chapter of *An Experiment* Milner writes explicitly about her "struggle for a sense of identity" which also "foreshadowed the long struggle to develop an inner life that was not just an escape from reality, but the only means by which I could face it" (161).

These are the personal struggles expressed in *A Life* and *An Experiment* that motivate Milner to engage with writing techniques that might give knowledge of her inner world and a sense of who she is. These books chart the development of a method for self-cure that the reader might also want to follow. *A Life*, for example, promises the follower of its methods a way of getting in touch with their authentic desires, and by extension, their authentic selves. The "need for such a method in these days is obvious" she claims, "for finding and setting up a standard of values that is truly one's own and not a borrowed mass-produced ideal" (xxxiv).[1] And she claims a universality for her method in its ability to effect change in different kinds of people: "The reason for publishing the book is that although what I found is probably peculiar to my own temperament and circumstances, I think the method by which I found it may be useful to others, even to those whose discoveries about themselves may be the opposite of my own" (xxxiii–xxxv). If "tempted to try the same experiment," she tells the reader, they "may discover as I did myself that they are quite different creatures from what they had imagined" (xxxiv). This is a confident claim for a method that has the potential to profoundly alter the reader's sense of themselves. Follow Milner and you will explore the unchartered hinterlands of the inner reaches of your mind, brushing aside the false ideals pressed upon you to learn who you really are and what you value. The preface of the book ends with a delicious invitation and challenge to the reader: "let no one undertake such an experiment who is not prepared to find himself more of a fool than he thought" (xxxvii).

Writing and diary keeping to reflect the self

Rather than presenting the reader with the finalised methods for self-transformation, *A Life of One's Own* charts Milner's own trial and error journey for finding ways of writing that put her in touch with herself. We first learn of the myriad ways in which particular types of reading and writing fail to provide her with the clarifying insights into herself that she is in search of. Although Milner is both a student and teacher of psychology, she nevertheless feels that whatever she has learnt from others has left her ill-equipped:

> The more I read scientific books on psychology the more I felt that the essential facts of experience were being missed out. In order to show how far it is possible to handle ideas with apparent competence and yet be utterly at sea in trying to live one's knowledge, I would like the reader to bear in mind, when reading the first few chapters, that I had a First Class Honours Degree in Psychology, and was also, during the time of this experiment, earning my living by applying my so-called psychological knowledge to others, in lecturing, research, and other ways.
>
> (*LOO*, xxxiv)

Some of the lecturing and research work to which Milner refers here would have likely been part of a Laura Spelman Rockefeller Scholarship, granted to support her attendance at the renowned Australian psychologist Elton Mayo's seminars in Boston between 1927 and 1928 (Letley 18). During the fellowship, Milner and the other research students spent most of their time reading the work of psychologists Jean Piaget and Pierre Janet, as well as some early Freud (19). Reading works by these psychological and psychoanalytic thinkers is felt to give her some insight into mind in general, but they do not seem to provide the knowledge about herself that she is searching for. At points aligned with a rigid and prescriptive science, Milner despairs that she did not gain from psychology books "any more help in scientific explanations than I had done before. I had of course heard a lot of talk which purported to explain such attitudes in terms of current psychological doctrine— 'unconscious guilt feelings', 'inferiority complex' and the like" (*LOO* 83). Felt to be doctrinal and reductive, they inhibit her coming to know more about her subjective experience.

Milner's frustrations with these "scientific explanations" is later encapsulated in a vignette she writes, reminiscent of Virginia Woolf's "Mr Bennett and Mrs Brown" (1924) in its advocating for new ways of representing human subjectivity. She recalls how one summer evening, whilst observing a woman from her train carriage window she came to realize how reading scientific books about human behaviour could never fulfil her wish to know what she wanted to know about this woman:

> At once I was seized with an impulse to know more about her, and then began wondering what the scientists who deal with different phases of social

life could tell me. I had even got as far as resolving to read some books on sociology, when it suddenly dawned on me that that was not at all what I wanted. I wanted to know that woman as a person, as a unique individual, not a specimen. It was only later, when I read that science is concerned, not with individuals but only with specimens, that I began to realize why I could not find what I wanted in science. For it seemed to be just the unique qualities of particular experiences which I wanted.

(158)

Science is here equated with that which dissects, depersonalises, categorises, and thus kills the uniqueness of individual identity. For Milner, to look at human subjectivity and turn it into a type through the cold eye of science wipes out the entire goal of her enterprise. Trying to understand this woman's subjectivity, and by extension her own through the books of sociology cannot provide the knowledge about the self that Milner aches to possess. At "one stage" Milner writes, "I had become disgusted with science for not giving me what was not in its power to give" (158). This powerful emotional reaction stems, perhaps, from that original feeling of having her identity wiped out or withheld from her, science reducing her feelings to nothingness in its furnishing material for categorisation. Searching in these books for knowledge about herself inevitably proves futile, "since it was my own mind I needed to understand, not mind in general" (34).

Freud himself might not have disagreed with Milner's frustrations levied at reading books likes his—as he writes in "Wild Psychoanalysis" (1910):

If knowledge about the unconscious were as important for the patient as people inexperienced in psychoanalysis imagine, listening to lectures or reading books would be enough to cure him. Such measures, however, have as much influence on the symptoms of nervous illness as a distribution of menu-cards in a time of famine has upon hunger.

(Freud, " 'Wild' Psycho-Analysis" 225)

In defence of her own self-analytical methods, Milner arrives at the "firm conclusion that reading must come after one had learnt the tricks for observing one's own mind, not before; since if it comes before it is only too easy to accept technical concepts intellectually and use them as jargon, not as instruments for the real understanding of experience" (*LOO* 159).

In the same way reading sociology and psychology books fails to provide the quality of self-knowledge she is searching for, so the self-help mental training systems popular at the time are felt to have produced disappointing results.[2] She tells us:

I had not been able to make more use of the mental training systems that offered such glowing rewards in efficiency and success. They were interested only in the development of maleness, of objectivity; and it was perhaps because the unconscious urge that I was blindly trying to express was to do with femaleness, with subjectivity, that I got little help from them and had had to develop my own method.

(168)

The only solution is to develop a method that is radically different, a method that must do away with the methodologies, abstract theories, and concepts of others, particularly of the authoritative objectivising of the rational male voice. Milner writes how following the spirit of Descartes' philosophical scepticism, "I set out to doubt everything I had been taught, but I did not try to rebuild my knowledge in a structure of logic and argument. I tried to learn, not from reason but from my senses" (xxxv).

It is the creative writer who Milner turns to specifically as someone who might possess the appropriate tools for her task. For she "had often thought that novelists and poets had a special advantage in learning how to live, their writings provided them with an instrument that most of us were denied. By being able to dramatize their own difficulties they were in a far better position for solving them" (11).

The power to cure oneself through one's own creations is irresistibly attractive. But "if one had no gift for creating imaginative truth," as Milner seems to charge herself with, and no talent "for symbolizing the stresses and strains of one's own inner life in terms of sound and shape or invented happenings in others, was there no way of dealing with them?" (11). The keeping of a diary, a quotidian, accessible form of writing, seems to offer a glimmer of hope to the laywoman: "I thought the best way to begin was to keep a diary, noting in it every day when I had been particularly happy and anything I wanted" (7).

Milner's decision to begin keeping a diary is significant considering the genre has been historically considered a female, domestic form. In *An Experiment*, the difficulties around maintaining a sense of identity are explicitly linked to her being a woman, for she writes: "I thought that this finding of self in oneself was perhaps harder for a woman than a man" (156). This statement certainly chimes with some later object-relations understanding of the mother-daughter relationship. Nancy Chodorow in her book suggests that the female child has an intrinsic difficulty in forming a sense of separate identity from her mother because of their being of the same sex (166–7). Accordingly, LuAnn McCraken contends that women are "less likely than men to have a stable self-image, and as a consequence are more likely to write fragmented narratives about their lives, as in the fragmented nature in which the sense of a stable identity recedes" (60). *A Life* and *An Experiment* certainly express a sense of identity that is at risk of receding, but they also demonstrate how through acts of writing about the self a more stable and more truthful self-image might be nurtured.

In her first forays into diary writing, however, Milner seems to find herself stuck in performing her own acts of ratiocination. She begins by "look[ing] at the facts of my own life, to see if I could find out what I wanted to know simply by observation and experiment. I thought that I would try to observe what my wants were and whether I got them and whether it made me happy or not" (Milner, *LOO* 7).

This first form of diary writing involves the deceptively straightforward method of picking "out those moments in my daily life which had been particularly happy and try to record them in words" (xxxiii). It is, however, a decided failure. She is struck by a sense of deep embarrassment at discovering in these diaries what she describes as the "depths of my own self-absorption," and little else beyond this (7). This type of writing reflects little of herself back to her apart from a censorious, inhibitive self-consciousness.

The search for the right technique continues. Hoping to procure greater insight into herself, she experiments next with making lists in her diary based on what she loves and hates and recording the significant events of each day. But once again this technique seems only to make her feel less known to herself:

> when I actually began to keep a record of daily concerns I was disappointed. . . . For then I came to realize that the facts of my life were not so many fixed items which only needed adding up and balancing. They were rather the continually receding horizons of the traveller who climbs the mountain.
>
> (23)

Self and mind slip away from view when she engages with this summative approach, the landscape of her inner world made to feel remote and out of reach. Finding herself becoming ever more elusive to herself, she laments how: "Diary-keeping had not brought me as far on my way as I had hoped," since the "more I had tried to find the facts the more I had become convinced that my own mind was something quite unknown to me" (34). Writing accounts of a life lived in the daily concerns of the external world bars her from the vistas of her inner world.

In a change of tactic, Milner tries writing "not just the things I wanted or liked, but whatever came into my head" (36). Following this practice, her diary entries start to shift to looser and more free associative forms of writing. Here we are witness to the beginning of a technique for writing that she calls "free writing," a narrative mode akin to stream-of-consciousness writing. Milner describes how significant this way of writing became, for:

> writing down my experiences then seemed to be a creative act which continually lit up new possibilities in what I had seen. . . . I merely felt that it was useless to go over these records as I had originally planned in order to balance the happiness and make decisions on how to act in the future. Instead I felt an urge to go on and on writing.
>
> (23)

As she starts free writing "only the first sentence or two were concerned with the present and then I had plunged into memories of fifteen or twenty years ago, memories of things I had not consciously thought of for all those years, memories that I never knew I had remembered" (38). That which was once unremembered and unconscious is suddenly brought to awareness, the temporal horizons of her subjectivity expanding and unfolding before her. The "act of writing a thought was a plunge which at once took me into a different element" (60). This form of writing allows the temporary bracketing of her everyday consciousness, providing an immersive entry into the depths of her mind.

She proceeds with this way of diary keeping, feeling that "every effort to articulate desires, however incoherent, was a step forward" (59). Writing in this way begins to provide her with a greater sense of who she is, apart from the pressures of other's definitions. Her true self, desires, and needs come to gain clarity:

> When I had first started free writing as an experiment . . . I had been forced to realize that my mind had thoughts I did not know about. Now I was being made to recognize that without any doubt I also had needs which might be quite different from those my everyday conscious self regarded as important. At first I had not known at all how to distinguish between things that I thought I ought to want because other people did, and those that were fundamentally appropriate to my own situation and nature. I had been very much inclined to intellectualize my wants, to try to decide what it might be good to want and then assume that I did want it.
>
> (128–9)

Free writing not only reveals to Milner a level of her unconscious mental life that she was previously unaware of, it also provides her with a burgeoning and expanded sense of her own identity. By routinely keeping up the practice of writing free written diary entries, she equips herself with a diurnal strategy for keeping her inner life and sense of self alive.

Milner is, she writes, "forced to realize the importance of making my thought see itself" (137). This sense of oneself becoming visible is also recapitulated in an epigraph to one of the chapters in *A Life* where the words of E. M. Forster proclaim: "How can I tell what I think till I see what I say?", a confirmation of Milner's recognition that having herself reflected back to her through her writing is of the utmost importance (Forster qtd. in *LOO* 116). These metaphors of visibility, of the self becoming seeable as she engages with this technique for diary writing, extends also to the terminology Milner invents to describe her psychic processes. Her terms "wide focus" and "narrow focus"—photographic and cinematic metaphors—for example, describe two different ways of being engaged with oneself, the former providing her access to what she calls her "back-of-my-mind thoughts," a term that describes something resembling the unconscious (xxxv). Another term she uses, "blind thinking," is understood by Rachel Bowlby as describing the "operation of a censorious primary consciousness which cannot and does not want to 'see' what is going on elsewhere, in the 'back of the mind'" (Bowlby xvii). Writing helps to illuminate these tenebrous areas of the mind. "Particularly was I struck by the effect of writing things down," she tells us. "It was as if I were trying to catch something and the written word provided a net which for a moment entangled a shadowy form which was other than the meaning of the words" (Milner, *LOO* 46–47).

Capturing her mind and its thoughts through free writing is credited with the capacity to give an otherwise slippery sense of self a visibility and tangibility. She writes how before developing this therapeutic writing technique, when she was "concerned only with [her] inner cogitations . . . what passed before me was so ethereal as to be almost invisible unless I gave it form. I could not stand back and look at it, because I hardly knew it was there" (102). Mind and its contents hardly feel like they exist. Upon writing, "Not only did I find that trying to describe my experience enhanced the quality of it, but also this effort to describe had made me more observant of the small movements of the mind" (71). The practice of free writing shows her that "words, pictures and all symbols helped me . . . in giving thought concrete form" (102). In another metaphor for this form-giving process, Milner writes how her autobiographical acts gave "outcast thoughts . . . seeking expression for themselves . . . indirect and symbolic language in which to clothe themselves" (116–17).

The most enduring set of metaphors Milner uses to describe her newly discovered inner life is that of the creatures of the animal world. In beginning her journey of giving written expression to her mind, she comes to imagine her psyche as an exotic, far-away place, "an unexplored jungle" teeming with various flora and fauna ripe for discovery (122). She describes her mind's "herds" of "special experiences" and gesturing to her unconscious, writes that "[f]or each thought which I kept domesticated and rational in my garden there might be a wild mate lurking outside the walls and howling at nights" (122). Butterflies give body to those "little movements going on in the back of my mind, passing ideas which were often quite irrelevant to my task of the moment and which I could never have noticed in the ordinary way. I called these 'butterflies', for they silently fluttered in from nowhere and were gone in a moment" (87).

Milner paints for the reader a picture of an alive inner world, a self-image in complete contrast with the annihilatory blankness and nothingness that would previously threaten to take over. In her method, "words run freely in writing to give shape to fears and overcome it" (148).

Animals continue to help Milner symbolise her psychic life in her later books, *An Experiment in Leisure, On Not Being Able to Paint,* and *Eternity's Sunrise: A Way of Keeping a Diary* through the various forms of tadpoles, serpents, goats, and ducks, to name but a few. In *An Experiment*, a centipede comes to portray and give body and life to something akin to a bad internal object, which she describes in the following passage: "When in bed I turned inwards to find my spacious inner fact, but in place of the usual feeling of delight I saw the image of a huge stinging centipede. I tried not to shrink from it but to accept it, there, at the heart of what I felt to be most intimately me" (47). This cast of animal forms bestows a representability to the psyche, literally animating the mind and objects of the inner world. "So vivacious are these images," writes Maud Ellmann about these animals in *An Experiment*, that for Ellmann "they upstage their referents, and we remember Milner's eagles, goats, bulls, fish, rhinoceros, and butterflies more vividly than what they stand for" (xxxiii). These portraits of her mental life themselves come to take on a life of their own.

In *A Life* Milner presents herself as something of a trailblazing lone explorer, discovering the techniques of free writing for the first time. Milner, however, along with her contemporaries would have been well acquainted with the techniques of automatic writing and drawing that the Surrealists adopting Freud's technique of free association had earlier applied to their methods for artistic creation. (Milner's use of the term "automatic self" to describe something akin to her unconscious processes certainly seems like a nod to André Breton's notion of psychic automatism (*LOO*, 40)). More contemporaneous to Milner was the publication of Dorothea Brande's *Becoming a Writer* in the same year as *A Life* in 1934. An early proponent of what she called "freewriting," Brande encouraged aspiring writers to write continuously whatever came into their mind for 30 minutes every morning in order to help kickstart the creative process (53). There is also evidence that modernist authors experimenting with stream of consciousness writing before and during this period had a direct influence on Milner. Helen Tyson's archival research has uncovered Milner's making reference in her diaries to the writing styles of T.S. Eliot and Dorothy Richardson, the latter celebrated as one of the earliest modernist novelists to use stream of consciousness as a narrative technique (7).

Milner's indebtedness to these popular techniques of her time is not lost on the poet W.H Auden in his review of *A Life of One's Own*. In his piece "To Unravel Unhappiness" published in *The Listener* in 1934 Auden situates Milner's book within the contemporary writing techniques of their time. He writes how Milner:

> set out first to discover the nature and objects of . . . [her] . . . unhappiness and then its remedy. The technique of discovery is nothing very new and exciting now: free association writing, either off the reel or on a set subject, automatic drawings, catching the wandering thought of the moment and putting it into words, transcribing dreams and so on.
>
> (Auden, "To Unravel Unhappiness" 40)

Despite the unoriginality of these techniques, it is Milner's application of them as a psychotherapeutic method that impresses Auden, who had a life-long interest in psychoanalysis.[3] Milner's methods produce "results . . . as startling to the subject as they would be to any of us who choose to apply them" (40). "This is a remarkable, and, I think, important book" he continues, "best described as a record of auto-analysis, a detailed account of a series of experiments in minor psychotherapy" (40). Amongst his many commendations of the book, Auden finds Milner's study "throws some light on literature—that the expression of thought in words, becoming aware of it, was the beginning of a process of development and enrichment" (43). Auden picks up on what is "new" in Milner: the use of aesthetic techniques, themselves influenced by psychoanalysis, to democratise the resources of psychoanalysis.

A method to rival psychoanalysis

A Life of One's Own markets itself as a book that is both influenced by, and at odds with, the practitioners of psychoanalysis, and deeply preoccupied with staking a claim for its own distinctive therapeutic method. In her acknowledgements, Milner gives thanks to "Mary Dalston, Jan and Cora Gordon, S.G.H. Burger, and my husband, for continual help and encouragement" (*LOO* vii). Dalston was a long-standing friend, Burger the architect husband of Milner's sister Winifred, and the Gordons artists and critics whose friendship and writings on art she found influential. Finally, she thanks "Dr Elton Mayo and Dr Irma Putnam for inspiration" (vii). During her time in Boston working on the psychology fellowship with Mayo, Milner had her first experience of psychoanalysis with Dr Putnam whom she saw "two or three times a week for three months" (Letley 19). Milner provides Mayo and Putnam with a curious kind of acknowledgement, however, by adding that these two figures "were not responsible for the use to which their wisdom was put and may even be embarrassed by this acknowledgement" (*LOO* vii). In doing so, she seems to suggest that her book does something that Mayo and Putnam, figures belonging to the institutions of academic psychology and of psychoanalysis, might not entirely approve of. But in anticipating the potential for disapproval from these two figures, Milner is also making a claim for her book as doing something new and different from the methods of conventional psychological and psychoanalytic work.

The potential for disruption that Milner claims for her work loses any remnants of coy embarrassment a few pages later in her Preface. It is here that the Preface functions, not unlike Wordsworth and Coleridge's Preface to the *Lyrical Ballads* (1801), as a de facto manifesto. As Wordsworth and Coleridge's romantic exhortations for a poetry that took as its subject ordinary life—expressed in ordinary language—paved the way for a new kind of poetic sensibility, so Milner's Preface similarly claims a new method for knowing the self and one's experience. She tells us how "in connexion with my professional work I had read many descriptions of the contents and habits of the 'unconscious mind'," but "by definition [this] was something I could never by unaided effort know in myself" (xxxv). In defiance of this insistence that knowledge about oneself and one's unconscious must come via the psychoanalytic relationship, Milner presents to her reader the possibility of another, self-administered method of her own creation. She comes to find how

> the no-man's land which lay between the dark kingdom of the psychoanalyst and the cultivated domain of my conscious thought was one which I could most profitably explore for myself. I had not realized that by a few simple tricks of observation I could become aware of quite unexpected things in myself.
>
> (xxxv)

Moreover, her method is presented as providing a self-knowledge equivalent to psychoanalysis. As she "realize[s] the importance of making my thought see itself," "writing my thoughts" is considered as effective as "talking out my blind desires to someone who could give them back to me afterwards in their true light and point out to me the absurdities of what I had said" (139).

In the Retrospect to the book, Milner not only suggests the therapeutic effects of her method are comparable to that of psychoanalysis, but they are also arguably superior. For her "method might be available for anyone, quite apart from whether opportunity or intellectual capacity inclined them to the task of wading through psycho-analytic literature or their income made it possible for them to submit themselves as a patient" (159). Hers is a method available to anybody, the therapeutic practices of written expression a method with the same outcomes as psychoanalysis, but demanding only paper, pen, and some time.

Milner's own experience as a patient of talking therapy is briefly recounted in the Retrospect of the book. For the first time she reveals to her reader she has herself undergone a psychoanalysis, albeit a limited one by other's standards: "As for admitting myself as a patient, I had once managed to do that for several months, a period which would of course be considered only a preliminary stroll by the Freudian school" (159–60). But she is anxious to assure her reader that her method is not fundamentally influenced by her own short experience on the couch:

> As this analysis occurred shortly after I had begun the undertaking described in this book, I cannot in fairness omit mention of it; but I do not think it materially affected the development of my method, or that the lack of it would make such a method impossible for anyone else.
>
> (159–60)

Knowing what we do about Milner's life prior to the publication of the book in 1934, this brief, nameless description of analysis relates to Milner's only experience of being a patient of Dr Ira Putnam's in 1927. She tells the reader: "I cannot tell exactly what happened, but I certainly found it an immensely interesting experience, and it had the concrete result that before I began I had often wished that I were a man, and that after it I never had such a wish again" (159–60).[4] Despite the effectiveness that Milner claims for this analysis here—that it seems to almost miraculously cure her problem of wanting to be a man—she offers the reader little information about the methods of this analysis. She "cannot tell exactly what happened," and how she got to such a "concrete" therapeutic resolution of no longer wishing to be a man is also not divulged (159–60).

Milner writes to her mother in a letter dated February 1927 how "extraordinarily interesting" she had found the analysis with Putnam, since "one can't hope to do much with other people, unless one explores one's own unconscious a bit" (Milner qtd. in Letley 19). But by 1934 Milner wants to make clear that it is her own method for the exploration of her unconscious through self-analytical techniques that can help "other people," her reader. Indeed, the problem of getting in touch with and privileging her own psyche as a woman—which might also be understood as the cure for not wanting to be a man anymore—is shown to be achieved through her methods of self-exploration. Much later in *Bothered by Alligators*, Milner attributes the therapeutic resolution of reclaiming her identity as a woman not to the talking cure, but to *A Life*: "my writing that book showed me that I am very glad to be a woman, and not the boy I had secretly thought I was" (238). Such a transformation of being, she makes clear, is within the remits of her own methods too.

We also see dream interpretation—whether via self-analysis or the analyst's interpretations—side-lined as a therapeutic technique for self-knowledge in *A Life*. Although Milner does not explicitly reference *The Interpretation of Dreams* as part of her study, she does express an awareness of Freud's belief in dreams as the royal road to the unconscious when trying to understand her own dreams. She tells us: "In another dream I experienced feelings immediately arousing thoughts of birth and this was before I had discovered, through reading, that so-called 'birth dreams' are very common" (Milner, *LOO* 126). In her description of the book's chapter "More outcasts of thought," it is described as being about "discover[ing] that dreams can provide clues" (xi). In actuality, however, Milner turns to her dreams as a source for self-knowledge in only a handful of instances. She finds the work of dream interpretation difficult and unrewarding. "It was only occasionally, however, that I could guess at any definite meaning in my dreams" she tells us, when attempting to understand the latent preoccupations of one particular dream she calls the "White Grebe" (125). She describes how "the White Grebe dream interested me first because of the conflict of mood, ecstatic self-surrender followed by scoffing comment, but I had no idea what it meant. Then I happened to tell it to someone, who said at once, 'It meant you wanted a child.'" (125). Whilst Milner agrees with this interpretation (by a friend or her analyst at the time, Dr Putnam?—she doesn't tell us), she finds that "it puzzles me a little that I could have failed to see for myself the suggested central theme. I suppose I must have guessed that it referred to some sacrifice that I might be demanding of myself, but I had failed to interpret it in specific terms because I did not really want to face the problem" (125).

But undertaking her own dream analysis in the way Freud does so comprehensively evades her. Consequently, her failure to analyse her own dreams leads her to develop her own technique for dream interpretation. "After a time," she tells us, "I learnt how to explore for myself dreams that felt emotionally important. I learnt how, while writing down the dream, to record also the first trains of thought which thrust themselves into my mind while I wrote" (125). We observe this technique in action as Milner analyses a recurring theme that crops up in her dreaming life. She begins as the Freudian analyst might, telling us how: "I observed . . . certain recurring themes in my dreaming. One, which I have already noted, was of being overwhelmed by a tidal wave" (126). Her technique parts ways with the Freudian, however, when she goes on to write how this "was a theme which eventually pushed its way into expression through drawing" (126). For "feeling it stood for something important, [I] cast about for ways of representing it" (126). After reflecting on these drawings, insight strikes: "My mind jumped to the thought that it stood for the panic dread of being overwhelmed by the boundless sea of what was not myself" (128). Diverging from Freud's dream analysis in which he attends to mental dream-images and to the patient's associations, for Milner insight is derived from her representations of the dream in her writing and drawing about it (we see this extended in her experiments with free drawing and the creation of images for understanding herself in her later book *On Not Being Able to Paint*, explored in Chapter 2). It is in this way that her unconscious, inner world is revealed and reflected back to her via her own acts of autobiographical mark-making. Writing about the dream seems to bypass the problem of resistance of "not really want[ing] to face the problem," the meaning of the dream elucidated not through Freudian methods for dream interpretation, but through her own aesthetic techniques (125).

There is no evidence that Freud ever read or wrote about Milner's books—the majority of reviews of *A Life* at its time of publication came from newspapers and literary magazines (e.g., *The New Statesman* and *The Times Literary Supplement*), and the book did not seem to circulate amongst the contemporary psychoanalytic world of the time. Milner's method for self-analysis and therapeutic cure, however, might not have landed so unfavourably with Freud himself. As John Forrester recounts, even as psychoanalysis was a much more established profession by the 1920s, "Freud retained a sympathy for the lone dream analyst" (Forrester 115). Freud's defence of a man called E. Pickworth Farrow and his ventures into his own self-analysis following failed experiences with two London analysts, for example, went against Ernest Jones's desire to dismiss him as a maverick writer on psychoanalysis (115–16). Forrester writes that in 1926 Freud "felt sufficiently kindly towards Farrow to write a preface for his self-analytic writings, where he implicitly admonished analysts like Jones who thought the heroic times of self-analysis were thankfully over, replaced with an efficiently policed hierarchical system of professionally run analyses" (115–16).[5]

Milner's repeated characterisation of psychoanalysts in *A Life* as possessively guarding the exploration of the unconscious for themselves and their own methods might be understood in part as a response to the increasing institutionalisation of psychoanalysis in the 1930s. We might even consider Milner's project as an attempt at resuscitating the autobiographical origins of Freud's own psychoanalytic work in *The Interpretation of Dreams* with its encouragement of the layperson's forays into self-analysis. But most importantly, perhaps Milner's need to create her own method is also part of the cure for self-constitution and self-definition, a method of one's own for a life of one's own.

As we know, Milner does eventually join the institutions of psychoanalysis in completing her training with the British Psychoanalytic Society in 1943, though she was never free from a degree of ambivalence towards this parent body. In an afterword to *A Life* written in 1986, she describes the influence of her discoveries in this book and their influence on deciding to become a psychoanalyst:

> As for . . . the impact on my life and future writings, I suppose it can be said that I was so astonished at what my diary keeping had shown about the power of the unconscious aspects of one's mind, both for good and for ill, that I eventually became a psychoanalyst. As regards my writings, I could say that, with one exception, all subsequent books and articles were concerned with this aspect of human life, either with my own or with my patients.
>
> (174)

This statement almost echoes Freud's evaluation of his work in *The Interpretation of Dreams* in the preface to the third English edition in 1932, where he writes how this autobiographical book: "contains, even according to my present-day judgement, the most valuable of all the discoveries it has been my good fortune to make. Insight such as this falls to one's lot but once in a lifetime" (xxxii). Both Milner and Freud held their explorations into their own psyches through autobiographical writing in the highest esteem. Freud's career, however, was ultimately dedicated to the development of psychoanalysis as a therapeutic and psychological research endeavour. *A Life of One's Own*, on the other hand, marks the birth of a life-long engagement with the site of autobiographical mark-making that endures throughout Milner's life, and as we shall see in the next chapter, directly influences Milner's psychoanalytic thinking and clinical technique in her work with patients.

Freud did himself speak of the merits of diary keeping for the work of psychological insight. In 1915 he wrote a preface to a diary of an unnamed young girl entitled "A Young Girl's Diary," written from when she was eleven to fourteen growing up in a middle-class family in Vienna before the First World War. He testifies to the value of the document in the following passage, where he is interested in what the diary reveals about the girl's development:

> This diary is a gem. Never before, I believe, has anything been written enabling us to see so clearly into the soul of a young girl, belonging to our social and cultural stratum, during the years of puberal development. We are shown how the sentiments pass from the simple egoism of childhood to attain maturity; how the relationships to parents and other members of the family first shape themselves, and how they gradually become more serious and more intimate; how friendships are formed and broken. We are shown the dawn of love, feeling out towards its first objects. Above all, we are shown how the mystery of the sexual life first presses itself vaguely on the attention, and then takes entire possession of the growing intelligence, so that the child suffers under the load of secret knowledge but gradually becomes enabled to shoulder the burden. Of all these things we have a description at once so charming, so serious, and so artless, that it cannot fail to be of supreme interest to educationists and psychologists.
>
> (Freud, "Preface")

Here the diary is appreciated for what it can reveal about adolescent development, providing the psychologist with a tool through which to better understand the burgeoning sense of self and sexuality. In Milner's method, however, the art of diary keeping also involves the art of interpretation, the work of diarist and psychologist taken simultaneously into one's own hands.

Perhaps the most striking way of illustrating the differences in approach between Milner's method and Freudian psychoanalysis is by attending to the metaphors each uses in their work to describe their psychological endeavour. Throughout the course of his life's work, Freud, in his efforts to conceptualise his work unearthing the hidden depths of his own and his patient's psyches, frequently used archaeology as a metaphor for the work of psychoanalysis. Peter Gay considers this Freud's "master metaphor," which is evocatively described in his paper "The Aetiology of Hysteria" (1896) (Gay 16). Freud describes the process by which the analyst-archaeologist works in the following passage:

> Imagine that an explorer arrives in a little-known region where his interest is aroused by an expanse of ruins with remains of walls, fragments of columns, and tablets with half-effaced and unread-able inscriptions. He may content himself with inspecting what lies exposed to view, with questioning the inhabitants—perhaps semi-barbaric people—who live in the vicinity, about what tradition tells them of the history and meaning of these archaeological remains, and with noting down what they tell him—and he may then proceed on his journey. But he may act differently. He may have brought picks, shovels and spades with him, and he may set the inhabitants to work with these implements. Together with them he may start upon the ruins, clear away the rubbish, and, beginning from the visible remains, uncover what is buried.
>
> (Freud, "The Aetiology of Hysteria" 1)

In this description, Freud paints a picture of the archaeologist, and by implication the psychoanalyst, who with the help of the local "barbarians"—presumably parts of the patient and their unconscious—employs the tools for discovering the hidden unconscious depths of the mind's terrain. This excavation is here depicted as a work of joint effort between the patient/local barbarian who inhabits this land and the archaeologist/analyst. Despite the colonial imagery and pejorative terms that Freud uses to characterise this local other, the imagery nonetheless implies the necessity for this kind of work to be done within some kind of relationship. But if we were to identify the "master metaphor" that defines Milner's project in *A Life of One's Own*, we would find an entirely different scene to that of Freud's in the scenes of Robinson Crusoe's adventures, where the solitary act of journal writing is the most powerful tool in the explorer's arsenal.

An Experiment in Leisure (1937)

A Life's successor, *An Experiment in Leisure*, follows a similar narrative arc to *A Life* in recounting how different ways of writing, but also reading, and in some instances, drawing is able to enhance therapeutic self-insight. Like its predecessor, *An Experiment* establishes itself as a method to rival that of the psychoanalytic talking cure. "Of course I knew that such a method would bring to light material that the psycho-analyst would claim was only his to interpret," she tells us, but in defence of her method "as most of us have to learn to reflect upon our lives without a daily hour of help from the psychoanalyst, I did not let this knowledge daunt me" (Milner, *EIL* xliv).

In this book Milner continues to explore the therapeutic powers of free associative diary writing, but she also extends her experimentations to the writing of a long-form fairy tale, titled "The Death's Head Emperor" and reproduced in its entirety in the book. In *A Life* Milner tells us of her uninterest in reading "fairy tales and stories of fantasy written for adults," which "rather bored me," though she recognises they can reflect her unconscious inner workings, since "I only had to scratch the surface of my thinking in order to slip through to mythological levels" (122). In *An Experiment* Milner takes the leap into writing her own fairy tale to see whether she might learn something about her own mythic depths, citing the advice of an (unnamed) man "who had especially studied the habits of this thing called the ID" (49). This unnamed expert of the ID that Milner references seems to have taken Freud's principles of free association in the consulting room and applied it to the writing of a fairy tale. Accordingly, "if an adult could bring himself to write a fairy tale, simply letting the story flow and describing whatever impossible happenings occurred to him, without any forethought or criticism, then the story would show in allegorical terms just what was going on in the deeper levels of his mind" (49).

Although she finds she can neither fully understand nor explain what the fairy tale she eventually produces is about, writing the story is felt to be helpful as it too reveals to her a deeper level of her psyche and inner world. As another technique for reflecting herself, storytelling gives Milner a new source by which she can give birth to her inner contents. As we have seen, however, the pleasure is not in the act of creation itself, that is to say, to give expression to an imaginative vision, but to produce further material for self-reflection—and by self-reflection, to gain greater awareness of the vividness of her own subjectivity. It is bringing the vividness of herself into being, rather than the artwork as such, that is Milner's primary aim. It is nonetheless the poet W.B. Yeats who affirms for her this finding—she writes how: "Yeats was right: forms of which man expresses his being alive are as powerful a force for change, though in a different way, as any deliberate attempt to get things done, because it is these which change men's hearts—particularly one's own heart" (140).

As we have seen, Milner's methods in *A Life* resist certain types of reading, especially the reading of psychology and sociology books. In *An Experiment,* however, the status of reading shifts drastically as Milner turns to different kinds of texts. Reading books about mythology, novels, and plays comes to feed the self-insight she craves. In magpie-fashion, she tells us how her new technique is to "pick whatever stood out in my memory, not just after each day, as I had tried to do once before, but for the whole of my life, from hobbies, from journeys, from books I had read, plays I had seen, as well as from moments of everyday living" (xliv). For example, for some time she finds herself greatly preoccupied by the image of a sacrificial horned goat creature. Her reading of mythological stories and texts on witchcraft triggers thoughts about her conflicted desires for submission, coming to see "the intimate problems of everyday living and loving and perceiving in terms of witchcraft and pagan ritual" (111). This is a way of reading that reliably reflects the self, her subjectivity dramatised on the page even in the writings and images of others. In this book, whatever Milner reads, writes, or draws has a way of leading back to herself and her inner conflicts.

Another example is her reading of Sean O'Casey's play *Within the Gates*. A well-known play, it is chosen as another source used to inform her about her own subjectivity. Having enjoyed seeing a performance of the play Milner is left puzzled as to its meaning. She thinks she might achieve some understanding by writing down a summary of the play for herself (74). But as writing down the facts of her life failed to generate insight, writing down the facts of the plot also falls short. She dismisses other interpretations of the play she comes across, believing that O'Casey must be doing more than simply using "a clever formalized and poetic technique to convey a picture of modern life as he sees it" (78). She then decides that

> Whether all this was the "true" interpretation of the play or not, was no concern of mine; I thought there might be several other versions—for instance, the purely psycho-analytic one, or the author's own account of what he meant, which I thought would most likely be quite different from the one I had given. But this did not worry me, since my sole concern at the moment was to borrow forms, no matter from where, by means of which my own obscure preoccupations could declare themselves.
>
> (81)

In her urgency to see herself represented in the O'Casey work, Milner interprets the play as an allegory of the inner struggle of the character of the Dreamer: "the Dreamer and the Prostitute would be the two sides of himself, and the Prostitute would stand for his sense of his own weakness, for the part of his mind that was receptive and therefore continually possessed by others" (81). This method of reading is an act of projection that uses O'Casey's play in such a way as to allow her to see herself—her reading of the play defined by her own preoccupations with feeling possessed by others. The stresses and strains of her inner life are superimposed on the playwright's creation, his work like a screen for hire.

The answering activity

It is in *An Experiment in Leisure* that Milner first conceives of "the answering activity," a term that I think clarifies the aims of Milner's therapeutic project in both this book and its predecessor, *A Life of One's Own*. Borne out of the techniques

Milner develops for representing parts of her mind on the page through various ways of writing, and some drawing, the answering activity is first described in *An Experiment in Leisure* (1937) as the following:

> Just in so far as I held myself still and watched the flickering movements of the mind, trying to give them expression in words or drawings, just so far would I become aware of some answering activity, an activity that I can only describe as a knowing, yet a knowing that was nothing to do with me; it was a knowing that could see forwards and backwards and in a flash give form to the confusions of everyday living and to the chaos of sensation. I still felt I was being lived by something not myself, but now it seemed like something I could trust, something that knew better than I did where I was going.
>
> (138)

In this passage, the only description of the term in the book, the answering activity seems to embody an important function for psychic health. It describes the capacity for the transformation of feelings of chaos and confusion into a trusted sense of organised knowledge about self and world.

It is only in 1987 in her book *Eternity's Sunrise: A Way of Keeping a Diary*, written after almost 45 years of practicing as a psychoanalyst, that Milner resumes her work developing and conceptualising a cure that takes place at the site of diary keeping, specifically the travel diary, and where she reengages with the term answering activity. Here, she places it within the framework of Kleinian terminology, writing how as a "a well-trained psychoanalyst I have learned to use that clumsy name for it, 'the good internalised object'" (Milner, *ES* 57). Apart from expressing resentment, perhaps, at having other people's ideas foisted on her, the answering activity from this perspective seems to embody the qualities of the experience of a good relationship to an external figure, which becomes internalised as the good object. Milner's earlier, pre-psychoanalytic description of the answering activity in *An Experiment* is, I think, a prescient description of a particular psychic function that bears a striking resemblance to later post-Kleinian object relations theory about the role of the mother in providing psychic functions to ensure the healthy growth of the infant's cognitive and emotional capacities. Wilfred Bion's theory of container and contained comes immediately to mind. The mother, through her acts of free-floating emotional receptivity (what Bion calls "reverie") to the baby's emotional condition, contains the baby's projected nonverbal feelings of intolerable fear or distress. By metabolising and processing these projections through attentive care, she hands them back to the infant in such a way that these emotions can be reintegrated by the child with some degree of meaning. In Milner's description of what the answering activity does, in "giving form to the confusions of everyday living and to the chaos of sensation," her description is suggestive of a similar kind of function (138).

This reference to trusting something knowing is also reminiscent of Winnicott's later paper "Mind and its relation to the psyche-soma" (1954). Here Winnicott links one of his patient's fear of death to a fear of "not-knowing" (206). Knowl-edge in this paper is about the infant's having experienced reliable behaviour from its caregiver; in other words, an environment in which one can have confidence in and going on being. Eventually, through the course of the analysis, "[a]cceptance of not-knowing produced tremendous relief" since ' "[k]nowing" became trans-formed into "the analyst knows," that is to say, "behaves reliably in active adapta-tion to the patient's needs" (206). To be known is to exist, in the same way that to be seen is to exist. Winnicott as the adaptive analyst can, in knowing and seeing the patient, reflect back the patient's existence, making up for early environmental failures that failed to support a sense of continuity of being. This is a description that resonates with the answering activity and its ability to provide a sense of "knowing, yet a knowing that was nothing to do with me; it was a knowing that could see forwards and backwards" (Milner, *EIL* 138).

Milner's description of the answering activity also bears similarity to another psychoanalytic concept that comes decades after the genesis of Milner's term: Winnicott's notion of mirroring, theorised in his chapter "Mirror-role of Mother and Family in Child Development" in *Playing and Reality* (1971). Winnicott's mirror function emphasises how the infant's emotional development and sense of self or sense of continuity of being is predicated on the mother being able to reflect "back to the baby the baby's own self" (5). It is the adaptive, good enough mother who can allow the infant to see itself reflected in its mother's gaze: "The mother is looking at the baby and what she looks like is related to what she sees there" (2). If instead the mother reflects back to the baby her own moods and defences this "brings a threat of chaos, and the baby will organize withdrawal, or will not look except to perceive, as a defence" (2). Similar to the function of mirroring, the answering activity describes an experience of a relationship that involves an agreeable responsiveness, the fruits of a relationship with another that is receptive, engaged and attuned with oneself. Milner's answering activ-ity seems to provide an equivalent function to mirroring, plus a sense of being known, understood, and accepted without judgement. Acts of writing and drawing thus help to ameliorate feelings of chaos, reflecting—answering—back a clearer sense of self and world.

Both the functions of containment and mirroring are to be provided within the context of intersubjective relations. It is the mother in early life who contains or mirrors the infant, and it is also the psychoanalyst who can provide for the patient in later life these caring functions. As Milner writes in *An Experiment*, however, it is by attending to "the flickering movements of the mind, trying to give them expression in words or drawings" that she "become[s] aware of some answering activity" (138). Crucially, it is autobiographical expression that puts one in contact with the answering activity. Whereas Winnicott locates the mirroring function in the face of the mother, Milner's answering activity isn't to be searched for in the visages of caregivers. In *Eternity's Sunrise* she writes how the answering activ-ity, perhaps invoking a comparison with Winnicott's mirror role of the mother, "does seem such a bodily thing, one's own body, not up there, not sought for in one's mother's (or father's) loving face looking down on one." (57). Whilst she concedes that "[s]omeone, even if not actually one's mother, must have given a minimum of mercy, pity, peace and love or else one would not be alive at all," the attuning, mirroring, and containing functions of the answering activity are to be found in one's own creative acts, away from the other (57). The answering activity is, I think, a term that embodies Milner's own failed search for "peace and love" in the faces of her caregivers, a search that instead turns to her own autobiographical acts of mark-making for emotional nourishment (57).

It is striking then that Milner's metaphor of answering invokes more powerfully than other object relations terms the dialogue and conversation that takes place within a relationship. In a diary note reproduced in *Eternity's Sunrise* Milner wonders: "Can I talk to it, this Answering Activity? More than just saying, 'I leave it to you', or 'Please help,' which I did as far back as I can remember" (57). In another diary entry the answering activity is personified further as Milner wonders "what it might be like to live in constant reference to this 'other', this answering activity?" (52). The answering activity gives a "feeling of partnership, of plugging into a presence, an active 'something' that is both 'I' and 'not I' and which gives me the feeling that I am not alone" (57). What if, Milner asks, "first thing on waking, one could plug in to the answering activity—or the Answering Activity?" Given the proper noun of a person, it would be "like waking and finding the person you love beside you" (97). Writing and drawing about the self is felt to powerfully put one in touch with an internalised experience of a good object relation. Whilst it may not originate itself from within a good relationship, it has the capacity to invoke it. As we have seen, this also applies to how Milner understands her autobiographical acts in *A Life* and *An Experiment* as providing an equivalent therapeutic function to the "talking cure" between patient and analyst.

In *An Experiment* these answering techniques are again championed and defended on the grounds of their therapeutic efficacy. Milner does concede that "since living is such a complicated business, it was of course very difficult to prove whether any of the changes I observed were definitely the result of the method I had adopted" (*EIL* 165). But she attributes to her auto-reflective methods her growing capacity to learn "how to experience more fully . . . to get closer in touch with what was going on around as well as inside me" (165). She continues: "I had discovered that, not through deliberate reasoning, logic, argument, but by another process that I can only call 'image-finding', I could come closer in touch with the movement of life" (165). This term "image-finding" is used only once in this book and never again, but I think it describes a similar function as the answering activity in the ability of certain types of autobiographical acts to provide a reflection and knowledge about the self, and that ensure a fuller and more solid sense of being. The term image-finding comes even closer perhaps than the answering activity to describing something akin to the function of mirroring. "Answering" evokes the register of voice, of language; "image-finding" on the other hand evokes images of the self that are reflected from the page rather than in the facial expressions of another. Milner's reading of literature, myths, and biblical stories provides her with "storehouses of vital images" (144). It is particularly in religious imagery that she finds "images that seemed to me to be concerned with finding out the truth of the experience of being alive" (109).

Eternity's Sunrise focuses on the genre of the travel diary, where ways of getting in touch with the answering activity are sought for in writing about the sights and landscapes of her adventures. Her attentions turn to the sights of the ancient ruins of Greece, the mountainous terrains of Kashmir and the biblical landscapes of Israel. In one free written diary note, Milner meditates on the vision of a tent she saw on a hillside during a car journey back to the Israeli city of Tiberius. She describes the significance of "the idea of a woven tent somehow linked up with . . . my own struggles to weave the cocoon or bodily tent containing the dark inner states" (Milner, *ES* 151). She also records the many souvenirs and relics she picks up on her travels, a motley assortment of objects used to stimulate memories, springboards for imaginative conjecture. A reliquary from Mykonos, a carved life-size duck from Torcello, and a piece of asphodel from Delphi, amongst others, inspire free written diary notes that provide self-insight. The world becomes something like a mirror ball, answering and reflecting her wherever she chooses to go.

I am not sure that Milner's descriptions of the answering activity amount to a definitive or comprehensive definition of the term. Her slippery, very personal writings about the answering activity suggest that she was not aiming to formulate a cohesive and comprehensive psychological concept as such. Perhaps it follows, then, that the term has received scant commentary from other psychoanalytic thinkers. The only psychoanalyst I am aware of who has written about the term, Michael Parsons, finds it evades simple definition, writing how "the nature of the Answering Activity is a question with no simple answer" (219). But he recognises that "Milner is in no doubt that the development of an inner relationship to something which is both oneself and other than oneself can produce a transformation of one's being" (219). As I have suggested, this transformation of being is for Milner produced by acts of written expression. Since Milner's concept shifts the psychic functions of the answering activity away from the site of intersubjectivity to that of autobiographical activity, it is unsurprising that the term has slipped through the net of psychoanalytic attention. In my reading of her work, however, the answering activity is central to an understanding of Milner as a thinker and as a psychoanalyst. It is a term that helps us to understand what kind of therapeutic work Milner understands as taking place within the pages of her autobiographical books.

Milner herself recognises having for a long time overlooked the importance of the answering activity in her thinking about her work. Reflecting on the term in *Eternity's Sunrise*, she writes:

> my mind went back to *An Experiment in Leisure* and a term that I supposed I must have first used then, the term "answering activity". I could not remember just when it had appeared and, although I had at times tried to make a kind of index of the main ideas in that book, when I now looked through this

I could not find that the term "answering activity" was even referred to, much less given pride of place. This was surprising because it seemed to me now that this was really what the whole book was about.

(51)

In her final book, *Bothered by Alligators*, she goes even further in recognising the importance of the term, defining all her books about diary writing (what she calls here her "three Joanna Field-type books," *A Life of One's Own, An Experiment in Leisure,* and *Eternity's Sunrise* as involving the answering activity (267)). She tells us how: "my struggle to trust the A.A., the answering activity, or whatever one chooses to call this something that I knew from experiences does need to be trusted, in spite of its being so hidden . . . this is what my books have been about" (267). These are books, therefore, about getting in touch with this internal goodness that answers through acts of autobiographical mark-making, through capturing self and mind on paper. Drawing from both Milner's own descriptions of the term and my own analysis of Milner's work, I understand the answering activity as describing a particular caring function that aids self-definition and provides a sense of "continuity of being," in Winnicott's terms, of a sense of self as existing across time.

Bead memories

As well as attending to the answering activity in *Eternity's Sunrise*, much of the book is dedicated to recording in her diary particular moments of personal significance, what Milner terms "bead memories." Her definition of a bead memory is characteristically enigmatic. She describes them as "being rooted in sensory experience, yet having a particular feeling quality, a warmth or glow, something which came in response to my asking myself the simple question, 'What is the most important thing that has happened today?'" (Milner, *ES* 172). As writing provides an answering activity that organises the chaos of experience into knowledge about the self that can be known, the bead memories seem to denote a function where subjective experience is made tangible and intelligible. Her concept of the bead memory emerges from thinking about the various "trophies and keepsakes," such as the clay life-size duck she picked up on her travels in Italy (3). From here, Milner turns to creating something like her own psychic objects that might be collected as one collects souvenirs, but which tell you more about the landscape and culture of the inner world than that of the external. These psychic objects, gathered and recorded in diaries, are felt to helpfully provide evidence of a self— souvenirs of selfhood, if you like.

Milner writes of her efforts to "collect" the bead memories to provide herself with "a little string of beads" (164).[6] In this way, memories are conceived as having the qualities of the material world, and the psychic creation of a bead is likened to the process of creating an aesthetic object from clay. In turning to free writing to explore what the word "bead" means to her, she remembers the following episode from her childhood:

Finding yellow clay in the ditch at the bottom of our garden, rolling it into beads and then baking them in the sun and painting them in bright colours. And then, too, making the clay into a little pot and burying it overnight in the ashes of the nursery fire. In the morning, raking it out, what astonishment, it had turned from a dirty yellow into a lovely pinkish red. Yes, out of the ashes comes the transformation.

(171)

Here the mental activity of creating a bead is given the physicality of the artisan's creative labour. Memory and subjective experience are something to be made, composed, and crafted. Hugh Haughton, in his introduction to *Eternity's Sunrise*, understands the beads as "enigmatic moments of importance," akin to Virginia Woolf's moments of being ("New Introduction" xxx). To this we might also add Wordsworth's "spots of time"—another term that aims to describe moments of significant experience captured in words. Milner's bead memory I think places a particular emphasis on endowing memory and experience with a solidly material and physical quality. Haughton's take on the nature of the beads picks up on this: "When something becomes a 'bead' . . . it can be fingered and stroked and reflected upon and moved from one place to another, long after the journey it is encountered on is over" (Haughton, "New Introduction" xxx). In recording the beads Milner provides herself with "the launch-pad for the metamorphosis of the moment into an object in the psychic afterlife, place where memory can be polished up into something aesthetically satisfying, ontologically charged and intellectually questioning" (Haughton, "The Milner Experiment: Psychoanalysis and the Diary" 357).

John Fielding's review of *Eternity's Sunrise* also observes the importance of the tactile nature of Milner's efforts in the book more generally, writing how: "extracts from her diaries or notebooks are quoted and meditated on, or rather, turned over, handled—one wants a word that conveys the physicality of the activity" (66). Her practice of recording subjective experience in writing, and then treating these written experiences as if they possess a material quality seems to be a powerful way of providing her subjectivity with a sense of form, shape, and in her earlier words, with "crystallization" (Milner, *EIL* 129). This is, I think, another strategy for giving form to a sense of self that threatens to feel formless, the feeling that "you are as nothing" with "nothing to say, nothing to feel, nothing to be" (195). Milner's collecting of bead memories in her diaries and notebooks is thus another technique for providing the fledgling self with a sense of selfhood, identity, being.

In his new introduction to *Eternity's Sunrise,* Haughton likens the bead memories to a "tourist equivalent of Winnicott's transitional objects" (xxvii). The bead memories "help you leave home, but also to find representations of a larger psychic home on your travels, to take back home with you, and to assert your fundamental belonging to a holding environment which is simultaneously culture and nature, cosmic and personal" (xxvii). Whichever way we might understand or interpret the nature of Milner's term, the bead memory is undoubtedly another term that fits in the psychoanalytically inflected, object relations framework of

Milner's thinking. Along with the answering activity, the bead memory is a term that describes different curative functions of autobiographical mark-making. The act of collecting bead memories through diary writing and the diary as receptacle or container for the beads introduces another way in which the therapeutic potential of diary keeping is explored.

This way of understanding the diary's potential for emotional transformation is not dissimilar from later psychologists Wendy Wiener and George Rosenwald who in their study, "A Moment's Monument: The Psychology of Keeping a Diary" (1993), consider how the diarist is provided with a continuous sense of self and a way objectifying their experiences. In a summary of their findings, we learn how:

> As the diary permits the evocation of fantasies about the self and the sedimentation of these fantasies on the written (and thus readable) page, the diary functions for the objectivation as well as transformation of the self. The keeping of a diary is an activity that binds self in time, not only across the span of a long-term diary, but also within each entry. Each entry is made with an intention to read it later and to add further entries, to return as reader and writer. The diary-writing thus serves as an instrument of self-continuity.
>
> (Paperno 564)

Here we find another description of the varieties of psychological functions of diary keeping Milner champions in her concept of the bead memory. The term bead memory embodies this notion of the diary providing an objectification of the self that then leads to a kind of transformation.

Milner's acknowledgements to *Eternity's Sunrise* are as revealing as those she provides in *A Life*, both addressing the disconnect between her autobiographical work and that of psychoanalysis. The acknowledgements in *Eternity's Sunrise* read as follows:

> The list of people I have to thank for, indirectly, making this book possible, both the living and the dead, would make another book and would include all those from whom I have learned how to become a psychoanalyst. All I can name here are the few friends, not themselves psychoanalysts, who have actually read the manuscript. They are: Jean Kadmon, Mary Dalston, Alexander Newman, Mary Pears and Susannah Richmond. Their response to it convinced me that I should try to make public this account of what has been an essentially private enterprise, one growing out of my own need to try and sort out what being alive really means to me.
>
> (viii)

This book then is essentially borne out of the encouragement of non-analysts and her own personal experimentations at the site of autobiographical writing. This other book that would need to be written to include acknowledgements from those she "learned how to become a psychoanalyst" is perhaps not as imaginary as Milner suggests here (viii). In the same year *Eternity's Sunrise* is published in 1987, the collection of her psychoanalytic papers *The Suppressed Madness of Sane Men: Forty-Four Years of Exploring Psychoanalysis* is also published. Her dedication in this latter book does in one fell swoop address the world of psychoanalysis— she writes: "*To the British Psycho-Analytical Society Warts and all—gratefully*" (Milner, *SMSM* v). This dedication to psychoanalysis, spiced with a pinch of reticence, is a sentiment that laces itself throughout Milner's writing.

In *Eternity's Sunrise* there is a "central image" Milner refers to that I think embodies her project in this book and her work as a whole (Milner, *ES* 42). It is an image she takes from an account of the art critic John Ruskin's travels across Europe, where during one journey Ruskin had "felt so ill that he had lain down by the roadside and thought he would die, but then found himself staring at an aspen tree and felt impelled to draw it. Having done so he then found himself totally recovered and able to continue his journey" (49). Ruskin's means of self-recuperation strikes a chord with Milner. Like her identification with Robinson Crusoe in *A Life*, it depicts an explorer whose solo acts of mark-making prove resuscitative and lifesaving. The creative gesture is imbued with the almost miraculous power to bring back the self from near psychic death.

* * *

How might the concepts of the answering activity and bead memory enrich our understanding of the autobiographical subject, and of the autobiographical act? Writers, and those engaged with life writing and autobiographical expression, have long connected the work of writing about the self with procuring self-knowledge and fostering self-development. In this sense, the notion of the "writing cure" is nothing new. But Milner's work, and her notions of the answering activity and bead memory elevate the therapeutic powers of writing, particularly diary keeping, to the equivalent heights of what object relations theory understands a caring relationship as providing. We might then call the answering activity an intrasubjective internal object relations concept for the work of writing and drawing, involving relations to oneself and a medium, rather than intersubjective relations with another.

The concept of the answering activity, I think, provides us with a new way of thinking about the nature of the autobiographical subject. For a long time, autobiography was characterised as a monologic form of expression, a solipsistic genre of writing. Applications of work by thinkers like Mikhail Bakhtin and his notion of the dialogic, have, however, shifted our understanding of the autobiographer as necessarily writing within a relational framework. The autobiographer always writes for an interlocutor, imagined reader, or audience. Eva Karpinski writes how "Bakhtin's understanding that one is a self only vis-a-vis another epitomizes both the constitution of the autobiographical subject and the social life of autobiography" (Karpinski 202–3). So much of one's sense of self is unavoidably "received [and mediated] through the consciousness and thought of others (one's birth, external appearance, and so forth)" (293). If the writer is always in dialogue with another, the answering activity describes the particular, important qualities of what that which answers can do for one emotionally. In essence, the answering activity provides an object relations understanding of the relational through which to understand the act of writing about the self. If, as scholars like Harris Williams understand autobiography as a form of writing which like psychoanalysis attempts to answer the question of 'who am I?', then the answering activity is a compelling way of understanding autobiographical writing and drawing as an intrinsically relational mode for constituting identity.

My reading of the answering activity as embodying something akin to Winnicott's idea of mirroring also provides a new perspective on a metaphor that has long been associated with the work of autobiography, that of the mirror. Charles Rycroft, in his essay "On Autobiography" (1983) employs the metaphor to describe how the autobiographer's work involves a confrontation not with a single, unitary self, but with multiple selves, so that for the work of autobiography the "appropriate visual analogy ceases to be that of a painter painting a self-portrait and becomes that of someone occupying a temporal corridor of mirrors and communing in turn with images of past and present selves" (Rycroft qtd. in Marcus, "Autobiography and Psychoanalysis" 259). Implied is a sense of gradually discovering different aspects of the self through writing, that can become integrated into a fuller sense of identity.[7]

Susanna Egan's *Mirror Talk: Genres of Crisis in Contemporary Autobiography* (1999) reinterprets the metaphor of the mirror for which to describe contemporary autobiography as involving dialogue and reflexivity—what she describes as "mirror talk" which involves "a two-way reflection" by which the autobiographer engages intersubjectively with the reader and audience "so as to overcome the other's alterity and enter into dialogue" (193). Autobiography is for Egan "an interactive genre even at the very simple level of what one might call 'interpersonal relations'" (qtd. in Eakin 56). In a closer vein to Milner, Marilyn Chandler emphasises how writing about the self can provide an intrasubjective, mirroring dialogue. For the autobiographer, "the written page is his mirror. In that dialogue he discovers a self that comes into being in the act of writing. The contents of the unconscious may first appear there in a form that allows them to be recognized and dealt with" (Chandler 117). The concept of the answering activity along with Milner's insights into the capacity for writing to bring self into being does, I think, deepen such analyses.

The genre of diary writing can be seen as an address to the self and the medium of the diary, rather than with another person. As the cliched address "Dear Diary" suggests, the diary itself has long been spoken to by diarists as a friend or intimate and trusted interlocutor. Whilst Milner does not explicitly do this, the diary does intermittently provide her contact with a good, trustworthy object. Her particular method of free written diary keeping and its capacity to put her in touch with the answering activity expands our understanding of the ways in which diary keeping might be considered a therapeutic practice. Philippe Lejeune's pioneering work on diaries resonates with what Milner claims her work does. Lejeune writes in his chapter, "The Continuous and Discontinuous" in *On Diary,* how: "the diary creates continuity, not only between today and yesterday, but also across the whole span of one's life. Can it give us access to a fundamental permanence?", he wonders (184). Certainly, the diary can help "to build a memory out of paper, to create archives from lived experience, to accumulate traces, prevent forgetting, to give life the consistency and continuity it lacks" (195). Milner's notion of the bead memory I think embodies Lejeune's sense of how a diary can aid in the objectification of the self and create something like a souvenir for one's being.

Lejeune identifies the four main functions of diary keeping as "expression, reflection, memory, and the pleasure of writing" (194). Concerning reflection, the "diary offers a space and time protected from the pressures of life. You take refuge in its calm to 'develop the image of what you have just lived through and to meditate upon it, and to examine the choices to be made'" (195). Lejeune makes an interesting comparison between diary writing and psychoanalysis. He states: "It is said that psychoanalysis is 'interminable.' But it is also said that you can do it in 'pieces.' These pieces must certainly be cut somewhere. Surely then, you leave a diary the way you leave an analyst" (195). The analogy stops short here in Lejeune's writing, but I think he touches upon a quality of diary keeping, that if sustained, can help with gathering up the self in its many parts—not dissimilar to work that can be done on the psychoanalytic couch. This is a comparison that *A Life of One's Own* certainly upholds, launching Milner into the world as a thinker and practitioner of her own autobiographical cure.

In 1939 Milner begins training in London to become a psychoanalyst, taking on two patients five times a week for the first time, and becoming a patient herself over a number of years as part of her own training analysis. Whilst 1939 might mark the beginning of her institutional psychoanalytic life, the publication of *A Life* in 1934 marks the beginning of her other therapeutic endeavour. A little note of Milner's on this period captures the extent to which she continued in the spirit of *A Life* despite joining the ranks of the psychoanalysts she had once competed with. On being accepted for training she "tried to keep a diary of misgivings about the theory I was trying to learn and when I came to give seminars myself I sometimes advised my students to do the same" (Milner, *ES* 9). We shall see this spirit of playful irreverence that we first encounter in *A Life* continue to flourish throughout her subsequent works, spurring on her commitment to her own therapeutic methods.

Notes

1   Helen Tyson has read Milner's rhetoric here as connected to a modernist fear of masses, mass commodification, and the rise of fascism. See "'Catching butterflies': Marion Milner and stream of consciousness writing" (2020).

2   Though Milner does not name this mental training system in *A Life*, it is likely she is referring to Pelmanism, a mnemonic self-help method taught by correspondence which she started whilst working under the industrial psychologist Cyril Burt (Letley 17). The Pelman system promised to cure such problems as a "grasshopper mind," depression, phobia, procrastination and, most tellingly, a "Lack of System" in its participants ("The Man with the 'Grasshopper Mind'" 33). In an interview Milner states she tried "'Pelmanism'. . . it said you've got to know what your aim in life is. And I got stuck there because I hadn't any idea what my aim in life was. So I decided the best thing to do was to make a diary" ("Me and Not Me").

3 Auden's poem "In Memory of Sigmund Freud" (1939) reflects upon the death of Sigmund Freud.
4 The psychoanalytic account of the wish to be a man be in the 1930s would likely have been through Freud's theory of penis envy and Daniel Paul Schreber's account of transsexualism in his book *Memoirs of My Nervous Illness*. During the 1920s and 1930s there was also much written about the feminine superego and the vicissitudes of the Oedipus complex.
5 The psychoanalyst Theodore Reik who was one of Freud's first students in Vienna proposed in 1949 in his work *The Inner Experience of a Psychoanalyst* that his reader might engage with free associative writing experiments to come to know the self, reminiscent of Milner's:
   The reader is invited to take paper and pencil and to write down whatever occurs to him during the next half-hour. He should eliminate all censorship of his thoughts while he writes. . . . He should then put the written sheets into a drawer and leave the room. When he takes them out the next day, he will meet a person there who reminds him of himself in many ways but is in other ways an unknown man. Was it he who thought all that? Here is a new I to whom he gets introduced." (Reik qtd. in Marcus, "Autobiography and Psychoanalysis" 264)
6 This is reminiscent of Freud's likening memories to "a string of pearls" in his paper "The Aetiology of Hysteria" (196).
7 There is a long tradition of using mirrors to reflect on the self: see Sabine Melchior-Bonnet's *The Mirror: A History* (1994).

References

Auden, W.H. "To Unravel Unhappiness." *The Listener*, vol. 12, no. 307, 1934, pp. 40–43.
Bowlby, Rachel. "New Introduction." *A Life of One's Own*, edited by Marion Milner. Routledge, 2011. http://dx.doi.org/10.4324/9780203817193
Chandler, Marilyn. *A Healing Art: Regeneration through Autobiography*. Routledge, 1990. http://dx.doi.org/10.4324/9781315673837
Chodorow, Nancy. *The Reproduction of Mothering: Psychoanalysis and the Sociology of Gender*. California University Press, 1999. http://dx.doi.org/10.1525/9780520924086
Eakin, Paul John. *How Our Lives Become Stories*. Cornell, 1999. http://dx.doi.org/10.7591/9781501711831
Egan, Susanna. *Mirror Talk: Genres of Crisis in Contemporary Autobiography*. North Carolina University Press, 1999.
Ellmann, Maud. "New Introduction." *An Experiment in Leisure*, edited by Marion Milner. Routledge, 2011. http://dx.doi.org/10.4324/9780203816769
Fielding, John. "Telling the Beads: A Review of Eternity's Sunrise by John Fielding." *A Celebration of the Life and Work of Marion Milner, Special Issue of Winnicott Studies: The Journal of the Squiggle Foundation*, vol. 3, 1988, pp. 64–68.
Forrester, John. "Dream Readers." *Sigmund Freud's the Interpretation of Dreams: New Interdisciplinary Essays*, edited by Laura Marcus, Manchester University Press, 1999, pp. 83–122.
Freud, Sigmund. "Preface." *A Young Girl's Diary* (translated by Eden, and Cedar Paul), *Project Gutenberg*, 1919. www.gutenberg.org/files/752/752-h/752-h.htm. Accessed 7 May 2021.
Freud, Sigmund. "The Aetiology of Hysteria." *The Standard Edition of the Complete Psychological Works of Sigmund Freud*, edited by J. Strachey, translated by J. Strachey, and A. Freud (24 vols., vol. III). The Hogarth Press and the Institute of Psychoanalysis, 1896/1962.

Freud, Sigmund. ""Wild" psycho-analysis." *The Standard Edition of the Complete Psychological Works of Sigmund Freud*, edited by J. Strachey, translated by J. Strachey, and A. Freud (24 vols., vol. XI). The Hogarth Press and the Institute of Psychoanalysis, 1910/1957.

Gay, Peter. *Freud: A Life for Our Time*. W.W. Norton, 1988.

Haughton, Hugh. "New Introduction." *Eternity's Sunrise: A Way of Keeping a Diary*, edited by Marion Milner. Routledge, 2011. http://dx.doi.org/10.4324/9780203720677

Haughton, Hugh. "The Milner Experiment: Psychoanalysis and the Diary." *British Journal of Psychotherapy*, vol. 30, no. 3, 2014, pp. 349–362. http://dx.doi.org/10.1111/bjp.12097

Karpinski, E.C. ""Broken Dialogues," or Finding Bakhtin in Auto|Biography Studies." *A/B: Auto/Biography Studies*, vol. 30, no. 2, 2015, pp. 199–215. http://dx.doi.org/10.1080/08989575.2015.1088714

Lejeune, Philippe. *On Diary* (edited by Jeremy D. Popkin, and Julie Rak, translated by Kathy Durnin). Hawai'i University Press, 2009. http://dx.doi.org/10.1515/9780824863784

Letley, Emma. *Marion Milner: The Life*. Routledge, 2014. http://dx.doi.org/10.4324/9780203767122

Marcus, Laura. "Autobiography and Psychoanalysis." *On Life-writing*, edited by Zachary Leader. Oxford University Press, 2015, pp. 257–283.

McCraken, LuAnn. " 'The Synthesis of My Being': Autobiography and the Reproduction of Identity in Virginia Woolf." *Tulsa Studies in Women's Literature*, vol. 9, no. 1, 1900, pp. 58–78. http://dx.doi.org/10.2307/464181

Milner, Marion. *A Life of One's Own*. Routledge, 1934/2011. http://dx.doi.org/10.4324/9780203817193

Milner, Marion. *An Experiment in Leisure*. Routledge, 1937/2011. http://dx.doi.org/10.4324/9780203816769

Milner, Marion. *Bothered by Alligators*. Routledge, 2013. http://dx.doi.org/10.4324/9780203140147

Milner, Marion. *Eternity's Sunrise: A Way of Keeping a Diary*. Routledge, 1987/2011. http://dx.doi.org/10.4324/9780203720677

Milner, Marion. "Me and Not Me." *Interview with Chris Crickmay. Typed Transcript of the Interview. P01-B-B-05, Marion Milner collection*. Archives of the British Psychoanalytical Society, 1975/2020.

Milner, Marion. *The Supressed Madness of Sane Men: Forty-Four Years of Exploring Psychoanalysis*. Routledge, 1987.

Paperno, Irina. "What Can Be Done with Diaries?" *The Russian Review*, vol. 63, no. 4, 2004, pp. 561–573. http://dx.doi.org/10.1111/j.1467-9434.2004.00332.x

Parsons, Michael. "Marion Milner's 'Answering Activity' and the Question of Psychoanalytic Creativity." *International Review of Psycho-Analysis*, vol. 17, 1990, pp. 413–424.

"The Man with the 'Grasshopper Mind'." *Popular Mechanics*, vol. 53, no. 6, 1930, p. 33.

Watsky, Paul. "Marion Milner's Pre-Freudian Writings, 1926–1938: The Originality and Origins of Her Creative Model." *Journal of Analytical Psychology*, vol. 37, no. 4, 1992, pp. 455–473. http://dx.doi.org/10.1111/j.1465-5922.1992.00455.x

Winnicott, D.W. "Mind and Its Relation to the Psyche-Soma." *British Journal of Medical Psychology*, vol. 27, no. 4, 1954, pp. 201–209. http://dx.doi.org/10.1111/j.2044-8341.1954.tb00864.x

Winnicott, D.W. "Mirror-Role of Mother and Family in Child Development." *The Predicament of the Family: A Psycho-Analytical Symposium*, edited by Peter Lomas. International University Press, 1967, pp. 26–31.

Chapter 2

On Not Being Able to Paint and drawing and painting for psychoanalysis

Visitors to the Marion Milner archive at the Institute of Psychoanalysis can find, if curiosity leads them, to a small leather-bound notebook belonging to Milner when she was a child.[1] In this notebook are three handwritten short stories accompanied by illustrations, entitled "The Golden Cockle Shell," "Tootles Turn Here," and "The Kitchen Room," each telling a different tale of worlds filled with adventures with talking dogs and clothed mice. At the end of the final story is a page of faintly drawn sketches of what appear to resemble picture frames. Whilst not obviously connected with the themes of the stories, they introduce the reader to an early iteration of an engagement around frames and the scene of writing and drawing that would endure throughout the course of Milner's life and work. Almost seventy years after these childish marks are made, we meet Milner in a video-recorded interview in 1975, where she states:

> The world comes alive when we invest it with something of our inner selves. . . . To achieve this we require the temporary protection of a frame. The frame in painting is a special case of general necessity. To preserve a space in which our imagination can operate on the world as is the case when we indulge in daydreaming.
>
> (Milner with Chris Crickmay, "Me and Not Me")

The frames to which Milner refers are the literal picture frames that provide a tangible boundary to the painting, but it is also a term, as this chapter will trace, that Milner uses to describe a particular quality of emotional experience that the act of creativity as well as the psychoanalytic session can provide.[2]

On occasion, *A Life of One's Own* and *An Experiment in Leisure* mention instances of drawing as part of their methods. Their primary focus however is on free writing and diary keeping. It is in her subsequent book, *On Not Being Able to Paint* (1950), where we see Milner turn her attentions most fully to the acts of visual-marking, devising a technique for doodling or free associative drawing and painting that she terms "free drawing" (xix). In this book we find Milner, now a psychoanalyst, continuing to look beyond the psychoanalytic setting to the site of creative, autobiographical activity to come to know about her early experiences. It

DOI: 10.4324/9781003296720-4

is also in this book that we are introduced to two other terms of Milner's making: the "frame" and the "pliable medium." These two concepts reflect Milner's commitment to the curative potential of visual mark-making, and how a relationship to the artist's mediums of paper and paint, for example, can provide a reparative, substitutive experience of an attuned relationship.

This chapter will also trace in Milner's clinical papers from the 1950s and 1960s and in her case study *The Hands of the Living God: An Account of a Psycho-analytic Treatment* (1969), the influence of her findings in *On Not Being Able to Paint* on her thinking and technique as a psychoanalyst. We shall come to see how the book influences Milner's introduction of a new element into the patient–analyst relationship whereby the patient's drawing acts become a part of the analytic treatment. Milner's psychoanalytic thinking and technique thus shifts the work of psychoanalysis away from the analyst–patient relationship to the relationship of analyst and patient to the patient's creative productions. Accordingly, her method is less preoccupied with the analyst–patient dyad (the transference and countertransference) that other psychoanalysts understand as the fulcrum of insight and therapy. Milner's clinical technique, as we shall see, attends instead to the set of relations between analyst, patient, and the patient's artistic medium to understand therapeutic transformation. These innovations in the next stage of Milner's autobiographical cure are shown to be of influence and closely tied up with the development and theory-building of other object relations thinkers, including Winnicott.

In her foreword to *On Not Being Able to Paint*, Anna Freud compares Milner's findings from her study of the amateur painter's experiences to that of the analysand in their initial period on the couch. "Both ventures," writes Freud, "the analytic as well as the creative one, seem to demand similar external and internal conditions" (xiii). These include, "above all, the same terror of the unknown" (xiii). Both painter and patient must be able to tolerate a plunge into the unconscious and be able to tolerate the uncertainty of where the brush may take them, or what psychic material might arise out of the analytic encounter. The essential difference between the analytic process and the process of creation is, however, that the "legitimate result of analysis is the inner experience of formerly unknown affects and impulses which find their final outlet in the ego-processes of verbalisation and deliberate action," whereas the creative process "remains within the realm in which unknown affects and impulses find their outlet, through the way in which the artist arranges his medium . . . whether deliberate action is affected or not is the last issue" (xiv). In contrast to Freud's claims, however, this chapter will show how Milner proposes painting and drawing enacts for her and her patients a transformation of action comparable to that of the analytic process. As part of a performative, critical engagement with Milner and her patients' own heuristic methods, this chapter will be structured around a handful of images.

Exploring early infantile experience through drawing and painting

When Milner was accepted to train at the Institute of Psychoanalysis in London in 1939 training involved three components of learning and practice, the modus operandi of the British Psychoanalytic Association that continues to this day. Milner underwent a training analysis with Sylvia Payne, received supervision for her work with patients from Ella Sharpe and Melanie Klein, and attended theoretical and clinical seminars led by psychoanalysts including Anna Freud and James Strachey. This institutional training was also accompanied, I want to suggest, by an exploration—a kind of training in its own right—into the use of images to explore the unconscious and its therapeutic potential, which was then applied to her work with patients.

In the same year that Milner began her training at the Institute of Psychoanalysis, she recounts attending an exhibition of paintings by the psychoanalyst Grace Pailthorpe and her partner Reuben Mednikoff held at the Guggenheim Jeune gallery in Cork Street in London. The duo were infamous in London at the time for their surrealist artworks created out of the intention of making visible their unconscious desires through paint, symbolism, and form. The pair would analyse and interpret their own and each other's pictures, taking turns in performing the role of analyst and analysand.[3] In this way, infantile fantasies were brought to consciousness via their expression on the canvas and mutual interpretation (Remy, "Lives of the Artists Grace Pailthorpe and Reuben Mednikoff"). Pailthorpe and Mednikoff's loose application of psychoanalytic techniques to creative work seems to have inspired Milner to turn her attentions to engaging with painting and drawing as another technique for exploring her mind. It was coming home from one of their exhibitions that Milner asked herself, "I wonder if I could do that too?" (*BBA* 9).

Billed as a study of painting and creativity and the psychic forces that make creativity possible or impossible, *On Not Being Able to Paint* is less ostensibly a work of personal self-exploration or self-analysis than *A Life* or *An Experiment*. Nevertheless, Milner's insights into painting and the creative process originate from her own very personal researches into her psyche, which continue to reveal to her her own struggles around identity and intersubjectivity. If *A Life* and *An Experiment* express an adult woman's struggles with her identity and capacity to maintain a sense of self whilst in relationship to others, *On Not Being Able to Paint* explicitly explores these adult struggles around the relationship between self and other as it originates in early life. *On Not Being Able to Paint* is, ultimately, about not being able to be. Milner's understanding in the book that the infant's relationship with the mother primarily determines the formation of its personality in adult life reflects her immersion in object relations theory that was continuing to consolidate itself as a significant strand of psychoanalytic thinking during this period. Taking on the practices and techniques of the artist through which to study her own psyche, Milner's experiments with visual mark-making in *On Not Being Able to Paint* provide a creative site for the coming to awareness and reconstruction of early emotional life.[4]

In a similar narrative arc to her discovery of free writing in *A Life of One's Own*, Milner takes us on a journey of discovery for coming to find a way of drawing that reflects her psyche, answering back to her knowledge about her unconscious and providing her with a way of coming to know the inner reaches of her emotional experience. At the beginning of *On Not Being Able to Paint* we are presented with Milner's drawings created from early on in her study, drawings created out of a desire to improve her technique of drawing from life, to better portray perspective when drawing landscape and still life compositions. Her frustration with these early drawings echoes those of her first diary writing attempts: "There was no doubt that drawings which were a fairly accurate copy of an object could produce an almost despairing boredom; so I was forced to the conclusion that copies of appearances were not what my eye liked, even though what it did like was not at all clear" (Milner, *ONBAP* 4). It is only when one day, whilst attempting to paint a peaceful summer landscape in the English countryside, that in a mood of absent-mindedness she startled herself when she finds she has drawn "a blazing heath fire, its roaring flames leaping from the earth in a funnel of fire, its black smoke blotting out the sky" (7). Drawing in this more freely associative way begins to reveal something about herself, her unconscious smouldering on the surface of the page.

After discovering this way of absentminded drawing, her pictures quickly start to move from attempts at drawing from life to expressing increasingly symbolic and phantastic images. By Chapter 6 of the book, her pictures are no longer studied for their capacity to capture the external world realistically, nor is their aesthetic value her concern anymore. Instead, her focus shifts from questions about painting, to the questions these paintings generate about her psyche. The early landscape paintings of the outside world come to be replaced with drawings that capture the landscape of her inner world, with Milner increasingly preoccupied by what they reveal to her about her "monsters within and without" (41). Like the free associative techniques adopted in *A Life*, free drawing proves very illuminative, and the book revolves around the analysis of 49 drawings created in this manner. Drawing provides her with a way of coming to know about her unconscious, pen and paper like a spiritual medium summoning the creatures of the inner world so that they might take life on the external world of the page.

Importantly, Milner credits her experiments with drawing and painting in *On Not Being Able to Paint*, alongside the psychoanalytic theories of other authors, with her coming to recognise the importance of the mother-infant relationship in shaping and unconsciously determining one's later relationships to other people and external reality. She tells us how

> psycho-analysis and the content of the drawings had forced me to face the fact that the relationship of oneself to the external world is basically and

originally a relationship of one person to another, even though it does eventually become differentiated into relations to living beings and relations to things, inanimate nature. In other words, in the beginning one's mother is, literally, the whole world.

(Milner, *ONBAP* 134)

Drawing is understood as being able to provide a deep insight into our very earliest object relations and the failures of attunement that might occur in this developmental stage. The "problem of the relation between the painter and his world" is, Milner continues, "basically a problem of one's own need and the needs of the 'other', a problem of reciprocity between 'you' and 'me'; with 'you' and 'me' meaning originally mother and child" (134).

In this way, *On Not Being Able to Paint* proposes a strikingly different medium for the restaging of the drama between mother and infant. During the time in which the book was written, psychoanalysts in the wake of Klein turned to child analysis and the child's play with toys and objects in the session as a way to gain insight into their inner dramas and earliest object relations. Analysts were also exploring how the adult patient's earliest experiences were restaged in the analytic relationship. Esther Bick's development of infant and mother observation as a method for gaining insight into the relationship between mother and baby and the infant psyche was also gaining traction in this period. Infant observation was included as part of the training course for psychotherapists in 1948 at the Tavistock Clinic, later incorporated into the analytic training at the Institute of Psycho-Analysis in London in 1960. Diverging from Klein and Bick's practices, *On Not Being Able to Paint* presents the reader with a method for coming to understand the qualities of infantile life and its early relationships not through an observation of the baby in its home environment, or of the child or adult patient in the consulting room, but through the exploration of art-making.

We see Milner's distinctive approach in her analysis of one of her free drawings, titled "Drawing without a Name." This drawing, surrealist in style (depicting a woman's head and torso made out of various cog-like and vegetal shapes) seems to inspire what might be considered a Kleinian understanding of infantile aggression towards the mother's breast. The drawing is described as:

A reference to the fact that the first contact with the 'other' is with the mother's breast seemed to be given by the round breast-like shape on the left; but this is shown surrounded by a shape which my first thought said was the handle of a crutch, as if the breast might have become injured by all these biting mouths. And here I remembered Blake's words:

"The caterpillar on the leaf
Repeats to thee thy mother's grief,"

a remark which had always before seemed quite meaningless; but now I thought it expressed the fear that one's babyhood greedy kind of loving could have injured the life-giving breast.

(71)

In what sounds like a recapitulation of Klein's depressive position and the guilt that arises out of having done damage to the mother's breast, it is nonetheless Milner's own drawing, along with Blake's poetry, that are credited with helping her to think about the infant's own impulses that might complicate the relationship between mother and baby.

Two other drawings, "The Angry Parrot" and "The Angry Ape," lead Milner to the "consideration of this one central hypothesis: that there might be some acute and critical moments in the history of one's power to accept, emotionally as well as intellectually, the distinction between subjective and objective, self and other, wish and what happens" (65). Moreover they alert her to the "emotional disaster . . . if the bridge were broken too soon and the change from innocence to experience not accomplished in the child's own time" (63).[5] This is an emotional disaster that Milner later connects to existing psychoanalytic thinking, namely, to Clifford Scott's terms "cosmic bliss" and "catastrophic chaos" to describe contrasting emotional experiences some infants feel when in fusion with the mother (Milner, *SMSM* 116).[6]

Whilst the free drawings might provide insights into a more generalised understanding of the universal aspects and experiences of infancy, they are still ultimately an autobiographical tool in Milner's quest for knowledge of her own unconscious experience. Her conceptualisations of early inner life are borne out of her own creations, and accordingly, reveal to us her own feelings of not having been provided with a sufficient sense of the "illusion" of oneness when mother and infant are a harmonic whole (65). She finds the free drawings help to reveal her own "disillusionments, firmly hidden away and either actively forgotten or perhaps themselves belonging to the time before the remembered years" (65).

We come to see some of these disillusionments dramatised in the free drawing "Horrified Tadpole" (Figure 2.1). In this striking picture, the visual drama between tadpole, teeth, and ball powerfully expresses the feelings of terror of a relationship in which one party is devoured and destroyed. In her notes about the drawing, Milner writes: "Here again are teeth, they are flame-coloured and about to close on the black ball in the middle. The little red tadpole creature on the right has his hair standing on end in fear and astonishment at witnessing such a relationship" (68). This drawing is just one of many that through pictorial expression helps to bring conscious awareness to ever-present concerns around relationship and identity.

We might understand Milner's free drawings as providing herself and her reader with portraits of her internal objects, if you will, portraits that come to provide a new understanding of her self-image and that give a new depth and colour to the self-portrait she slowly paints for us across her autobiographical books.

Figure 2.1 "Horrified Tadpole" by Marion Milner.

Source: By permission of The Marsh Agency Ltd., on behalf of The Estate of Marion Milner.

It is thus the language of pictures in *On Not Being Able to Paint* that is the primary source for insight into fears and desires around the relationship between self and other, subjective and objective—ultimately, questions around ego boundaries and separation. Milner states how her experiments with drawing and painting "had led me to suspect that painting goes deeper in its roots than restoring to immortal life one's lost loves, it goes right back to the stage before one had found a love to lose" (79). Painting is felt to put one in contact with a stage in the emotional life of the infant that, in Milner's understanding of infant development, comes before the baby begins to relate to its mother as a separate object, where fleeting object separateness is lost to undifferentiated sensations and before the body ego has clear boundaries.

In order to understand the effects of free drawing more fully, this "private language" of hers, Milner finds it "necessary to try to compare the relative advantages of thinking in words used logically versus thinking in non-logical imagery, whether in words used poetically or in quite non-verbal imagery such as in the free drawings" (142). The kinds of writing and drawing that facilitate greater contact with the unconscious is preferred, and making "statements in pictures" seems to offer a particularly rich representation of experience, since pictures:

> were much more comprehensive than verbal statements, meanings that stretched back through the whole of one's experience could be presented to a single glance of the eye. And not only did they bring so much of the past into a single moment of present experience, they also embraced a wider range of bodily experience than intellectual verbal statements can; by stimulating the sense of rhythm, balance, colour, movement, they seemed to give the sense of a solider, deeper-rooted kind of knowing than any purely logical statement ever did.
>
> (142)

Pictures are the ultimate autogenerated autobiographical medium, capturing the essence of life in one space and moment in time. We might understand Milner as overplaying the "logical" in the verbal here—certainly Freud's own theory of verbal free association was not limited to "intellectual" verbal statements, nor was Milner's own experiments with free associative writing. The powers of the pictorial in this book seem to embody a fantasy of wordless communication, a longing perhaps for that form of preverbal communication between mother and baby.[7]

Indeed, it is the painter and their particular engagement with the wordless realm of the visual and spatial that provides insight into the registers of early experience. Milner tells us how:

> Somewhere in the books it was stated that painting is concerned with the feelings conveyed by space. This was surprising at first, up to now I had taken for granted and never reflected upon what it might mean in terms of feeling. But as soon as I did begin to think about it, it was clear that very intense feelings might be stirred. If one saw it as the primary reality to be manipulated for the satisfaction of all one's basic needs, beginning with the babyhood problem of reaching for one's mother, leading through all the separation from what one loves that the business of living brings, then it was not surprising that it should be the main preoccupation of the painter.
>
> (13)

Taking up some of Milner's thinking in his book *Art and Psychoanalysis* (1980), Peter Fuller writes of his "deeply held feeling that there are moments . . . genuine extensions of the capacity of *painted* images, and spatial organisations, to speak of certain aspects of human experience in ways which simply could not be reproduced in other media, where space cannot be imaginatively and affectively *constituted* in the same way" (164). The particular spatial formal quality of visual art seems to speak for Milner with eloquence about the self within relationship, and the issues of union and separateness with the mother in early life.

Indeed, it is the impressionist painter Paul Cézanne's remarks on the power of the painted image to stir certain feelings that deeply affects Milner in *On Not Being Able to Paint*. She quotes a description by Cézanne of the ideal engagement of spectator and painting:

> This is what a picture should give us, a warm harmony, an abyss in which the eye is lost, a secret germination, a coloured state of grace. All these tones circulate in the blood, don't they . . . to love a painting, one must first have drunk deeply of it in long draughts. Lose consciousness. Descend with the painter into the dim tangled roots of things, and rise again from them in colours, be steeped in the light of them.
>
> (Gasquet and Cézanne qtd. in Milner, *ONBAP* 29)

This is a troubling description for Milner, for "This idea of the very eye which sees being lost, drowned in the flood of colour, sounded all right, as long as it was a coloured state of grace and one did rise again. But supposing one did not?" What if "it was not a picture but a person that was loved like this?" (*ONBAP* 30). Fears of loving or being loved like this are brought to consciousness through Cézanne's unproblematic relationship to colour, powerfully embodying for Milner an experience of losing oneself in relation to someone else. Cézanne's artistic aesthetic, with its ambivalent differentiations between foreground and background, figure and environment, certainly embodies pictorially this merger of self and other.

Playing with form, colour, and line

It is also through formal experimentation with colour and outline that Milner finds a way of restaging these early disillusionments in *On Not Being Able to Paint*. The chapters "Being Separate and Being Together," "Outline and the Solid Earth," and "The Plunge into Colour" record Milner's acts of painting and drawing that put her in touch with powerful, deep-seated feelings around the relationship between self and other. Reflecting on her early drawings that tried to depict objects and scenery in the external world, Milner comes to realise that she had been misguidedly trying to represent objects by enclosing them in sharp outlines. This clarity of outline however captures a false reality, since "When really looked at in relation to each other their outlines were not clear and compact, as I had always supposed them to be, they continually became lost in shadow" (18). But trying to represent the reality of these objects in drawing threatens to disturb her emotionally, for she "noticed that the effort needed in order to see the edges of objects as they really look stirred a dim fear, a fear of what might happen if one let go of one's mental hold on the outline which kept everything separate and in its place" (18). These fears are linked to a fear of madness, and she writes how:

> I could only suppose that, in one part of the mind, there really could be a fear of losing all sense of separating boundaries; particularly the boundaries between the tangible realities of the external world and the imaginative realities of the inner world of feeling and idea; in fact a fear of being mad.
>
> (19)

Here is an adult's mind put in contact with infantile terrors. Losing boundaries in her painting has the effect of triggering all these terrors around losing the boundaries of herself and being engulfed by another. Playing with making and undoing boundary on the page translates to the experience of boundary making and undoing in the mind.

The use of colour when painting, the merging and bleeding of one pigment into another similarly evokes these anxieties around the loss of boundaries between self and other. The contrast between the chapter titles "The Plunge into Colour" and "Outline and the Solid Earth" is revealing: in the latter, Milner's free drawings depict landscapes that she understands as trying to achieve a "relation to the inevitable 'otherness' of what is outside one, to the reality of the solid earth" (24). Earth is the ultimate outline, the base line beneath our feet that keeps us oriented; in life we maintain a separation from it but in death we merge with it. If line is solid earth, then colours in painting that seep into one another are like the formless open space of water in which one becomes submerged. These experiments with painting stimulate a reliving of her fears around her early traumas, yet they also provide an opportunity to work them through by making them conscious and known.

There is one drawing, however, that stands out for representing a playful and pleasant interchange where relationship is depicted as something balanced, where separateness and togetherness can occur in simultaneity (Figure 2.2). Milner describes the creation of her "Two Jugs" drawing in this passage:

> I woke one morning and saw two jugs on the table; without any mental struggle I saw the edges in relation to each other, and how gaily they seemed almost to ripple now that they were freed from this grimly practical business of enclosing an object and keeping them in its place. This was surely what painters meant about the *play* of edges; certainly they did play and I tried a five-minute sketch of the jugs. . . . Now also it was easier to understand what painters meant by the phrase "freedom of line" because here surely was a reason for its opposite; that is, the emotional need to imprison objects rigidly within themselves.
>
> (19)

This free interrelatedness of both jugs is described as a relationship of gaiety because they can momentarily mingle and merge, then detach and regain their original shape without losing their own forms—in other words, they can still

Figure 2.2 "Two Jugs" by Marion Milner.
Source: By permission of The Marsh Agency Ltd., on behalf of The Estate of Marion Milner.

return to being two jugs. Rather than depicting relationship as something maddening and frightful where boundaries and outlines are muddled and lost, it is instead a lack of relationship that comes from rigid separateness, the absence of interplay, that is felt to be "grim." Here is a pictorial symbol for the kind of relatedness that is possible, not only between objects, but between two people.

This drawing is directly attributed with influencing Winnicott's thinking. In his paper "The Location of Cultural Experience" (1967) Winnicott writes how Milner's "Two Jugs" drawing "conveyed to him the tremendous significance there can be in the interplay of edges" (369). The jugs provide a helpful symbol for the necessary interplay of separation and union between the infant and its environment that Winnicott explores in this paper. We might also consider Winnicott's doodles (one of which is reproduced in *Bothered by Alligators*, p. 243) that depict the mother–infant relationship and transitional space, as representing something similar to that which Milner's two jugs picture did many years earlier in depicting the boundaries between one figure and another.

There is also evidence that *On Not Being Able to Paint* had considerable influence on the work of other Independent Group thinkers. In Benjamin Poore's study of Masud Khan's work and life, he writes that a key theoretical question for Khan, Winnicott, Michael Balint, and Milner became: "what is the relationship of pictorial expression and psychic life, and what aspects of self experience are actualised by the pictorial in a way that is not possible through verbalisation alone?" (230). Poore understands these analysts as each turning to a visual register for thinking about subjectivity, the self-other relationship, and ego boundaries.[8] Published in 1950, *On Not Being Able to Paint* was the first publication in what might be understood as this turn to the pictorial by these mid-century thinkers. Two years after its publication, Balint published his paper "Notes on the Dissolution of Object Representation in Modern Art" (1952), taking as its subject the dissolution of boundaries dividing and separating objects in modern art. Emma Letley understands Balint's paper as being directly influenced by both Ella Sharpe and Milner's ideas (101). Writing about the history of object representation in art and science, Balint notes how "In earlier times objects were represented as isolated entities; nature (or life) was conceived as a collection or a conglomerate of separate, clearly defined, and sharply delineated objects" (323). This was eroded by the impressionists who (resonating with Milner's engagement with Cézanne) "dissolved the hard contours of the objects. One of their most important discoveries was that it is not the contour that makes the object, but the contrast of its tones, shades, and colors to those of its environment" (324). Balint states that modernist artists took this one step further, showing a fascination for the disintegration of the secure outside dividing subject from object and objects from one another. Taking as an example lithographs by Picasso, Balint writes how,

> The sovereign, sharply defined, and delineated object disappeared. It was no longer possible to project ourselves into the objects, to see in them our cherished phantasy about our independent, uninfluenceable, imperishable selves; we had to learn to represent the objects *as we saw them* (not as we wanted to see ourselves): merged into and inseparable from their environment.
>
> (324)

Much like Milner and Winnicott through Milner, Balint uses art as a visual metaphor for thinking psychoanalytically about subject–object relations.

The turn to drawing and painting in *On Not Being Able to Paint* as a site for the examination and insight into the psyche evidently drew interest from other psychoanalytic thinkers. As Rye Dag Holmboe attests, it "is important to recognise . . . that drawing does not emerge in the history of British psycho-analysis as an illustration of this or that theory, but rather as primary, as the material and generative ground of theory" (64). But as we shall see, Milner's psychoanalytic engagement with drawing and painting goes a step further. *On Not Being Able to Paint* also proposes the act of picture-making as providing a reparative experience of an attuned, reciprocal relationship with another. Milner's terms the "pliable medium" and the "frame," which she coins in this book, reflect her commitment to art-making as an explicitly therapeutic activity.

The pliable medium

Milner first uses the term "pliant medium" to describe a particular quality of mediums like pencil, chalk, paint, and paper (*ONBAP* 136). She comes to find that in her work with these materials one could find an "other", a public reality, that was very pliant and unde-manding; pencil and chalk and paper provided a simplified situation in which the other gave of itself easily and immediately to take the form of the dream, it did not stridently insist on its own public nature, as I had found natural objects were inclined to do.

(136)

By free drawing with these materials, she "succeed[ed] in discovering a primitive reciprocity" (139). She wonders whether the failures of reciprocity between child and caregiver might simply be for reasons such as the child's wishes being differ-ent from the adult's, or from failures in communication between them. "Of course this failure of relationship is inevitable at times, it is part of the agonising side of being a child," writes Milner, but the "free drawing method . . . apparently made it partly able to compensate for that failure" (136).

The free drawings are felt to provide an "essential basis" for an experience of intersubjectivity where for both self and other there is "equal claim to the recogni-tion of needs and individuality" of both parties (136). This finding is elaborated in the following passage:

> Could one say that by finding a bit of the outside world, whether in chalk or paper, or in one's analyst, that was willing to temporarily to fit in with one's dreams, a moment of illusion was made possible, a moment in which inner and outer seemed to coincide? Was it also true to say that it was by these moments that one was able to re-establish the bridge, mend the broken boat, and so be re-awakened at least to the possibility of creative life in the real world? Was it not a legitimate hypothesis to suppose that by these moments of achieved fusions between inner and outer one was at least restored poten-tially to a life of action, a life in which one could seek to rebuild, restore, re-create what one loved, in actual achievement?
>
> (138)

Like the analyst, these artistic mediums are felt to be able to repair the disillusion-ments of childhood. I understand these fusions that Milner speaks of as an experi-ence of a relationship in which good enough care enables a creative relationship to oneself and the world, something like Winnicott's notion of creative apperception which he would later conceptualise in *Playing and Reality*.

This pliant medium comes later to be referred to as the "pliable medium" in her clinical writing, notably in in her paper "The Role of Illusion in Symbol Forma-tion" (1952), published two years after *On Not Being Able to Paint*, where Milner explicitly links the act of painting with the qualities of a good mother:

> I had come to see how the medium, for instance, paint, by its special quali-ties of spreadability and the way it allows one colour to mix up with another and so make a new one, and because it does not intrude its demands, but just

waits, submitting to things done to it, waits for the painter to become more and more sensitive to its real qualities and capacities; by this means it does for the painter, I believed, some of the things that a good mother does for her baby.

(108)

Here, the mixing of colour is experienced as a benign fusion. Milner also suggests that this kind of relationship can be found in the psychoanalytic setting in the "analyst acting as a pliant medium, giving back the patient's own thought to him, in a clarified form, rather than intruding his own needs and ideas" (118). Here, it is a real separate person, the analyst, that can embody the therapeutic qualities of the free drawings so long as they remain in a receptive mode, giving back to the patient their original thoughts in clarified form.

In this way, we see Milner not only using the qualities of the medium of paint as a metaphor for the kind of care the good enough mother should ideally provide its baby with but also that the analyst can provide the patient. For Milner, certain expressive mediums like painting and free drawing are also felt to provide a real corrective for early failures in attunement, with pen and paper helping to bring about or make up for an emotional reciprocity that was lost or never established in the original mother–infant relationship.

In an interview with artist and educator Chris Crickmay in 1975, Milner elaborates on the nature of the pliable medium, making sure to emphasise the extent of its capacity for flexibility and adaptability that another person is ultimately not able to provide to the same extent. She states:

because it's pliable it doesn't insist. It's got the minimum of character of its own so that it makes a kind of bridge between us and the world, where the world has its own nature. And if it's people, they've got their own character and one's got to recognise that they don't always fit in with what one wants. But the medium, although it's got certain character—and one mustn't go against that character and make it try and do something it can't do—still it does, as it were, make a bridge so that it takes its form from one's inner life. And yet it's outside.

(Milner with Chris Crickmay, "Me and Not Me")

The pliable medium seems to possess qualities that another person could never provide in the same way. Crucially, the pliable medium supplies a therapeutic relationship that can only be provided by the self and for the self, bypassing the interfering complexities of interpersonal relationships.

In relation to Milner's pliable medium, Alberto Stefana wonders whether "considering the wide variety of expressive media" Milner ignores "certain materials [which] are hostile, as those who have carved wood or stone, tried to fashion a figure from warm wax, or used watercolours on a textured surface with brushes are well aware" (142–3). Certainly, Milner seems to be describing only one kind of experience the artist might have with their medium. As a counterpoint to Milner's thinking, Eve Kosofky Sedgwick offers an interesting psychoanalytically informed analysis of her own experiences making art with textiles. In *The Weather in Proust* (2011) she describes how in her experience of working with "paper, fabric, thread, and other supplies," these materials "press back so reliably, so palpably, against my efforts to shape them according to models I've conceived" (Sedgwick 79). This gives her a "reassuring sense of grounding reality" in this pressing back, which she connects back to Melanie Klein's argument that the infant feels relief "rather than a big tragedy in the way it is in Freud, when one manages to get disabused of the fantasy of omnipotence, together with the reflex fantasy of utter impotence" (83). She writes how "In these circumstances perfectionism, for me, would make no sense at all, and the disturbing fantasy of omnipotence has no opportunity to arise" (83). Instead, "second-by-second negotiations with the material properties of whatever I'm working on, and the questions 'What will it let me do?' and 'What does it want to do?' are in constant, three-way conversation with 'What is it I want to do?'" (83). Whereas for Milner the "pliant and understanding" mediums of pencil, chalk, and paper are essential for her emotional health, Sedgwick finds relief precisely in the demands her materials make of her (Milner, *ONBAP* 117). The qualities of the pliant, pliable medium, however, are required to be much more "compliant," we might say, to Milner's needs.

The frame

The other term Milner conceives in *On Not Being Able to Paint* is that of the frame. First mentioned in the first edition of the book in 1950, Milner continues to write about the frame in her 1956 postscript to the second edition of the book, as well as in a retrospective description of the concept in "1952: The Framed Gap," one of the papers included in *The Supressed Madness of Sane Men: Forty-Four Years of Exploring Psychoanalysis* (1987). Her thinking on the frame in this paper dates back to a lecture she delivered in 1952, only coming to write about it in essay form in 1987. As one of the slighter papers in the collection, this paper might seem at first glance to be on fringes of Milner's body of work, compared to her longer and more theoretically dense papers of later years. She admits that the concept is essentially described in retrospection since "What I said was never published, and my notes are by now somewhat disremembered" (Milner, *SMSM* 79). But this is no old, abandoned concept; it is described with a relevance and liveliness that, as Claire Pajaczkowska writes, "Milner retrospectively identified as a unifying concept across her clinical and cultural work" (35).

Recounting her lecture on the concept of the frame from 1952, Milner describes how she explained the term to her audience in the following way:

> I told how I saw the frame as something that marked off what's inside it from what's outside it, and to think of other human activities where the frame is

essential, a frame in time as well as in space; for instance the acted play, cer-emonies, rituals, processions, even poems framed in silence when spoken and the space of the paper when written. Also the psychoanalytic session framed in both space and time. I said I thought that all these frames show that what is inside has to be perceived, interpreted in a different way from what is out-side; they mark off an area within which what we perceive has to be taken as symbol, as metaphor, not literally.

(*SMSM* 80–81)

And when painting, the frame is "that limited space . . . the edge of the paper, even a wall" (80). The frame is the boundary and setting for a particular kind of activity that includes the analytic encounter as well as aesthetic, creative experiences. Along with these frames of creative activity, Milner also understands art school as providing a frame:

It is said that no art school can teach you how to paint, in the real sense. But the art school can and does provide the frame, it offers regular times and places and materials for creation. And by the willed act of registering as a student and attending at the proper time one can, as by a protective frame, free oneself from the many distractions of trying to paint at home.

(*ONBAP* 121)

The frame, in Milner's description, allows for the self to get "lost in a moment of intense activity in which awareness of self and awareness of the object are somehow fused, and one emerges to separateness again to find that there is some new entity on the paper" (80).[9] In many respects, this is exactly what had ear-lier so frightened Milner in Cézanne's description where the viewer of a painting should: "Lose consciousness. Descend with the painter into the dim tangled roots of things" (Gasquet and Cézanne qtd. in Milner, *ONBAP* 29). However, instead of entering the painting and getting lost inside it, the frame is like an anchorage that guarantees a safe return, where entering and exiting, and remaining intact from such an experience is now possible. The frame seems to describe a safe setting in which self and other can enter into a creative, reciprocal relationship. Whether this takes place within the time and place of the psychoanalytic setting, the frame of the paper, or in art school, Milner is suggesting that both psychoanalysis and creative activity can provide a caring function, akin perhaps to the good environ-ment, or the holding environment, that Winnicott wrote about in the same period, in his paper "Transitional Objects and Transitional Phenomena—A Study of the First Not-Me Possession" in 1953. In this way, Milner and Winnicott's theories seem to delineate and demarcate the inner world from the outer in such a way that Kleinian theory does not. As Lyndsey Stonebridge writes, "[w]here the Kleinians seem to engulf the child in a phantasy world, Milner, in both her autobiographies and her psychoanalytic work, attempts to construct a 'frame' for phantasy and illusion: a space where the inside can traffic with the outside, where the self can meet the not-self" (*The Destructive Element* 144).

In her interview with Chris Crickmay, Milner also uses the term "cocoon" to describe the frame, telling Crickmay that to allow for a state of absentmindedness, creative reverie, "I think you need a protective cocoon. The artist needs a studio. And a child needs a playroom. And the analyst needs a consulting room. It needs a safe place" ("Me and Not Me"). The cocoon, with its more womb-like, enveloping evocations further emphasises Milner's expansion of the provision of a maternal function to different sites beyond that of the mother's care and the role of the analyst. As well as comfort, the cocoon has powerful associations with transformation, providing the conditions for the emergence of something new.

Crickmay goes on to ask Milner if "[s]upposing these conditions are not available, supposing the frame can't be got, what kind of consequences [might this have]" ("Me and Not Me"). Using herself as an example, she responds:

> People can suffer I think if they're not able to get at it. In fact "The Experiment in Leisure" [sic] I had a term off work in which I wrote that. It was I think it was boiling away inside me and a rather perceptive doctor said, why not take a term off. And I wrote it I think there are times when things required some time off from practicality for this creativeness to go on. And can make people quite almost physically ill I think at times when the thing is on the boil.
>
> ("Me and Not Me")

As the meta-frame that frames the frames, the writing of the autobiographical books themselves provide a frame for the frames provided by free associative writing, drawing, and painting. Milner's thinking then presents us with an ever-evolving expansion of the sites through which she can provide herself with an experience of an attuned, reciprocal relationship.

Crucially, Milner's work at the site of drawing and painting profoundly shapes her work with patients. In the years after *On Not Being Able to Paint*, Milner writes a number of papers detailing her analytic work with both child and adult patients. These case studies reflect the deep influence her drawing and painting experiments had on her clinical work, and they include: "The Role of Illusion in Symbol Formation" (1952), "The Communication of Primary Sensual Experience" (1955), and her book-length study, *The Hands of the Living God: An Account of a Psycho-analytic Treatment* (1969). In these analytic works, we shall see how Milner pays special attention to the creative play and visual acts of her child and adult patients (Simon, Ruth, and Susan), attending closely to their creations as part of the analytic process.

Simon, "The Role of Illusion in Symbol Formation" (1952)

Milner writes about the pliable medium and frame in relation to her clinical work for the first time in her paper "The Role of Illusion in Symbol Formation." Recapitulating her earlier findings, in this paper she tells us how "by the recurrent providing of a framed space and time and a pliable medium . . . from time to time, it will not be necessary for self-preservation's sake to distinguish clearly between inner and outer, self and not-self' (Milner, *SMSM* 75). We are presented with the case of Simon, who "was suffering from a loss talent for schoolwork" (88–89). From the ages of four to six Simon had been very interested in and successful at school, but now as an eleven-year-old, was close to failing his schoolwork and at times even unable to attend class. Milner carefully observes Simon's frequently aggressive play in the consulting room, where he would often wage a war on an imaginary village which in his mind belonged to Milner. Despite the ostensible violence of the play, Milner observes how when Simon could settle down "to using the toys as a pliable medium" which were "external to himself" but did not insist "on their own separate objective existence, then apparently he could treat me with friendliness and consideration, and even accept real frustration from me" (68). Only then would Simon drop the usually bullying, hectoring attitude he would adopt towards Milner, a sign that analyst as other is tolerated and accepted to some degree, the marker of some progress in the analysis. This leads Milner to consider the function of his play with these toys as equivalent to her own experiments with painting and free drawing— "on days when he did play with the toys, there seemed to develop a relationship between him and them which reminded me of the process I had myself tried to observe introspectively when doing 'free' drawings" (92). Indeed, Simon's play is attributed with an aesthetic quality: "the boy's play nearly became 'a play', in that there was a sense of pattern and dramatic form in what he produced" (72).

Analytic transformation is therefore understood as being produced via a relationship to an aesthetic medium; Simon's play provides him with the possibility for re-imagining reality "just as in free imaginative drawing the sight of a mark made on the paper provokes new associations, the line as it were answers back and functions as a very primitive type of external object" (92). Interestingly, Milner likens the pliable medium in this paper to an "intervening substance" in the analytic setting (following a dictionary definition of the word medium), writing how transformation occurred when Simon "had become able to use both me and the playroom equipment as this intervening pliable substance" (74). The pliable medium is felt to intervene in the relationship a positive way, precisely because of how little it is felt to intervene and impinge in the demanding way another person might.

Milner's account of play and creativity in her work with Simon is striking given a few biographical facts. Simon was in fact a pseudonym for Michael Clyne, Melanie Klein's own grandson. The account of this analysis was written as part of an edited collection of papers celebrating Klein's seventieth birthday, and Klein supervised Milner's handling of the analysis. We might then assume that Klein's thinking would permeate Milner's work—instead, we see Milner part ways with classic Kleinian analytic technique in her presentation of the analysis, her own thinking and techniques becoming visible. In a Kleinian manner, Milner does acknowledge Simon's violent and aggressive feelings towards his parental internal objects through his play, but she pays little attention to how they enter the transference, instead understanding Simon's struggles to be about the "problem of establishing object relationships at all, rather than on the restoration of the injured object once it is established" (97). Simon's play suggests to Milner that "Clearly . . . there was a great amount of resentment and fear to be worked through in the Oedipus situation," but diverting from the Kleinian narrative of reparation, this was not the only reason for the persistence of this type of play—it is related to something more basic, "to do with difficulties in establishing the relation to external reality as such" (92). In other words, Milner finds Simon is suffering from a difficulty of accepting the "not-me-ness" of his external reality (93). And it is the pliable medium of toys that provide a good enough experience of otherness, restoring his faith in having a creative relationship with his schoolwork, his relationship with his analyst and with his family and friends.

This case illustrates how in the analytic setting, the pliable medium plays a role in providing the patient with a simplified version of a good, attuned relationship, which then acts as a springboard for the patient to better engage with other interpersonal and external relations. Milner's role as analyst involves nurturing her patient's use of a pliable medium, and also taking on the qualities herself as much as possible of the pliable medium so that both can be put to use by the patient. Her understanding of the importance of the pliable medium thus shifts attention to the patient's use of a material object in the analysis, introducing another element into the attention customarily paid by psychoanalysis to the transference and countertransference. In Simon's case, it is the pliable medium of the toys that provides an essential foundation, a getting ready if you will, for the more daunting real relations between the self and another person.

Ruth and Susan, "The communication of primary sensual experience" (1955)

Another clinical paper published after *On Not Being Able to Paint*, "The Communication of Primary Sensual Experience" (1955), describes Milner's work with two patients, one a child called "Ruth" and another adult patient named "Miss. A," later appearing as "Susan" in *The Hands of the Living God*. Ruth's drawings were all made during the analytic sessions, with Susan's largely created in between sessions (Milner, *SMSM* 86). These patients' drawings take centre stage in Milner's clinical writing, the paper being about "what I had learnt from both Ruth and Susan through their drawings" (85). Rather than examining her patient's psyches through the prism of the transference and countertransference, Milner comes to knowledge about her patients' early relationships through their drawings. Once again she establishes this approach to thinking about her patients' creative products as differing from a Kleinian one, telling the reader:

> In discussing the drawings I shall not be talking about the reparative aspect of them, but about the light they throw on the specific problem of how love and joy is to be expressed, communicated. I shall be talking about the interplay between the wish to communicate, to share feelings, and the strivings after primary narcissistic states; and how this interplay is shown in the drawings.
>
> (86–87)

Milner's concern here is with how her patients' autobiographical drawings shed a light on their feelings around relating to others—she attends to how their conflicted desires around wanting to relate and communicate, and the desire to stay apart and withdrawn in a state of primary narcissism are expressed pictorially. As Milner's own free drawings are read for what they can reveal about her inner struggles with relationship, so her patients' drawings are subjected to a similar analysis. Their use of line reveals feelings that have their origins in preverbal and pre-oedipal experience before object separateness—of particular concern is the way in which both patients depict an "oscillation" in their drawings between one thing and another (116). For example, one of Susan's drawings depicts a face within a sphere that might be one face or two—a visual representation of an interplay between dualities. Ruth's drawing is strikingly similar to that of Susan's in its depiction of two faces that might also be viewed as one (Figure 2.3). Milner reads this oscillation as "the swing between: on the one hand, the wish for the discriminated state, recognition of separateness, and . . . on the other hand, the wish for fusion, oneness, the oceanic feeling, or the state of cosmic bliss" (116). This is a swing reminiscent of what Milner herself feels in her experiments with using and losing outline in *On Not Being Able to Paint*.

Importantly, Ruth and Susan's drawings provide a basis for communication with Milner. She writes how:

> I had been able to watch something of the process by which they externalized, threw out of themselves on to the paper, marks which, because of the pliable character of the medium, could take on an infinite variety of shape and thus provide a feedback, a basis for communication, both with the analyst and with themselves.
>
> (108)

The pliable medium of drawing provides a "bridge" between patient and analyst, rather than the potentially claustrophobic you–me entrapment. Milner's clinical technique seems to ensure that her patients are given the space to explore themselves in her presence without an insensitive imposition of her own presence or ideas. It provides a safe setting where no premature demand is made on the patient to engage with the analyst or themselves, letting the patient move at their own self-determined pace. With the help of the pliable medium and the analytic setting, the patient can build up a stable internal base, and only once this base is established can they step out into the world. The following passage in the paper encapsulates this work with Susan as well as with Simon, the cure of drawing once again championed:

> I have tried to show how these two patients could be seen as having been able to externalize this inner encounter, through their willingness to enter into an active relation with the blankness of the paper, as well as through the pliable medium of paint, chalk, water. Also, in the light of Susan's later drawings and

Figure 2.3 Ruth's drawing in "The Communication of Primary Sensual Experience" (1955).

Source: By permission of The Marsh Agency Ltd., on behalf of The Estate of Marion Milner.

my analysis of them, I had come to see how the drawings shown here did fore-
shadow the later working through of the problems they symbolized, but now
in relation to the more complex reality of encounter with me, the analyst, as
a whole person. Thus it could be said that, in order to achieve this, it had first
been necessary for her to go through the stage of relating to me as the primary
substances of the media she used, substances which, by their pliability, gave her
something near to the illusions of primary omnipotence, for here I remembered
Simon's insistence that I was his "lovely stuff" that he had made.

(108)

As many of Susan's drawings are created outside of the analytic session, bringing her creations to the analysis after they have been produced, the act of drawing seems to provide a frame for when the frame of the analysis is missing.

In this paper we also learn of another unusual and unorthodox technique that Milner employs. She gives copies of both Ruth and Susan's drawings to a number of anonymous commentators to help her understand their drawings in greater depth. These commentators include a variety of unnamed psychoanalysts from different schools—Independents, Jungians and Kleinians, but also an equal number of non-analysts, all of whom are involved with art in some way. They include a painter and head of an art school, a painter and an art teacher, a writer on art, and a professor and teacher of painting (140–52).

A comment from one painter simply commends one of Susan's drawings, the "Post-ECT drawing," praising it as "amazingly good, frightfully good, requires no comment. Absolutely original" (140). A writer and teacher of the psychology of art applauds Susan's drawing "Dancing figure among leaves," finding the picture's "very beautiful white spots well-conceived, spaces which result from brush strokes which coagulate as one goes in, convincingly, not scatteringly, to a centre, with a looseness of organization which still holds together marvellously, no stiffness of brush" (160). This commentary from anonymous psychoanalysts and non-analysts is accredited by Milner with making her more aware of certain theoretical preoccupations around the "concept of delusion as compared with that of illusion," which although not stated here, is perhaps a nod to Winnicott's writing on the necessary illusion of omnipotence in the earliest stages of life (165). This commentary, however, is mostly left in the paper without much further review or reflection, and it isn't clear how she derives from them these insights into illusion (165). Though not fully developed here in any clear way, it does indicate that Milner gives particular value to the artistic, aesthetic, and formal qualities of her patient's drawings as part of her psychoanalytic theorising. The painter and those involved in the milieu of the art world are considered to have the insight useful for her psychoanalytic project; in her technique the analysis of her patients' creations is an important component for understanding their struggles. In performing such an exercise, we see Milner continuing to forge her own very distinctive practice—one that is informed by, rather than in complete servitude to, the accepted parameters of psychoanalysis.

In the appendix to the second edition of *On Not Being Able to Paint* published in 1956, Milner mentions her work with two patients. Though she does not name them, given her description and time of writing, it is likely she is referring to Ruth and Susan. She describes both patients as having "had mothers who were mentally extremely ill" (Milner, *ONBAP* 192). "I suggest that such a human environment," Milner writes, "forces a child into desperate clinging to the phase of thinking that does distinguish between the 'me' and the 'not-me', because this is the only protection against an impossible confusion between their own and their parents' inner problem" (192–3). Based on what she has found in her own experiments, she writes:

> What they are essentially in need of is a setting in which it is safe to indulge in reverie, safe to permit a confusion of 'me' and 'not-me'. Such a setting, in which it is safe to indulge in reverie, is provided for the patient in analysis, and painting likewise provides such a setting, both for the painter of the picture and for the person who looks at it.
>
> (*ONBAP* 193)

In her work with these patients, Milner as analyst provides both frames—the frame of creative activity within the frame of the session or its encouragement outside of it. These structures, in turn, help to consolidate the framing capacities of the analyst.

Susan, *The Hands of the Living God: An Account of a Psycho-analytic Treatment* (1969)

Almost a decade later we come to meet Susan again in Milner's book-length case study, *The Hands of the Living God: An Account of a Psycho-analytic Treatment*. Here it is also visual art—its use by the patient and its interpretation by Milner—that forms the heart of the account of the analysis. The book charts the length of the treatment which began in 1943 when Susan was 23 years old, and ended decades later around 1958–60. Over the course of the analysis Susan created over 4,000 drawings, bringing up to 90 with her to a single session. This prolific creative output began a couple of years into the analysis, apparently out of Susan's own accord: "Susan was eventually to produce doodle drawings herself and to do this quite spontaneously, for I had neither suggested it nor did she know about my book, since I had not been able to find a publisher till 1950" (Milner, *HOLG* xlvii). In what seems an almost uncanny parallel between analyst and patient, Susan is presented as finding, on her own terms, a visual, autobiographical cure.[10]

The likeness between Susan and Milner extends to their emotional struggles. At the heart of Susan's analysis was Milner's belief that Susan needed to be reborn into her own separate identity. Much of Susan's suffering is attributed to her experience of never having felt herself to be a separate person from her mother who was mentally very unwell. In Susan, we might say, Milner finds a much more extreme version of her own suffering, and the intensity with which Susan draws and paints—the intensity of the creative cure—seems to match the intensity of her difficulties. In their first ever session, Susan tells Milner that she no longer felt she had a boundary to the back of her head and that the world was no longer outside of her (17). Having lived through the Blitz, the fear of air-raids became intolerable because "there was nowhere else for the bomb to fall except on her, since everything was her" (17). In his preface to *The Hands of the Living God*, Winnicott understands Susan as suffering from schizophrenia or a schizoid personality (ix). Though Milner does not use either term to describe Susan's suffering, she comes to find evidence that is highly suggestive of profound failures in Susan's infancy and childhood that prevented Susan from feeling herself to be a whole person with her own consolidated identity, separate from her mother, and separate from her external reality.

As with her work with Simon and Ruth, Milner finds herself having to forego Kleinian methods of interpretation, which are seemingly fruitless in their ability to help Susan. In the early years of Susan's treatment, Milner was also in weekly supervision with Klein, and initially fed Susan various interpretations about her infantile phantasy life. These interpretations continually fell flat, however, and provided Milner with little insight into her patient. When Milner tried to understand Susan through the concepts of fragmentation or projective identification, for instance, Susan bafflingly "continued to maintain that neither she nor I was there" (26). As Mary Jacobus describes the situation, this "brought Kleinian interpretation to a halt. Only gradually did Susan's own evolving drawings prove able to unlock her previously inaccessible bodily phantasies, while allowing Milner to develop her psychoanalytically based theories of creativity" (123).

It is instead Milner's creative, home-grown methods which start to make some difference. Commenting on one of Susan's paintings, Milner writes how Susan:

> achieved, through the medium of paint, such a momentary integration; I thought this because I had come to believe, through my own experiments with painting, that the pliability of the medium, the receptivity of the paper, and the willingness of paint to take on the form of one's visions, do provide a kind of ideal, but also in a sense real "other" with whom one can achieve a quick and subtle interchange.
>
> (*HOLG* 219)

Susan's prolific doodles are understood as a way of harnessing the emotional reciprocity of the pliable medium, aiding contact and communication between patient and analyst. In such a way, her drawings importantly help Susan to gain an awareness of both the analyst and the patient in the room that she previously lacked. Milner continues:

> My first way of looking at this sheer amount of them was in terms of what I saw as her desperate need for a continued contact with a bit of external reality which was "other" and yet completely responsive to what came from her; the paper became as it were a substitute for the responsive ideal mother. . . . Also I saw her as, through her drawings, constantly creating a bridge between me and herself, a basis for communication.
>
> (267)

Through the process of this treatment Milner also comes to observe Susan as growing her "own inner frame," facilitated by the external frames of the analysis and the act of drawing (277). We see this frame being literally represented in Susan's drawings, which towards the end of the treatment, start to feature ducks or boats on water that represent a baseline on which things can stand or be kept afloat without sinking or drowning (227). In this turn to her own methods, Milner observes Susan's slowly getting better, her suffering lessening, and her developing the capacity to "love and work" more happily (399).

In the preface to *The Hands of the Living God*, Milner writes about how she and Susan were involved in a "Freudian analysis . . . confronting each other in the crucible of the analytic room, engaged in the process, or working towards the process, of remaking each other through the confronting of the opposites of 'you' and 'me'" (xl).[11] This book however, as we have seen, presents a psychoanalytic treatment that is as much Milnerian as it is Freudian. Much of the confrontation of you and me, self and other, patient and analyst is conducted through relations that revolve around the patient's autobiographical acts of drawing. The way in which Milner organises her account of the treatment around Susan's drawing in this book is also indicative of this shift in attention. In the introduction to the book, she describes her difficulties in finding a way of narrating such a long and complicated analysis, explaining how:

> As for the method of writing the book, I had intended, in the beginning, to use my own diary notes of the experiences with this patient, together with her drawings, as the basis for a descriptive account of what had happened between us. Soon, however, I found that the problem of selection from verbal material collected over many years was too difficult; so I decided to make the account centre on the drawings, since I did come to look on these as containing, in highly condensed form, the essence of what we were trying to understand.
>
> (xxxix)

Susan's drawings and their analysis are used in the service of writing about the treatment and expressing and communicating the long encounter between analyst and patient, helping Milner to understand Susan and the nature of her problems better. It is also through Milner's attending to and discussing Susan's drawings with her in the analysis that Milner as analyst makes contact with her patient. She writes how she came to see Susan's drawings "as my patient's private language which anyone who tried to help her must learn how to read—and speak" (xxxix). This is a psychoanalytically informed treatment in which analyst and patient speak to one another not via the customary talking cure, but via the speaking and analysis of a visual, symbolic language.

There is one drawing of Susan's, the "Post-ECT drawing" that is particularly significant in Milner's coming to understand her patient. We learn that it was "within the framework of contemplating the post-E.C.T. drawing" (Figure 2.4) in the early stages of writing *The Hands of the Living God* that Milner "began to feel ready to face the task of looking through all the drawings, in order to try and understand more of this visual language through which Susan was seeking to communicate with me and herself" (288). As the drawing that sparks Milner's own act of relating to Susan, it embodies the central problems tackled in the

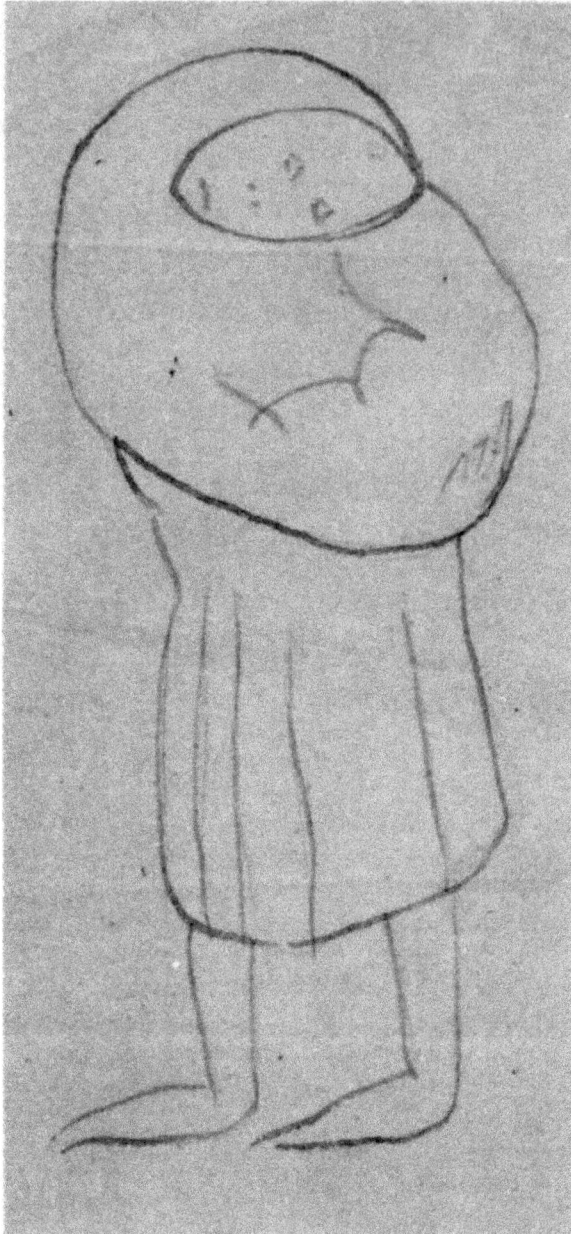

Figure 2.4 Susan's "The Post-E.C.T. drawing."

Source: By permission of The Marsh Agency Ltd., on behalf of The Estate of Marion Milner.

analysis: the picture powerfully represents the form of an infant held by an adult figure, likely the caregiver or mother. The form of the infant, however, could also be the figure's arm—it is unclear where one figure begins and the other ends, and whether both heads are connected or separate. As Milner suggests, there is "no clear distinction" for Susan "between the holder and the held" (279).

Milner is uniquely moved and unsettled by this drawing when she comes across it for a second time when in the process of gathering materials to write *The Hands of the Living God.* The drawing produces in her a kind of countertransference, where she feels "such a complex state of feeling to do with anguish and tragedy that it seems I did not really know what to do with it [the picture]" (277). She tells us how on "looking back I realized that the impact of this drawing had been so intense that I had been unable at first to bring myself to concentrate upon its meaning" (277). And what Milner finds herself doing next to Susan's picture is striking, shocking herself by her "cavalier treatment of someone else's drawing" (277). For she had

> inked it over—in order, I thought, to see it better since it was so faint—instead of, as I should have done, making a traced copy. I was to remember this action of mine as a warning of how too great enthusiasm for the clarity of a verbal interpretation can also, at times, disastrously distort what the patient is experiencing.
>
> (277–8)

In this act of drawn imposition, Milner seems to acquire insight into the countertransference, not through the lived here and now experience of being in the session with Susan, but through a retrospective relationship to Susan's drawings. This copying over of Susan's work seems to represent a dramatisation of Susan's difficulties in coming into her own being without the impingements of an other that fails to allow her a separate sense of self.

Does Milner's method help Susan to get better? *The Hands of the Living God* ends with Susan being able to live more independently and marrying her husband whom Milner describes as playing an increasingly vital part in her development (411). In one of his meetings with Milner towards the end of her life, Adam Phillips describes Milner's feelings about Susan's treatment:

> I asked her about Susan, about whether she thought the analysis had worked. "Of course she never got better", she said briskly and there was a pause. And then she said, "but we got somewhere, she got somewhere", and there was another pause, and she said, "better".
>
> (xxxiii)

Whilst Milner and her reader may be unable to definitively determine the efficacy of the treatment, certainly as Phillips adds, "Milner never takes for granted what it would be for Susan to be better. It is, that is to say, a work of (modern) literature not of propaganda" (xxxiv).

A distinctive theory of object relations

On only a couple of occasions does *The Hands of the Living God* explicitly connect Susan's acts of drawing to providing herself with the attuning functions described by Milner's colleagues, Winnicott and Bion. Milner mentions in the following passage the terms "mirror" and "contain" in relation to Susan's drawings, which although they remain uncited, are arguably in reference to these thinkers' concepts. She writes about Susan's drawings, how:

> even when the drawings were not interpreted, or even not seen, by me, they did seem to have provided some sort of substitute for the mirror that her mother had never been able to be to her; they did in a primitive way give her back to herself, as well as providing a substitute for me from one session to the next . . . there did seem to have been no hope whatever of a truly personal relationship with such a mother, an other who could never contain her and give her back to herself as the paper did, and as I was trying to do.
>
> (268)

Drawing between the sessions is another way of providing herself with a mirroring function when the analyst is not present. In a footnote on the page where this passage appears, Milner provides a reference to Winnicott's 1953 paper "Transitional Objects and Transitional Phenomena. A Study of the First Not-Me Possession," in a sense inviting the reader to bring her work into dialogue with these other Winnicottian theories. Certainly, the links between both thinkers' works do not end here.

As we have traced, the pliable medium and the frame are first described in 1950 in *On Not Being Able to Paint* and expanded in Milner's theoretical and clinical writing of the 1950s and 1960s. One year after the publication of *On Not Being Able to Paint*, Winnicott presents his concept of the transitional object in a paper read before the British Psychoanalytical Society in 1951 and later published in 1953 as the paper "Transitional Objects and Transitional Phenomena. A Study of the First Not-Me Possession." Bion's theory of containment is first introduced in published form in his book *Learning from Experience* in 1962, followed by Winnicott's paper "Mirror-Role of Mother and Family in Child Development" in 1967, two years prior to the publication of *The Hands of the Living God*.[12] Such chronology not only demonstrates the shared time frame these thinkers all belonging to the Institute of Psychoanalysis were working within, but that Milner's concepts of the frame and pliable medium preceded at the very least the public dissemination of both Bion and Winnicott's theories. Whilst it is impossible at the level of theory to precisely determine the degree to which one thinker was influenced by another, it is worthwhile nonetheless to introduce Milner's thinking into the mix, situating it within the object relations tradition, while also acknowledging her singular contribution.

In one of the few analyses of Milner's frame, Claire Pajaczkowska understands Milner's concept as sitting alongside those concepts "all developed by the same generation of analysts," namely Bion's theory of "containment," and to which I would add Winnicott's concept of the holding environment (36). These concepts—the container/contained of Bion's model, the holding environment of Winnicott's thinking, and the frame of Milner's—all describe a spatial setting of some sort in which a particular provision of care is provided for. Winnicott seems to share Milner's language of the frame when in his article "Additional Note on Psycho-Somatic Disorder" (1969) he makes an analogy between the picture frame and the infant's care. Although he does not make explicit any reference to Milner's thinking, Winnicott seems to allude to her notion of the frame, writing: "One example of . . . unthinkable anxiety is the state in which there is no frame to the picture; nothing to contain the interweaving of forces in the inner psychic reality, and in practical terms no-one to hold the baby" (*Psycho-Analytic Explorations* 115). In this statement we can trace an unspoken dialogue between Winnicott and Milner that likely demonstrates a mutual influence. These allusions to each other's concepts suggest a history of theory-building that sometimes involved a fusion, or loss of boundary between one thinker and another, making it difficult to trace the exact provenance of their ideas and journeys of influence, but that nonetheless suggest Milner's thinking around her autobiographical cure were at least somewhere in the background to Winnicott's thinking.

In describing the quality of relationship to an external, material object, Winnicott's transitional object bears comparison with Milner's pliable medium. Such a comparison, does, I think, highlight the distinctiveness of Milner's approach. For Winnicott, the transitional object is for the child a material object, typically something soft like a blanket to which the child attributes a special value, enabling it to make the necessary shift from the earliest oral relationship with the mother to genuine object-relationships ("Transitional Object"). As the first not-me possession the transitional object, like the pliable medium, provides an experience of object otherness that functions like a steppingstone for the move into relations with other people. Later on, the establishment of the reality principle and the inevitable disillusion associated with this will be tolerated by virtue of the transitional object, which allows the child to exercise its feelings of omnipotence in a playful manner ("Transitional Object"). As early as 1951, however, Winnicott warned against the risk of this thinking about the relationship to a real object being reified. And in 1971 in his introduction to *Playing and Reality* he wrote how "what I am referring to . . . is not so much the object used as the use of the object" (xii). It is the baby, not the object, who is in a state of transition. In the concept of the pliable medium, however, it is the qualities of the object, the material adaptability of paint, for example, and how this provides a tolerable experience of otherness that is of fundamental importance.[13] Winnicott's associated terms "transitional phenomena" and "potential space" denote even less of an interest with the material, bringing into greater relief Milner's singular interest in the external, concrete reality of the object and medium.

In relation to clinical technique, Milner's interest in images and their creation may have influenced that much more widely known use of drawing within the psychoanalytic session: Winnicott's squiggle game. "It is in Milner's free drawings that squiggles of Winnicott . . . are deeply rooted," writes Alberto Stefana (132). In this game, Winnicott would "squiggle" a simple form on a piece of paper and ask his child patient to "make it into anything," and the squiggle-making would be passed back and forth from analyst to child (*Psycho-Analytic Explorations* 302). Describing a typical session in which the squiggle game is played with a child patient, Winnicott writes how "Often in an hour we have done twenty to thirty drawings together, and gradually the significance of these composite drawings has become deeper and deeper" (302). Throughout the process, Winnicott would invite his patients to talk about the meaning of these collaborative constructions. The purpose of this game was to allow for the child's "communication of significance" with the analyst (302). (Prior to the development of the squiggle game, Winnicott also employed what he called the spatula game, described in his 1941 paper "The observation of infants in a set situation" which involved observing how an infant would play or react to a spatula to understand the mutuality between mother and baby. Winnicott's interest in Milner's free drawings can then be understood as building on this interest in the use of objects from within this observational setting).

In her article "Squiggle Evidence: The Child, the Canvas, and the 'Negative Labor' of History," Lisa Farley traces the history of the origins of the squiggle game. Though Winnicott's first published mention of the game appears in 1953 and the first case study is not published until 1965, Farley finds evidence in Winnicott's notebooks from 1945 that he was already drawing with children during this period (14). Like Stefana, Farley speculates that it was Milner who influenced Winnicott's use of drawing in the clinical setting. Considering Milner was a colleague of Winnicott's since 1939, "The significance of this relationship is that Milner, who was deeply interested in the place of the visual in communication, very likely influenced Winnicott's own visual turn" (19).

Despite the likelihood of Milner's influence, Milner and Winnicott each turn to the production of pictures in the consulting room for decidedly different purposes. Milner never tells us of her own participation in a creative game with the patient. Instead, her technique is to allow the patient (child or adult) to create independently in the room with her or outside of it, and she would attend to their drawings created both inside and outside the session. By contrast, the squiggle game produces composite drawings made up of both Winnicott and the patient's mark-making in the session, helping to foster a productive analytic relationship between analyst and patient. In the case study of one girl patient, "L," the squiggle game shows Winnicott that L is able to enjoy playing and is capable of entering into a playful relationship with him (*Psycho-Analytic Explorations* 311). Winnicott does briefly touch on what the symbols L draws might mean, a charging goat for example is understood as "a symbol of male instinct" (312). But Winnicott writes that the squiggle game "will not be found to dominate the scene for more than one session, or at most two or three . . . one can say that the Squiggle Game or its equivalent is useful as a first-session technique" (316–7). He distinguishes this kind of work from psychotherapy and psychoanalysis, preferring instead the term "psychotherapeutic consultation" to describe its use (299). Ultimately, the squiggle game is used as a way to make a preliminary contact with the child patient and, unlike Milner, Winnicott does not consider the curative qualities of the acts of drawing for the patient in and of itself. Ultimately, the squiggle game is a technique that helps foster a relationship between patient and analyst, which is where the main therapeutic relationship takes place.

As another way of demonstrating Milner's distinctive drawing and painting cure as part of, but also separate from the rest the psychoanalytic tradition, I want to end on a paper published in 1981 by the child analyst Lore Schact, entitled "The mirroring function of the child analyst." It helps, I think, to bring Milner's unique formulations greater clarity. Milner supervised Schact's work with a boy patient, Jasper, and Schact writes in her paper how: "I want to express my gratitude for the help given by Mrs. Marion Milner under whose supervision I was able to conduct this analysis" (79). Whilst it is to Winnicott's concept of the mirror role of the mother and analyst that Schact turns for analytic understanding, I think we can see some inflections of Milner's preoccupations around a relationship to a medium— in this case study, an actual mirror—in Schact's paper. Schact writes how in one significant session Jasper first engages with a "mirror in the lock of my handbag," but then quickly "prefers the living mirror and asks me: 'Can you see me?' Out of an experience of his relationship with me he demands my contribution" (84). Schact goes on to consider the meaning of a child's engagement with a real mirror versus the mirroring of mother or therapist:

> I assume that, amongst other things, a child who has to look time and again into a real mirror to find himself, has looked into "emptiness" when looking in mother's face. . . . A child who tries to arouse and to release the mirroring function of the mother or the therapist shows hope and trust in his mother and therapist. A child, however, who is exclusively dependent on the real mirror as such, has given up hope—he has to fill the emptiness himself by going to the mirror. But what he gains by it is not more than a self-made image which can dissolve itself again at any time and has therefore no reliable continuity.
>
> (84)

For Schact, a relationship to the object mirror cannot hope to provide a sufficient substitute for the mirror found within a relationship, in the mother or therapist's face. Milner I am sure would not disagree: the object of the mirror lock cannot provide an equivalent mirroring function. But by engaging with painting, drawing, and creativity more generally, pliable mediums might be found and paper mirrors created, all of which is felt to aid in providing the self with a sense of continuity. And while the influence of this autobiographical cure might be less apparent in other psychoanalysts' clinical technique, we shall see in Part 2 of the book how her methods are taken up by non-analysts elsewhere, beyond the confines of the consulting room.

* * *

Coming to appreciate the full force of her discoveries around painting, Milner writes in *On Not Being Able to Paint* how she had come to realise "how inadequate the phrase 'Art for Art's sake' became; it was rather 'Art for life's sake'" (162). Her experiments with visual art-making in this book expand the reach and depth of her therapeutic methods, whereby both types of line—the drawn line and the written line—come to be deeply explored in the service of a creative, autobiographical cure. Indeed, this chapter has traced the extent through which Milner's thinking though her own self-produced pictures, and those of her patients, contribute to a unique understanding as to how acts of drawing and painting about the self can provide psychoanalytic insight. Playing with visual line allows Milner and her patients to express a selfhood in all its complexity and disturbance, revealing the scars of early experience. But as well as aiding in the communication of psychic experience, Milner opens up the relational world of the artist as a site where these wounded psyches might be healed and transformed.

In the last chapter of *On Not Being Able to Paint*, Milner finds she is finally able to make sense of one of the free drawings that had previously eluded meaning. Called the "Bursting Seed-pod" (Figure 2.5), this drawing had "obvious symbolic reference to a personal theme of producing new life" (167). It is understood as a "picture both of the epoch I was living in and my own relation to that epoch. I saw it as showing the irresistible thrust of life that was giving birth to new ideas and also how they were bursting through the seed-pod of the old world that gave them birth" (167). How different this picture is to the devouring dentata bearing plant of the "Horrified Tadpole," in which terrified bystanders are helpless witnesses to the ball's engulfment. Whereas in this picture the ball is being swallowed whole, in the seed-pod drawing the old plant is producing new, whole seeds, springing forth from the old plant. The birth of these new ideas that can go forth separately into the world imagines a more solid, cohered sense of self, a self that doesn't feel like it will be destroyed or pulled apart into fragments. This is a hopeful vision of a post-war future in the mid-twentieth century, in which the ravages of the past can give way to new life and new beginnings. It is also Milner claiming the potential of her method, a method that can enact a profound transformation in herself, her patient, and her reader.

Figure 2.5 "Bursting Seed-pod" by Marion Milner.

Source: By permission of The Marsh Agency Ltd., on behalf of The Estate of Marion Milner.

Notes

1 This diary was likely written in from when she was eight to twelve years old. The diary is dated from between 1908–12 by the archives of the British Psychoanalytical Society ("Notebook containing a story written by Marion Milner as a child").

2 During her life, Milner exhibited her art in venues such as the former Drian Gallery in London, and a gallery in Shinjo, Japan. We now know that her art never permanently found its home in any art gallery, but one of her paintings did however eventually find itself in the halls of a psychoanalytic institution: "A thought too big for its concept" hangs today in the entrance to the Institute of Psychoanalysis in London.

3 On Pailthorpe and Mednikoff's practice of what they termed "psychorealism," see Hope Wolf's edited collection *A Tale of Mother's Bones: Grace Pailthrope, Reuben Mednikoff and the Birth of Psychorealism.*

4 With regards to Milner's relationship to the movement and discipline of art therapy, Milner never regarded herself as an art therapist although her work is often cited by art therapists including Rita Simon, David Edwards, and Tessa Rawcliffe. Milner succeeded Adrian Hill to become Honorary President of the British Association of Art Therapists, saying of her relationship with BAAT that "I don't do anything for them or with them but they use my name" (Milner qtd. in Hogan 84).

5 This is likely a reference to William Blake and his *Songs of Innocence and Experience* (1789). For further discussion of Blake's influence on Milner and her use of his "composite art," see Chapter 4.

6 Scott's notion of cosmic bliss is similar perhaps to Freud's oceanic feeling in primary narcissism where a feeling of oneness, a non-separation from self and other that is blissful, proceeds object awareness and therefore object separateness. But whereas Freud might have understood this sense of illusion as part of the phantasy of omnipotence that the infant has under the sway of the pleasure principle and must let go in relation to the reality principle, Milner seems to be more sympathetic to the need for such an illusion of omnipotence to be sustained for the right amount of time, similar to Winnicott's thinking on the matter.

7 This desire has been traced back to Romantic longings for wordless communication. See David Wellbery, *The Specular Moment: Goethe's Early Lyric and the Beginnings of Romanticism* (1996) for a discussion of how this longing is traced in the lyric poem from the eighteenth century.

8 Khan attended painting classes with Milner and was an avid collector of modernist works of art, including pieces by Miro and Georges Braque. Poore writes that for Khan, cubism offered a "striking picture of the constant negotiation between private unconscious, object, and outside world," turning to these artists to imagine the productive possibilities for subjective disintegration and disorganisation (210–11).

9 Jo Winning links Milner's concept of the frame to that of modernist painter Gluck's design of her own picture frame, which she called the "Gluck Frame" (120). "Predating Marion Milner by some years," Winning writes, "Gluck, in fact, was much exercised by the limitations of traditional picture frames. . . . Where the edge of the traditional frame usually builds to a deep outer edge, here, in its final wooden incarnation, the Gluck Frame diminishes, fading into the outside space in a way that allows the symbolic contents on the canvas to seep out, to slip off into the space beyond the frame" (120–21).

10 Julie Walsh has also noted the likeness between Milner's drawings of heads in her notebooks held in her archives of the British Psychoanalytical Society and those of Susan's drawings in *The Hands of the Living God* like "Squashed profile head"—with this copying and mimicry, is there a kind of dialogue in drawing between patient and analyst? ("Marion Milner: Modernism, Politics, Psychoanalysis Symposium," University of Sussex, June 21, 2022).

11 The book's title is taken from a line of D.H. Lawrence's poem *The Hands of God*: "It is a fearful thing to fall into the hands of the living God."

12 Winnicott's first published version of his paper "Mirror-Role of Mother and Family in Child Development" appeared in the edited collection by Peter Lomas, *The Predicament of the Family: A Psycho-Analytical Symposium* (1967). Its later publication in *Playing and Reality* (1971) arguably brought its ideas to greater awareness and a larger audience.

13 The concept of the pliable medium might make us consider Winnicott's one mention of a painter and painting in his paper "Mirror role of mother and family in child development" (1953/1971) differently. He finds in the British twentieth-century painter Francis Bacon's self-portrait an example of failure in mirroring the role of mother. For Winnicott, Bacon seeing himself in his mother's face, but with some twist in him or her that maddens both him and us. I know nothing of this artist's private life, and I bring him in only because he forces his way into any present day discussion of the face and the self. Bacon's faces seem to me to be far removed from perception of the actual; in looking at faces he seems to me to be painfully striving towards being seen, which is at the basis of creative looking (*Playing and Reality* 114).

From a Milnerian perspective, painting might have provided Bacon with a substitutive relationship to something more attuned and reciprocal.

References

Balint, Michael. "Notes on the Dissolution of Object-Representation in Modern Art." *Journal of Aesthetics and Art Criticism*, vol. 10, no. 4, 1952, pp. 323–327. http://dx.doi.org/10.2307/426062

Chandler, Marilyn. *A Healing Art: Regeneration through Autobiography*. Routledge, 1990. http://dx.doi.org/10.4324/9781315673837

Farley, Lisa. "Squiggle Evidence: The Child, the Canvas, and the 'Negative Labor' of History." *History and Memory*, vol. 23, no. 2, 2011, pp. 5–39. http://dx.doi.org/10.2979/histmemo.23.2.5

Freud, Anna. "Foreword." *On Not Being Able to Paint*, edited by Marion Milner. Routledge, 1950/2010. http://dx.doi.org/10.4324/9780203833650

Fuller, Peter. *Art and Psychoanalysis*. Writers and Readers Publishing Cooperative, 1980.

Hogan, Susan. *Healing Arts: The History of Art Therapy*. Jessica Kingsley, 2001.

Holmboe, Rye Dag. "A Line Around a Think" in "Special Issue: Marion Milner: Modernism, Politics, Psychoanalysis." *Critical Quarterly*, vol. 63, no. 4, 2021, pp. 51–72.

Jacobus, Mary. *The Poetics of Psychoanalysis*. Oxford University Press, 2005.

Kosofky Sedgwick, Eve. *The Weather in Proust*. Duke University Press, 2011.

Letley, Emma. *Marion Milner: The Life*. Routledge, 2014. http://dx.doi.org/10.4324/9780203767122

Milner, Marion. *Bothered by Alligators*. Routledge, 2013. http://dx.doi.org/10.4324/9780203140147

Milner, Marion. "Me and Not Me." *Interview with Chris Crickmay, Typed Transcript of the Interview. P01-B-B-05. Marion Milner Collection*. Archives of the British Psychoanalytical Society, 1975/2020.

Milner, Marion. "Notebook Containing a Story Written by Marion Milner as a Child." *P01-E-D-01. Marion Milner Collection*. Archives of the British Psychoanalytical Society, 1908–1912/2020.

Milner, Marion. *On Not Being Able to Paint*. Routledge, 1950/2010. http://dx.doi. org/10.4324/9780203833650

Milner, Marion. *The Hands of the Living God: An Account of a Psycho-analytic Treatment*. Routledge, 1969/2010. http://dx.doi.org/10.4324/9780203833643

Milner, Marion. *The Supressed Madness of Sane Men: Forty-Four Years of Exploring Psychoanalysis*. Routledge, 1987.

Pajaczkowska, Claire. "On Humming: Reflections on Marion Milner's Contribution to Psychoanalysis." *Winnicott and the Psychoanalytic Tradition: Interpretation and Other Psychoanalytic Issues*, edited by Lesley Caldwell. Routledge, 2018, pp. 33–48. http://dx.doi.org/10.4324/9780429485077-4

Parsons, William B. "The Oceanic Feeling Revisited." *The Journal of Religion*, vol. 78, no. 4, 1998, pp. 501–523. http://dx.doi.org/10.1086/490288

Poore, Benjamin. *Modernism and the Making of Masud Khan*. Dissertation. Queen Mary University, 2015.

Remy, Michel. "Lives of the Artists Grace Pailthorpe and Reuben Mednikoff." *Tate Etc.*, vol. 44, 2018.

Schact, Lore. "The Mirroring Function of the Child Analyst." *Journal of Child Psychotherapy*, vol. 7, no. 1, 1981, pp. 79–88. http://dx.doi.org/10.1080/00754178108255018

Stefana, Alberto. "Revisiting Marion Milner's Work on Creativity and Art." *The International Journal of Psychoanalysis*, vol. 100, no. 1, 2019, pp. 128–147. http://dx.doi.org/10.1080/00207578.2018.1533376

Stonebridge, Lyndsey. *The Destructive Element*. Routledge, 1998. http://dx.doi.org/10.1007/978-1-349-26721-7

Winnicott, D.W. *Playing and Reality*. Tavistock Publications, 1971. http://dx.doi.org/10.4324/9780203441022

Winnicott, D.W. *Psycho-Analytic Explorations*. Routledge, 1989. http://dx.doi.org/10.4324/9780429478932

Winnicott, D.W. "The Location of Cultural Experience." *International Journal of Psycho-Analysis*, vol. 48, 1967, pp. 368–372

Winnicott, D.W. "Transitional Objects and Transitional Phenomena—A Study of the First Not-Me Possession." *International Journal of Psycho-Analysis*, vol. 34, 1953, pp. 89–97. http://dx.doi.org/10.4324/9780429475931-14

Winning, Joanne. "Love and the Art Object." *Modernism and Affect*, edited by Julie Taylor. Edinburgh University Press, 2015, pp. 111–130. http://dx.doi.org/10.1515/9780748693269

Chapter 3

Bothered by Alligators and compensating for the failures of a "couch analysis"

Lively conversation and a glass of whiskey (or two) in the consulting room. This jovial scene is a familiar one painted by close friends and colleagues of Milner in the last years of her life. The art therapist Martina Thomson describes her meetings with Milner in her tribute, "Marion Milner Remembered" published in the *International Journal of Art Therapy* in 2001. She recalls fondly being welcomed into

> a light, spacious room on the upper ground floor which was then still her consulting room with its analytic couch "Would you like some tea?" She asked, "Or some whiskey?" "Whiskey, I think", I said. "Good", she said smiling openly and we never looked back. At the many meetings that followed, the bottle of Teacher's, the jug of water and two tiny glasses were ritual.
>
> (Thomson 83)

In his new introduction to *The Hands of the Living God* (2010), Adam Phillips also reminisces how "towards the end of her life I would sometimes go on a Saturday afternoon to talk with Marion Milner, and to drink whiskey. She would talk with wide attention about many things" ("Introduction" xxxiii). Philips notes, however, that one particular topic of conversation would often crop up, sobering the occasion. He remembers how in their meetings "she mostly wanted to talk to me about her relationship with Winnicott, partly, I think, because I had recently written a book about him and partly because her relationship with him had left her troubled" (xxxiii).

Linda Hopkins paints a similar picture when visiting Milner at her home, finding Milner preoccupied with her experience of being analysed by Winnicott and her earlier analysis with Sylvia Payne:

> I had the privilege of meeting with Milner in 1996, when she was 96 years old, and just a year and a half away from her death. I interviewed her in connection with research for a biography I am writing on Masud Khan, who had been her student, her editor, and her friend. As things turned out, she didn't have much to tell me about Khan, and she talked mostly about other parts of

DOI: 10.4324/9781003296720-5

her analytic life. . . . I was fascinated to hear that she felt that she had never been sufficiently analysed—that her own underlying "madness" had not been understood in her analyses with Payne and Winnicott.

(234–36)

This fixation with her past analyses, especially her analysis with Winnicott, is also given expression in her final book *Bothered by Alligators*, left unfinished at her death but posthumously published by Routledge in 2013. Suzanna Richards "remembers that Milner worked on the book for many years and became stuck and was often very upset when writing the chapter concerning her relationship and analysis with Winnicott" (Margaret Boyle Spelman 63). Martina Thomson also notes this distress in her final visit to Milner on the evening before her death, on 28 May 1998. Winnicott and her patient Susan "were much on Marion's mind. She wept and, out of her distress, found a last line for a chapter about Winnicott for *Bothered by Alligators*" (63).

Indeed, this charged emotional state, as we shall see, informs the mood of *Bothered by Alligators*, which involves a painful revising of her experiences of being a patient of Winnicott's, and attempts to compensate for these failures on the couch through her own autobiographical cure. Her ambivalence towards the institution and profession of psychoanalysis reaches a crescendo in this final autobiographical book, and it is here where we find Milner at her most critical of her own experiences as a psychoanalytic patient, and adamant in providing herself with her own autobiographical cures.

The failures of a "couch analysis"

Milner was working on the manuscript for *Bothered by Alligators* up until her death in 1998. Although she died before the book was fully edited and completed, its subsequent publication by Routledge in 2013 provides a valuable addition to Milner's corpus. Of all of Milner's books it is perhaps the most conventionally autobiographical in its accounts of her upbringing, providing biographies of her parents and family members, and details the events of a life lived out in the world. Nevertheless, like its predecessors, *Bothered by Alligators* is highly invested in continuing the search for and development of therapeutic cures at the site of different autobiographical and creative acts. As well as continuing to engage with the well-trodden methods of free associative diary keeping and free drawing, Milner turns to the analysis of a recently discovered story-book written by her son John when he was a child, along with the diaries she kept long ago recording John's early years. In addition, Milner develops a practice of making collages out of her old paintings which are explored as another creative, curative practice. If we can characterise *A Life* as presenting itself as providing a therapeutic method to rival psychoanalysis, with *On Not Being Able to Paint* influencing and adapting the clinical practice of psychoanalysis, *Bothered by Alligators* deliberately tasks itself with providing a compensation for her own failed experiences of being on the couch. Milner turns to her own methods in order "to make up for what had gone wrong in my own experience of being a patient in psychoanalysis" (Milner, *BBA* 12). And it is here that Milner simultaneously reflects on her own troubling experiences of care—of mothering, being mothered, and being a patient of psychoanalysis.

Milner uses the term "couch analysis" to refer to her experiences as a psychoanalytic patient (189). This term emphasises the site of the couch as distinct from that of the page or canvas, as alternatives "spaces" for where an analysis might take place. Milner does make some acknowledgement of what her couch analysis did for her—when analysing the image of a steamroller in John's storybook, she writes how she was now very much aware that "such a steamroller could still be at work inside me, even though much modified by the years on the psychoanalytic couch" (156). In general, however, *Bothered by Alligators* presents a picture of the many ways in which her experiences of analysis came up short at best, and at worst, left indelible wounds. Her autobiographical cure is presented as not only able to produce the same results as a psychoanalysis, but as capable of redressing the shortcomings of analysis. We learn that through the course of her explorations she was "discovering, through meditating on the diary and story book, something that had apparently not been adequately realised in my own couch analysis" (189).

What were Milner's experiences of a "couch analysis," and how does she understand these experiences from the vantage point of later life? As we know, her first experience of talking therapy was with Dr Irma Putnam in Boston for a period of several months. In *A Life* she considers how this was "a period which would of course be considered only a preliminary stroll by the Freudian school . . . but I certainly found it an immensely interesting experience" (159). Much later in her life Milner is more dismissive of the experience, sounding herself more like the Freudian school she once felt disregarded by—in an interview in 1989 she tells Janet Sayers how her experience was not "really analysis. In Boston I saw a Jungian two or three times a week for three months. I didn't know the difference then between Freud and Jung" (Milner qtd. in Letley 19).

Upon returning from the States to life back in London, Milner began to see the psychoanalyst Sylvia Payne about three times a week, with Payne eventually becoming her training analyst in 1939 as she embarked on qualifying to become a psychoanalyst in 1943. "My training analysis," she tells us in *Bothered by Alligators*, "was, I now think, rushed through, because of a shortage of analysts to take on the training of students, owing to many being away on war work" (233). Milner also mentions in *Bothered by Alligators* that when in analysis with a "Freudian" (whom she doesn't name, but the description fits Sylvia Payne best), she brought to one a session a drawing she had made. Recounting this session, she felt "fairly sure she [Payne] said nothing about it," an insinuation that suggests she would have welcomed an analyst's attention to her creations (Milner, *BBA* 174). Likely not helped by the war-time conditions, Payne as analyst does not seem to provide Milner with the understanding she needs. We might say that this oversight in the analysis is made up for in the same period with her engagement with drawing and the pliable medium in *On Not Being Able to Paint*.

Shortly after qualifying as a psychoanalyst and in the midst of the Second World War, Milner began an analysis with Winnicott in 1943, lasting until 1947.

This analysis preoccupied Milner long after it was over. Part 8 of *Bothered by Alligators*, entitled "D.W. Winnicott and me" reflects on her analytic, professional, and personal relationship with Winnicott. She describes the sequence of events that led her to commencing the analysis:

> It was only after a few years of practising with patients that I happened to hear D.W. Winnicott (probably on a radio broadcast) saying that having swollen finger joints might have some connection with a bit of madness. Since I noticed my own finger joints had become swollen, I rang him, to say that I did not think my own training analyst had understood my mad bit, and could he advise me about who I should go to for some more analysis. After a little time (I don't remember how long) he actually suggested himself.
>
> (Miner, *BBA* 233)

Winnicott offered to analyse Milner in her own home, which at the time she "assumed he did this out of kindness, to save me time" by avoiding the journey to Winnicott's consulting room (233). With hindsight she writes that "It seems I was grateful for this plan," but "surprisingly, did not question the arrangement by which he was to be sitting daily in my consulting room chair, and me lying on my own analytic couch" (233–34). These were not the only unusual arrangements between the two. To add to these professional and personal entanglements, Milner's husband, Dennis Milner, was also in analysis with Winnicott during this period, with sessions also held at the Milner family home.

Milner's patient Susan was referred to her for treatment by Winnicott and his wife. Winnicott's first wife Alice Buxton had taken an interest in Susan after meeting her in the hospital, eventually inviting her to live with Winnicott and herself, a set-up which continued for some time until the break-up of their marriage. In Milner's account of how she came to analyse Susan in *The Hands of the Living God* she refers to a "Mr. X," a thinly veiled disguise for Winnicott. Mr X is described by Milner as "a man of independent means, who was interested in problems to do with mental health. He asked if I would undertake a research-analysis with a girl, Susan, aged twenty-three, who was just about to come out of a hospital for functional and nervous diseases" (Milner, *HOLG* 3). Acknowledging that Milner "might not want to take on such a difficult problem," he reassures her that "the main treatment would be the fact that he and his wife were providing her with a home" (3). She tells us frankly how difficult the analysis was, and that "from time to time over the years she [Susan] would say I was crazy and that she was getting worse. . . . I certainly had no conviction at these times that I was really helping her and I frequently shared her doubts about whether the analysis should go on at all. . . . I think it was only Mr X's belief that it should which kept us at it" (30). Winnicott was then a central figure in the instigation and continuation of Milner and Susan's analytic relationship.

The Susan-Winnicott-Milner analytic triangle quickly became unsupportable in the aftermath of the dissolution of Winnicott's marriage. Susan suffered another breakdown, and something had to change. Milner recounts how "quite soon I could no longer manage the situation of having to analyse Susan in her temporary breakdown at the same time as being Winnicott's patient. Obviously I could not abandon Susan, so I left Winnicott and went for analysis to Clifford Scott" (*BBA* 225). One wonders what kind of accusation against Winnicott this conceals, since he was inarguably the more experienced analyst in the situation. As Emma Letley notes, this was an "unusual arrangement, to say the least (arguably more characteristic of their time than of ours)," the boundaries between the personal and the professional surely also exacerbated by the chaos of the wartime period (Letley 53).

For Milner, however productive and generative her intellectual relationship with Winnicott was later in their careers, her experience of Winnicott on the couch was troubling and failed to enact the inner transformation she was both hoping for and expecting. In *Bothered by Alligators* she reflects on moments of transgression in the analysis, with Winnicott on one occasion leaving her a gift of a crucifix after one session with no explanation (Milner, *BBA* 235). Sometime after the analysis ended, Winnicott tells Milner that he knew he shouldn't have done it, but he would not have done this with anyone else. She writes how on reflection "this being special was not what I really wanted, I wanted analysis" (235). Their close relationship, which at points seem to teeter perilously close into romantic territory, is revealed in their personal letters to one another.[1] In an unpublished letter from 22 March 1943, Winnicott tells Milner that he had read her recent letter several times and tells her "I very easily see in you something very loveable, and tantalisingly unfathomable," but adds that he "could not have too much of you . . . as I cannot eat you I shall probably want to choose from among the possibilities which leave life manageable as a going concern" (Winnicott qtd. in Letley 55). These romantic intimations also invite the idea that Winnicott and Milner were like "parents" to Susan, further blurring the boundaries between the personal and professional. Upon the termination of the analysis, Milner writes how:

> Certainly I remember that in my last sessions as Winnicott's patient, in 1947, I could not stop crying at having felt I must stop the analysis, just as I had been, according to my family, unable to stop crying when the nanny, who admitted having spoilt me, left us. What Winnicott did say seems to indicate that he was forgetting what Freud had discovered about how his patients transferred their feelings about childhood figures onto him. What Winnicott said to me, was that he did not know I felt so strongly about him.
>
> (*BBA* 237)

It seems that the struggle to maintain appropriate professional analytic boundaries also haunted Winnicott. He would later tell Milner that he thought she was "a casualty of analysis" but added that "anyway the period with him was far too short, lasting only four years" (235). In her interview with Linda Hopkins in 1996 Milner describes the limitations of the analysis for both herself and Winnicott: "the analysis was a failure. Once after we had ended, he said to me, 'You'll be on my conscience until my dying day.' But I never asked him why! I think it's because there was no use of the countertransference in the analysis—that's what I needed to find my 'madness.'" (Milner qtd. in Hopkins 238). As Winnicott himself wrote in an essay in 1955, "Clinical varieties of transference," that "every failed analysis is a failure not of the patient but of the analyst," he would likely have been acutely aware of his own shortcomings in the analytic relation (257).

Milner also casts doubt on the interpretations she recalls Winnicott making during the course of her analysis, painting him in a light in which he appears much closer to the Freudian analyst's role as interpretative master than mirroring presence. She describes in *Bothered by Alligators* how:

> The main interpretation that I remember he made was that I have been spending the rest of my life trying to deal with my father's schizophrenia. Was he right in what he said? Surely it depends on how you define the term schizophrenia? I do remember telling Winnicott that once, when we were living at Hindhead, my father, who sat at the head of the table in his Windsor chair, and was standing beside it just before a meal, suddenly bent over, put his hands on the arms of the chair, lent forward and kicked his heels up in the air. Winnicott said, "OK, if you thought it was funny (which I did) but it might have seemed a bit mad." He also said he thought my sister must have looked down upon me in my cot and hated me. It has taken me all these years to try to work out just what he meant by saying these things, in fact, to wonder if they were true.
>
> (237)

In this description Winnicott seems to embody what he himself refuted in the figure of the psychoanalyst that concerns himself with "making clever and apt interpretations" at the expense of the patient (*Playing and Reality* 5). His belief that an analysis should involve the "long-term giving the patient back what the patient brings" is brought into question by Milner in her description of her experiences with him (5).

After the termination of the analysis with Winnicott, Milner went on to have what she considered was a more effective analysis with Clifford Scott. She reports that his first comment to her was that the analysis with Winnicott "had all been a travesty of psychoanalysis" (Milner *BBA* 235).[2] Despite this new start, the analysis was prematurely cut short when Scott returned to live in his native Canada. Ultimately, these experiences of a "couch analysis" were frustrating at best and disturbing at their worst. Milner partly attributes this to the analytic techniques of her era; in an interview she reveals how "I envy people in analysis now, because today's analysts know how to find the aggression and work with it" (Milner qtd. in Hopkins 238). As Winnicott outlines in his 1969 paper "The Use of an Object," the analyst/object must be able to survive the destructiveness of the patient/subject in order for the patient to feel trustworthily held. It seems that for Milner, her aggression towards Winnicott was not able to be "found" or appropriately used in the analytic relationship. We see this anger towards Winnicott in some degree expressed in her later writing on him in *Bothered by Alligators* (we also learn that shortly after writing about her analysis with Winnicott in this book she experiences an "eye burst," a burst blood vessel in the eye, which Milner describes as sparked by "a terror that a split-off and angrily rebellious bit of myself would emerge with disastrous results" (251)).

In her description of the analysis with Winnicott, Milner seems to reexperience a relationship in which the other is felt to impinge and interfere. One of Milner's closest friends, the analyst Nina Farhi suggests that Milner herself always retained a resistance to being in analysis. Letley writes how in personal communication with Farhi, "One of Milner's close friends has said that the trouble with her analyses was that she caused each of her analysts to fall in love with her— 'thus remaining outside the experience—deeply lonely but formidably independent. She both did and did not seek 'to be found'" (Letley 54). Milner's autobiographical books and their independent search for self-cure resonate deeply with this picture. Perhaps involving a scotomization of the relational, the autobiographical cure avoids the complicated realm of interpersonal relations and the transferences and countertransferences that might prove harmful.

Creating her own "inner analysts"

We find then that the main effective analytic presences in Milner's later life are not another psychoanalyst or indeed another person; they are instead attributed in *Bothered by Alligators* to her self-created forms or the childish works of her son, John. These self-created forms, such as the collages she creates later in life, are directly referred to as analysts, described as aesthetic objects with interpretive powers. These collages which she writes about in the chapter "Play of making collages from my old failed paintings" are made out of her older paintings which are cut up into fragments and reassembled into new configurations. In an interview with Elizabeth Meakins, Milner characterises these collages in the following way: "They are not planned at all, just playing with colours and shapes. Only when finished do they tell me what they are about. Then they become a kind of inner analyst" (Milner qtd. in Meakins 132).

In *Bothered by Alligators* she describes the analytic capacities of her collages in greater detail: "There was yet another collage amongst the twenty or so which I had got framed and hung on my studio wall so that they could talk to me or to any of my friends who might have ideas about what they are saying. This was one that I myself kept putting off listening to" (196). Eventually taking note of her evasion, she forces herself to listen to what the collage had to "say." She finds that in terms reminiscent of the answering activity, this speaking collage, which she titles "Woebegone" helpfully makes her aware of her need to "trust in what one does not yet know; in fact, once more, trust in emptiness, trust in the gap in knowing" (197).

Another collage, "The Green Baby" (Figure 3.1) depicts the shapes of two figures cut out of an old painting and superimposed onto a watercolour background next to the figure of a cradle. This collage she sees as coming to represent a "double hole" that had been left from "the feelings of emptiness when my parents were away together after my father's breakdown. . . . Also could it even be that behind this feeling of loss

Figure 3.1 "The Green Baby" by Marion Milner.

Source: By permission of The Marsh Agency Ltd., on behalf of The Estate of Marion Milner.

there was also a more deeply hidden memory of the sudden loss of warm contact of my infant lips with my mother's breast?" (195). The collage provides Milner with her own understanding of what was psychically most impactful about her relationship with her father and mother, with Winnicott's interpretation of her father's schizophrenia and its effect on her seemingly fading into the background.

Figure 3.2 Photo of a selection of Marion Milner's clay heads in Giles Milner's personal collection. Titles and dates unknown.

Source: By permission of The Marsh Agency Ltd., on behalf of The Estate of Marion Milner.

Martina Thomson describes seeing in Milner's home a number of clay figures made by Milner and arranged in different rooms of the house. To one of these clay heads, Milner gave the name "Sad Mr. Freud." These figures were, according to Thompson, "her witnesses and were often consulted" (qtd. in Caldwell 146). I myself met some of these silent analytic figures when I visited Milner's grandson's personal collection of her work. They were also reminiscent, I think, of the many sculptures and figures that populated Freud's study (Figure 3.2).[3]

Unlike her experiences on the couch, Milner's speaking collages and consulting clay heads come closest to an analytic presence like that of the pliable medium.

These clay forms and collages are literal manifestations of the analyst as pliable medium, standing in stark contrast to Winnicott's interpretations which are felt to be a form of analytic intrusion and demand compliance. In the analytic powers that Milner ascribes to these earthy, nonhuman objects, they bypass the problematic otherness of analyst and countertransference, as well as providing an experience of the attuning, adaptive pliable medium in the process of their being created.

The other creations that Milner attributes with providing her with an experience of being analysed are those of her son John's creations. John's story-book, created when he was seven years old, is composed of words and drawings that narrate a number of short stories (the story-book is reproduced in its entirety in Part 3 of *Bothered by Alligators*) (Figure 3.3). Milner painfully admits she hadn't paid much attention to the story-book when John first gave it to her in 1939. Only at the age of 90, when she re-discovered it amongst her papers and looked at it more attentively, did she find it deeply moving. She finds it helps her understand her son and a child's experience more generally, suggesting how a child can "struggle with the interplay of his own and parents' problems, and how he can do this by using his poetic intuition long before he can express the problems in direct logical speech" (Milner, *BBA* 2).

By attending to John's story-book, however, she "kept finding that deep psychoanalytic ideas kept cropping up, and this made me anxious that I might really be trying to analyse my own child," a discomfort at her own potential to inappropriately blur relationship boundaries and become mother as analyst (2). But she then goes on to shift the focus of the analysis in Part 4 of the book, "Towards a change of aim," writing how "I slowly came to realise that it was not a question of me analysing him, but rather of his images analysing me" (2). Milner reminds herself of this again later in the book, proclaiming: "No, it's his images analysing me, helping me to find out what had been left out of my own couch analysis" (145). Turning to her son's story-book becomes, in her words, an "attempt to see if I could use J's images to make up for what had gone wrong in my own experience of being a patient in psychoanalysis, and to see how far this could be done without the help of the analyst and the psychoanalytic couch" (12). A strange analytic substitute, perhaps, but one that Milner assures herself is tempered by the impersonality of paper and the passing of time. At the time during which Milner was writing *Bothered by Alligators* in the late 1990s, John was now well into adulthood, holding the position of Senior Fellow at his university (2). The John that is engaged with in the book, however, is between the ages of two and nine. The only mention in the book of John in his adult, contemporary form is when Milner describes his reaction to her plans for writing about the story-book and diary after re-discovering them:

> He had chuckled at a few of the items but said he had no memory at all of making the story book. Later when I sent him a note telling him of the plan to publish it and the diary together with my own comments, he had phoned and said simply, "No problem."

(2)

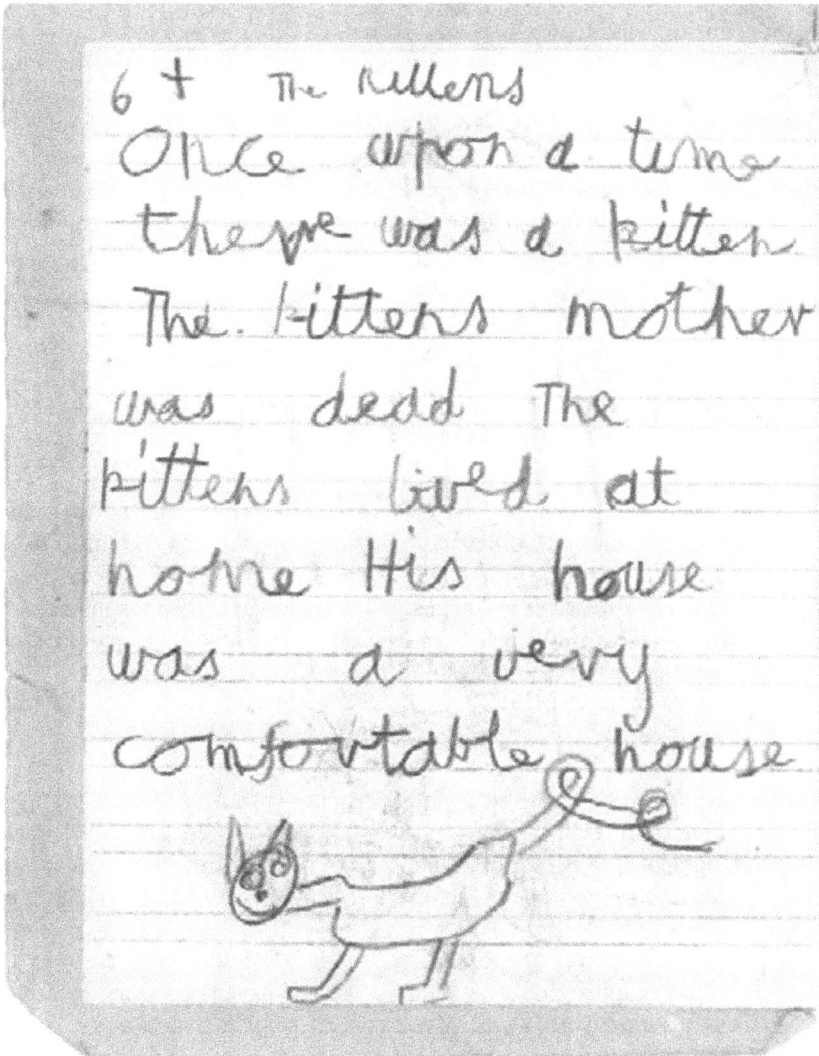

Figure 3.3 Page from John Milner's story-book.
Source: By permission of The Marsh Agency Ltd., on behalf of The Estate of Marion Milner.

No other mention is made of her son or their relationship in the years beyond those attended to here. This gives the curious feeling in the book of their relationship as existing primarily through the historical documents associated with John in this period: the diary Milner kept about him, his story-book, and a picture letter he sent to her. Milner puts the reader at a distance from the living and breathing John, mediating their relationship through time and text, communicating instead with her son's creative productions. Again, we see Milner designate the work of the flesh and blood analyst to that of the site of paper, drawing, and writing—this time not to her own autobiographical creations, but that of someone else's. Margaret Walters writes in her introduction to *Bothered by Alligators* that Milner "never quite comes to a definite summation of her son's image-text" (xvi). But it is her method to keep "returning to it, teasing out more meanings from it, and using it as a springboard for musings about herself and the relationship with her own mother" (xvi). John's story-book seems to provide analytic insight that is difficult but digestible, and importantly devoid of any damaging countertransference.

One of John's stories in the story-book narrates in words and drawings the life of a kitten whose mother has died. This story provides Milner with distressing insight into herself during this time in her son's life and her "unadmitted depressive feelings about holding together the security" of her marriage with her husband, Dennis Milner (Milner, *BBA* 159). Meditating on a story, she wonders:

> Could it not also be that he [John] was trying to convey a feeling of something intermittently not sufficiently alive in me? This was painful to think about, but I did now have to face the fact that during some of those years there had certainly been a backdrop of anxiety about the security of our marriage, a preoccupation that could have been recurrently interfering with my sensitivity to his feelings, on a deep level.
>
> (158)

This passage is painfully reminiscent of Milner's own feelings about her mother's unhappiness in Milner's early life, and the struggles that impacted her capacity to care for Milner as a baby. Milner also suggests that John necessarily turned to his own autobiographical cure to provide himself with the maternal functions he was missing. Meditating on a story of John's about a bird building a nest, she tells us the following:

> [I] kept thinking that the nest building must also have to do with his feeling about all the times when I seemed to be not properly holding him: in my reveries, or too busy with my work. . . . Whatever the possible relevance of such an idea, I felt that the real culmination of all the nest building was the story book itself, a self-created container for his growing awareness of his separate and unique identity.
>
> (137)

Like mother, like son, it seems—the autobiographical cure turned to in the absence of a good enough relationship. In *Bothered by Alligators* we learn that in order to write *An Experiment in Leisure* in 1937, Milner left the country for a period, working on the manuscript in Spain away from Dennis and John, then aged seven. Re-reading John's story-book and a picture letter he sent her at the time leads her to wonder about the repercussions this time away had had on her son. She wonders if

> J must have managed to deal creatively with this shock through the gradual discovery that he could learn to make meaningful marks on paper, marks which in the end had become the story book, something live enough to make a bridge of communication both with other people and with hidden parts of himself.
>
> (157)

With autobiographical mark-making providing a kind of bridge, we are reminded of Milner's words in *On Not Being Able to Paint* when she writes how the parent–child relationship "could fail through inability to establish communication" but that "the free drawing method that apparently made it partly able to compensate for that failure, able to act as a bridge" (117). John's story-book is thus understood as attempt to find in his own acts of creation an ideal mother better than his own. But it is also a place whereby he can communicate his loving feelings. Milner writes how the story-book

> shows his capacity both to create and play with images of his own experience, including images for his feelings, conflicts, fears and enjoyment, all embodied in the stories he told himself, the story-telling in fact a loving gift of himself made by the integrating of work and play, the love shown in the care to produce what is obviously meant to be read, with its carefully numbered pages and beautifully painted cover.
>
> (*BBA* 158)

Milner's pride here is evident, her son's loving gift is sharing his inner world with his reader, his mother. The same might be said for Milner's own autobiographical books and creations. Whilst they might involve a defensive withdrawal from the figures of the analyst or mother, they also provide the reader with an object created out of love.

In defence of the autobiographical cure

If in later life we find Milner talking and writing openly about her misgivings towards Winnicott's practices as a psychoanalyst, we also come to learn that Winnicott may have had his own reservations about Milner's autobiographical works. At the end of the chapter "Being in Analysis with Winnicott" in *Bothered by Alligators*, Milner brings up a reference to *A Life of One's Own* that Winnicott makes in his chapter "Contemporary Concepts of Adolescent Development and their Implications for Higher Education" in *Playing and Reality* (1971). Based on a lecture he gave to the British Student Health Association, Winnicott explains his views on the development, growth, and immaturity experienced in adolescence.

Before turning to the psychological issues particular to this stage of life, Winnicott begins by establishing the importance of maternal care for helping to provide for the infant, child, and later the teenager a sense of continuity in being. He writes:

> Let me refer to the maternal provision. We now know that it does matter how a baby is held and handled, that it matters who it is that is caring for the baby, and whether this is in fact the mother, or someone else. In our theory of child care, continuity of care has become a central feature of the concept of the facilitating environment, and we see that by this continuity of environmental provision, and only by this, the new baby in dependence may have a continuity in the line of his or her life, not a pattern of reacting to the unpredictable and for ever starting again (cf. Milner, 1934).
>
> (Winnicott, *Playing and Reality* 141)

In referring here to Milner's 1934 book, *A Life of One's Own*, Winnicott seems to be suggesting that the book is itself an example of, or a reaction to, unpredictable care, part of a futile attempt at providing oneself with a sense of continuity of being. This is at least how Milner interprets the reference, writing in *Bothered by Alligators*: "Was Winnicott right in using my first book as an example of my 'for ever starting again'? I am still doubtful about this, for, as I see it, writing that book initiated change in my inner world that has been going on continuously ever since" (238). Milner does seem to share Winnicott's understanding that she experienced unpredictable care in early life (in *Bothered by Alligators*, as we know, she writes: "Very slowly I began to face the possibility that my mother had been secretly unhappy, in her marriage, perhaps from the very beginning of my life" (218) and "was it that I had always been trying not to see my mother's pain and woes because of my not yet having properly separated out hers from mine?" (220). Given this she wonders, "did this mean that I would never have any 'continuity of being'?" (238)). But for Winnicott, Milner's autobiographical book is a symptom, a product, of Milner's early traumas. *A Life* is therefore seen as an ultimately futile, doomed attempt in trying to find a sense of being and self. Milner's distrust of Winnicott's pronouncement of her book as symptom shows a clear parting of ways around whether this kind of autobiographical project is simply another manifestation of the problem or the means through which to resolve it.

We can glean more of Winnicott's views in this area in another chapter in *Playing and Reality*, "Playing: Creative Activity and the Search for the Self." Winnicott does not make any direct reference to Milner's therapeutic strategies, but he does make clear his stance on the creative artists' attempts to find themselves through their creation of emotionally resonant forms. Winnicott is of course a famous proponent of the importance of playing for the psychic health of both child and adult, the creativity of playing seen as facilitating mental growth and healthy development. He writes of the importance of play as enabling the individual "to use the whole personality, and it is only in being creative that the individual discovers the self" (Winnicott, *Playing and Reality* 54). This does not mean, however, that it is through one's creative products that a sense of self is forged. Winnicott goes on to explain that it "is a frequent experience in clinical work to meet with persons who want help and who are searching for the self and who are trying to find themselves in the products of their creative experiences" (54). But if "the artist (in whatever medium) is searching for the self," he concludes, "then it can be said that in all probability there is already some failure for that artist in the field of general creative living. The finished creation never heals the underlying lack of sense of self" (54–55). Instead, the only resolution for this kind of patient, Winnicott writes

> depends on there being a certain quantity of reflecting back to the individual on the part of the trusted therapist (or friend) who has taken the (indirect) communication. In these highly specialized conditions the individual can come together and exist as a unit, not as a defence against anxiety but as an expression of I AM, I am alive, I am myself. . . . From this position everything is creative.
>
> (55)

It is the reflection of the self within an interpersonal setting, not through searching for a reflection of the self in one's creative products, that is understood as being able to provide a person with a real and profound sense of self.

Winnicott's exploration of creativity and psychic health during this period also extends to another paper, "Living Creatively." Borne out of an amalgamation of two talks for the Progressive League in 1970 and published in the posthumous collection of his papers, *Home Is Where We Start From* (1990), Winnicott makes a similar argument about the artist and the search for self. Here he states even more emphatically how "life is worth living or not, according to whether creativity is or is not a part of an individual person's living experience" (Winnicott, "Living Creatively" 213). "To be creative a person must exist and have a feeling of existing, not in conscious awareness, but as a basic place to operate from," if not "[a] whole life may be built on the pattern of reacting to stimuli. Withdraw the stimuli and the individual has no life" (213–14). He explicitly defines creativity as "the doing that arises out of being," writing: "I come back to the maxim: Be before Do. Be has to develop behind Do. Then eventually the child rides even the instincts without loss of sense of self" (215).

We might compare this maxim of Winnicott's to the one Milner comes up with through the course of her explorations in *On Not Being Able to Paint*: "how inadequate the phrase 'Art for Art's sake' became; it was rather 'Art for Life's sake'" (140). Whereas for Winnicott, the child must feel it exists before it can live creatively, for Milner it is through creative activity and through the creation of her autobiographical books that self is felt to be able to be found. This stance is also reflected in one of Milner's own psychoanalytic writings, "Psychoanalysis and Art" (1956) published in *The Suppressed Madness of Sane Men* (1987). The statement "The sovereign awakening of creative subjectivity to itself" by the French Catholic philosopher Jacques Maritain captures what she wants to say about creativity and psychic health, another depiction of the self exclusively providing itself with a creative subjectivity, an intrasubjective rather than intersubjective provision of a sense of identity and selfhood (Milner, *SMSM* 156).

Some twenty-two years before the publication of *Playing and Reality* and Winnicott's reference to *A Life of One's* Own, another paper of Winnicott's, "Mind and its relation to the psyche-soma," engages with a patient's autobiographical writing, specifically, diary keeping. This paper was originally delivered as lecture in 1949, revised for publication in 1953 and published in the *British Journal of Medical Psychology* in 1954. To illustrate his thinking on the importance of a good environment in infancy for mental health in adulthood, Winnicott presents us with a case study of his psychoanalytic work with a forty-seven-year-old woman. He describes this patient as having:

> made what seemed to others but not to herself to be a good relationship to the world and had always been able to earn her own living. She had achieved a good education and was generally liked; in fact I think she was never actively disliked. She herself, however, felt completely dissatisfied, as if always aiming to find herself and never succeeding.
>
> (Winnicott, "Mind and Its Relation to the Psyche-Soma" 27)

Milner was forty-seven years old when she ended her analysis with Winnicott in 1947. Certainly, Winnicott's description of his patient in this passage has the emotional feel and shape of Milner. We also learn that the patient had undergone a Freudian "classical" analysis for some years before beginning analysis with Winnicott, which fits with Milner's period of analysis with Sylvia Payne. But perhaps most tellingly, Winnicott refers to how this patient kept a diary through much of the analysis, where the events of each session would be meticulously recorded. As we know, Milner was consistently keeping diaries throughout the period when Winnicott was writing and rewriting versions of "Mind and Its Relation to the Psyche-Soma," some of which are included in excerpts in books such as *A Life of One's Own* (1934), *Experiment in Leisure* (1937) and *On Not Being Able to Paint* (1950). If Winnicott was indeed writing about his analysis with Milner here, he does not do much to quash speculation that the patient is her—and one might wonder whether at the time this might have felt like a betrayal of confidence for Milner. Whilst we may never be able to confirm the true identity of this patient, Winnicott's understanding of the woman's diary keeping offers an interesting illustration of the differences between his and Milner's thinking.

Winnicott describes how his patient suffered from suicidal inclinations, but which were kept at bay by "her belief which dated from childhood that she would ultimately solve her problem and find herself" (205). Through the course of the analysis, Winnicott comes to find that the patient must make a "very severe regression or else give up the struggle" (205). This regression would come to take the form of episodes in which the patient would in the session throw herself off the couch and onto the floor. These episodes are understood as a regression to an early, prenatal stage of life in which the birth process, a painful, traumatic, existentially threatening experience, had to be re-enacted and re-experienced. Winnicott links the patient's fear of death during the re-enacted birth process to a fear of "not-knowing" (206). Knowledge is here understood as trust in a reliable environment, where one can have confidence in depending on the mind of another. Because of the early failures in the patient's environment, the patient's "whole life had been built up around mental functioning which had become falsely the place (in the head) from which she lived, and her life which had rightly seemed to her false had been developed out of this mental functioning" (206). Eventually through the course of the analysis, "[a]cceptance of not-knowing produced tremendous relief" since ' "[k]nowing" became transformed into "the analyst knows," that is to say 'behaves reliably in active adaptation to the patient's needs'" (206) To be known is to exist, in the same way that to be seen is to exist. Winnicott as the adaptive analyst can, in knowing and seeing the patient, reflect back her existence, making up for early environmental failures—what Winnicott would later consider failures in the mother's mirroring—to support the patient's continuity of being. (It is worth reminding ourselves that Milner's "answering activity" provides a function that is linked to knowing: It is "an activity that I can only describe as a knowing, yet a knowing that was nothing to do with me; it was a knowing that could see forwards and backwards and in a flash give form to the confusions of everyday living and to the chaos of sensation" (Milner, *EIL* 138). And it is her collage "Woebegone" that she tells us makes her conscient of the need to "trust in what one does not yet know; in fact, once more, trust in emptiness, trust in the gap in knowing" (197).)

Winnicott describes how his patient kept a diary "during the analysis, and it would be possible to reconstruct the whole of her analysis up to this time from it. There is little that the patient could perceive that has not been at least indicated in this diary" ("Mind and Its Relation to the Psyche-Soma" 207). As the analysis progressed, "the meaning of the diary now became clear—it was a projection of her mental apparatus, and not a picture of the true self, which, in fact, had never lived till, at the bottom of the regression, there came a new chance for the true self to start" (207). A thorough and all-consuming way of keeping a diary, diary writing here seems to function as an obsessive technique of recording that deadens lived experience. The patient's diary keeping is for Winnicott a symptom of early failures of continuity in being, a denial of depending on another mind for knowledge, or an effect of the fact that there was not another mind there to depend on. In other words, the activity of diary writing is understood as replacing the function of the good enough mother with one's own mind. For Winnicott, the diary at this point is unable to capture in words the quality of the true self because his patient is not yet in possession of a sense of a true self—instead, she can only represent her mental functioning and not the richness or truthfulness of her inner world.

Similar to his judgement of *A Life of One's Own*, Winnicott views the diary as a symptom of the patient's psychological struggles. There is, however, a short note in the text that suggests his views on diary keeping are potentially more multi-layered. An asterisk in the body of the text leads the reader to a short side note which states how the patient stopped writing her diary at a turning point of transformation in the analysis, this break considered to be a sign of her making progress. But Winnicott does add that "The diary was resumed at a later date, for a time, with a looser function, and a more positive aim including the idea of one day using her experiences profitably" (207). What Winnicott means by profitable diary keeping here is kept vague, but it does gesture towards recognising a particular practice of writing that is more conducive to emotional health, the "looser function" as distinct from using the diary to "confine" or limit her perception of the world (207).

Nevertheless, for Winnicott it is still the site of the analytic relationship that is felt to provide positive and profitable outcomes for the patient. By contrast, it is Milner's work that presents the reader with a comprehensive exploration of the positive effects of diary keeping. In *Bothered by Alligators* along with her other autobiographical books there is a drive to come off the couch in order to heal the self. In this final book particularly, such is Milner's commitment to her autobiographical cure and repudiation of analysis, that the picture of Winnicott's patient who would episodically throw herself off the couch in order to re-enact a pivotal scene of disturbance from her early life strikes me as an apt symbol for Milner's project in this book.[4] For this patient, too, perhaps, being "on the couch" was not enough?

Winnicott's own autobiographical cure?

Part 8 of *Bothered by Alligators*, "D.W. Winnicott and me" relates Milner's experience of analysis with Winnicott, but it also contains two other sections which I think coincide with two other key points of relation between them. Chapter 15, "A Winnicott paper on disillusion about what one gives," gives some insight into their mutual creative interaction in the development of their psychoanalytic theories, and the crossover of their ideas and concepts. In Chapter 16, "D.W.W.'s doodle drawings," we see Milner trying to understand Winnicott's own personal history better through his creative acts. Significantly, even though Milner perceives Winnicott in *Bothered by Alligators* as disparaging the work of her autobiographical books, Milner ups the ante by also suggesting that Winnicott himself might be engaging with his own forms of writing and drawing that have a therapeutic motivation.

In "D.W.W's doodle drawings," Milner turns her attention to a drawing made by Winnicott and a poem he wrote, both taking as their subject the mother–infant relationship. She writes how in his book *Winnicott*, Adam Phillips includes a transcription of a poem written by Winnicott and which he sent to his brother-in-law called "The Tree." Winnicott says in this letter to his brother-in-law that the poem "had come out of him and was very painful, and he hoped it would not happen again" (qtd. in Milner, *BBA* 235). The poem is reproduced in *Bothered by Alligators* as follows:

> Mother below is weeping
>   weeping

weeping
Thus I knew her
Once, stretched out on her lap
   as now on dead tree
I learned to make her smile
   to stem her tears
   to undo her guilt
   to cure her inward death
To enliven her was my living.
      (Winnicott qtd. in
      Milner *BBA* 236)

This poem reveals the painful struggles Winnicott himself experienced with a mother who was likely depressed. Milner wonders whether "his poem was about something that had been left out of his own analyses?" (236). The poem, Milner conjectures, brings to consciousness a painful understanding of the earliest relationship to his mother, a relationship seemingly tackled at the site of poetry rather than in the analyst–patient relationship.

Milner also attends to a drawing of Winnicott's which had been displayed in an exhibition of his doodle drawings in London in 1995. The image depicts a mother holding a baby with a black central column between them. At least three different versions of this drawing exist, Milner tells us, and she wonders: "Just what is D.W.W. trying to work out in these three drawings of a mother and a baby?" (244). She speculates about the quality of the mother–infant relationship depicted here and what it might tell us about Winnicott's own relationship to his mother: "what about that so black column coming between mother and baby, blotting out their contact, yet also being a kind of support for the whole picture?" (244). The quality of Winnicott's early relationship to his mother is thus cast as one of profound ambivalence.

In an emotionally charged but slightly less coherent passage in *Bothered by Alligators* Milner again suggests that Winnicott used the scene of writing as a form of therapeutic resolution:

Sometimes it occurs to me that his talking about a fresh start that never gets anywhere is his own wish to have actually been born a woman. In fact my writing that book showed me that I am very glad to be a woman, and not the boy I had secretly thought I was. Did Winnicott's writing all those voluminous papers make him glad to be an analyst? Certainly we have his second wife's assertion that he did become potent in his marriage with her, but it was by then too late for her to produce a child. Does this link up with the fact of there being so little about fathers in his papers?

(238)

As Milner presents Winnicott in this chapter, he is not so dissimilar from her in his personal problematics and gender confusions, and his working through of his own haunted psyche through the site of poetry, doodling, and analytic writing suggesting that these forms of mark-making were also a part of his personal therapeutic labour. Winnicott did himself write an autobiography, called *Nothing Short of Everything*. As it remains unpublished, and at the time of writing, restricted from public view in his archives, we do not yet know what this autobiography is about or what form it takes (Boyle Spelman 65–66). It would be interesting to see whether it reflects on whether the act of autobiographical writing arises out from any therapeutic motivation, as Milner suggests his other works do.

Despite Milner and Winnicott's complicated history, theirs was certainly a productive relationship, and one that allowed Milner to develop her own ideas within a psychoanalytic framework. As we know, Milner attributes her deciding to train to become a psychoanalyst to listening to a public lecture given by Winnicott in 1938. She writes how: "I do not remember at all what was said in the lecture, but I did get the feeling that, contrary to the impression that some Freudians had given me, the main ideas I was preoccupied with could be accommodated within the Freudian metapsychology" (Milner, *HOLG* xlvi). Milner perhaps found in Winnicott, professionally, a freeing figure, one that allowed her to explore her own interests on her own terms.

Winnicott evidently influenced Milner's thinking and development as a psychoanalyst, but her influence on him has also been recognised by various commentators. Margaret Boyle Spelman highlights the "incredible overlap" between Milner's thinking and that of Winnicott, predating Milner's candidacy at the Institute of Psychoanalysis, and preceding "her awareness of his writings, their friendship, and the much later analytic situation" (Boyle Spelman 44). For Boyle Spelman, Milner was a "like-minded peer, close friend, and female equivalent in whose company the seeds of many of Winnicott's ideas germinated with bidirectional influence on their respective thinking" (44). Winnicott himself pays tribute to the influence of Milner's thinking on his chapter, "Playing A Theoretical Statement" in *Playing and Reality*. He writes how: "I do wish to pay tribute to the work of Milner (1952, 1957, 1969), who has written brilliantly on the subject of symbol-formation" (Winnicott, *Playing and Reality* 38). And Milner too acknowledges Winnicott's influence on her book *On Not Being Able to Paint*. Emma Letley summarises an undated letter from Milner to Winnicott as showing how:

> She is herself anxious about his influence in the book, writing in an undated letter that she is concerned that it seems "full of things I've pinched from you" and worrying that on re-reading the text she finds "several phrases which I've definitely pinched from you, and that's real thieving. But I'll give them back."
>
> (Milner qtd. in Letley 62)

The pinching is perhaps mutual—the analyst Andreas Giannakoulas claims that many people were inspired by Milner's work, stating how "I think a lot of people just picked up her ideas without acknowledging that they did—including Winnicott" (qtd. in Boyle Spelman 186). In this way, the faint shadows of Milner's autobiographical cure on other psychoanalysts' work like Winnicott, and in turn his followers, might just be made out.

Conclusions and resolutions?

In the various documents held in Milner's archive at the Institute of Psychoanalysis we find a number of sketch pads and notebooks containing what appear to be free drawings created in the last years of her life. On one page of her "Windsor & Newton Cartridge Sketch Pad" we find a drawing accompanied with handwriting that reads: "It looks a bit smug, maybe it thinks it has swallowed its world" (Figure 3.4). On the top left-hand corner of the picture Milner has written "At Royal Free July 95," presumably referring to the Royal Free Hospital in London which was in close proximity to her Hampstead home. At this point in her life, at the age of 95, Milner's list of ailments was not inconsiderable: she had angina which prevented her from travelling very far from home, she was very deaf and almost blind, and so no longer able to paint.

Although I have been unable to find out the nature of Milner's visit to the Royal Free and for what reasons she may have been there and for how long, this visit to the hospital evidently stirred something within her which compelled her to produce a free drawing. In this picture, a single pen line jerks and curves to outline the form of what may resemble a hospital bed, with a head and what could be arms exposed above the folds of a bed sheet. Or we might also see the form of an infant in swaddling, Milner's annotations suggesting perhaps a sense of infantile omnipotence: "maybe it thinks it has swallowed the world" suggestive of the baby's illusion of the world as being an extension of itself. Whatever phantasies might be expressed in this picture in relation to the hospital, illness, or the possibility of impending death, this free drawing reveals how wedded Milner was to her drawing cures even at the end of life. Another drawing dated from 1994 (Figure 3.5) depicts a mass of scribbled entangled lines, portraying visually what its title "Chaos" describes in words. Perhaps there is a cathartic release in giving form to what Milner once described as her own feelings of formless confusion and chaos.

In the concluding pages of *Bothered by Alligators* we see Milner reflect on two of her dreams. In this first dream, which she calls "The three planks," she finds herself struggling to walk along an expanse of muddy water. Then, a person beside her turns to her and says "Ought you be doing it by yourself?," and in the dream Milner replies: "Yes, that's OK. I always do." (*BBA* 267). In characteristic fashion Milner engages in some free writing to better understand what the dream is telling her, which she summarises in the following passage:

> *Free thought:* The first thoughts that came were that the ledges that support my feet on the slippery bank are my three Joanna Field-type books that look for beads of memory. Slipping into thickly muddy water sounds like depression, terror of being swept away, drowned. But the bit about "always doing it

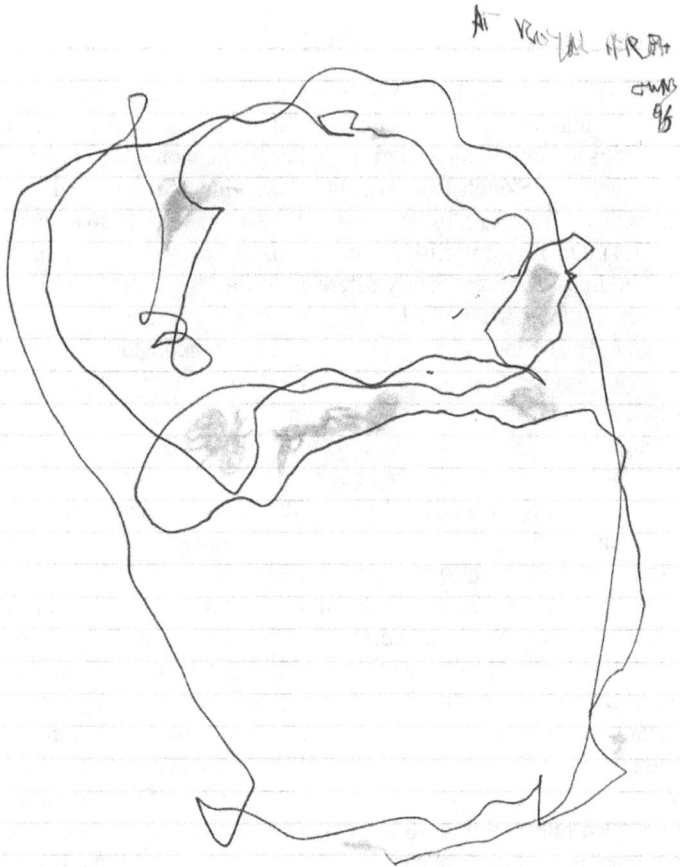

Figure 3.4 "At Royal Free July 95" by Marion Milner. Marion Milner's own art. P01-H-A. Marion Milner collection, Archives of the British Psycho-analytical Society, London.

Source: By permission of The Marsh Agency Ltd., on behalf of The Estate of Marion Milner.

Figure 3.5 "Chaos" by Marion Milner. Marion Milner's own art. P01-H-A. Marion
Milner collection, Archives of the British Psychoanalytical Society,
London.

Source: By permission of The Marsh Agency Ltd., on behalf of The Estate of Marion Milner.

myself" seems to link up with my recurrent awareness of holding my lower
jaw rigid, a kind of inability to let go, unable to trust any support.

(267)

This inability to trust in any support is "in total contrast with all those A.A. experiences I had had" (267). It is, indeed, she reflects, the drive to "find that trust,
which is the question that I have been trying to answer in the whole of this book"
(267). She continues:

So is not this dream really about my struggle to trust the A.A., the answering
activity, or whatever one chooses to call this something that I knew from experiences does need to be trusted, in spite of its being so hidden. Since this is what

my books have been about, then it is a question both about what happens when I do trust it, and exploring what interferes with that trust. Is it partly wanting to do it all myself? A kind of omnipotent wilfulness that wants to be in total control.

(267)

In this final consideration, Milner seems to cast into doubt the whole of her self-curative, solitary enterprise. Is it by engaging with an autobiographical cure, her do-it-yourself method, that in fact prevents her from ever really trusting in the answering activity, the good internalized object? Here, for the first, and last time, Milner betrays a vulnerability towards a method borne out of her own problematics. There is however, Milner might have been reminded, "no theory that is not a carefully prepared fragment of some autobiography," wrote the French poet and essayist Paul Valéry (213). According to Masud Khan (who seems to be the bearer (and indeed subject) of gossip in the ana-lytic world at this time), Winnicott's former analyst Joan Riviere reportedly said of Winnicott at one of his lectures: "He just makes theory out of his own sickness" (Anderson 24). Such a statement writes J.W. Anderson "from anyone is objectionable, but coming from Joan Riviere, who had been Winni-cott's analyst, it is unspeakable" (24). Yet Anderson accepts that "underneath her pathologising twist, there is an element of truth, in that all psychological theorists rely heavily on their most personal experience in developing their theories" (24). Winnicott's comments about his own analysand's work, *A Life of One's Own*, are perhaps a slightly more veiled version of the charge that Riviere aims at his own work. Freud himself has been levelled with having a fervid Oedipus complex, and Erik Erikson who explored the notion of identity crisis himself admitted: "If ever an identity crisis was central and long drawn out in somebody's life, it was so in mine" (qtd. in Anderson 25). Indeed, Milner's autobiographical cure is perhaps less sullied by an illusion that theo-rist and theory are separate, or should be considered separate, than by other psychological thinkers. Her cure and its accompanying theories are, after all, borne out precisely from an attempt to cure herself.

* * *

On the final page of *Bothered by Alligators*, Milner describes briefly the second dream of hers, which she calls "An Analyst's touch." Describing this dream, she simply writes: "D.W. putting his hand on my bare left shoulder. That's all the dream said" (Milner, *BBA* 268). Providing more context for the dream, she con-tinues by writing the following "free thought":

This is the shoulder that was hunched from the time of my father being away after his breakdown and me being diagnosed after a school gym class as hav-ing a crooked spine. In his analysis with me I did once put out a hand and he took it and held it for a few seconds.

(268)

Though *Bothered by Alligators* reflects a deep ambivalence and lack of resolution regarding the analysis with Winnicott, in this dream scene that ends the book Milner does seem to suggest an appreciation of some trusting hand, a support, afforded from their relationship. There is some real contact made, a touching, albeit brief, in a relationship, that can provide a trustworthy foundation. Perhaps in the final pages of this book there is also a recognition that an analysis could not be total or complete—an idealising phantasy of what an analysis can do and should do tempered, to some degree. And Milner I think does leave open the possibility that analysis, by developing her creative capacities, also helped her in developing her autobiographical cure.

Ultimately, neither the methods of autobiographical mark-making nor psychoanalysis can provide the miracle cure for infant disillusions. But Milner seems to find some form of resolution in how both these methods can go some way in doing something. This might be the only kind of resolution Milner, and we, can come to. Margaret Walters ends her introduction to *Bothered by Alligators* by acknowledging that Milner's "search for her own inner reality, which can help us find our own, was restless. It was never quite at peace, yet neither was it at war with itself. But it was certainly endowed with riches, riches which she shared generously with us all" (xxii). Perhaps we can see this is as evidence for what Winnicott meant by the ability of his female patient to keep a diary more "profitably." These creative forms might spring from an early pre-oedipal crisis in confidence in maternal care, in which relations fail and cannot be depended upon, but they can generate a productive and creative relationship to oneself and for the reader.

When asked about her intentions for writing the manuscript that would become *Bothered by Alligators*, Milner writes in a note dated from 1996 how: "I'm trying to finish this book, for all people who can't geographically access or afford analysis" ("Miscellaneous notes"). This statement echoes that of her first book *A Life of One's Own* when she writes of creating a method that "might be available for anyone, quite apart from whether opportunity or intellectual capacity inclined them to the task of wading through psycho-analytic literature or their income made it possible for them to submit themselves as a patient" (159). Milner's project, then, is a lifelong commitment to the democratisation of the resources of psychoanalysis, resources that might allow the reader to bring their own shovel and pick to mine the riches of their own inner reality.

Notes

1   These letters are held at the Winnicott papers in the Wellcome Collection. See Box 10, series PP/DWW/B/A/21.
2   There does not seem to be any direct statement from Scott himself about the Milner and Winnicott analysis. Before Scott departed for Canada permanently in the 1950s, Scott analysed Winnicott for one session as well as both of Winnicott's wives, Clare and Alice (exact dates unknown). Scott and Winnicott seemed to respect each other as colleagues based on their correspondence, with Winnicott asking for advice from Scott on various clinical matters.

3   In his description of the exhibition "Freud's Sculpture: A View from the Desk" held at the Freud Museum between 2005–6, the curator Dr Jon Wood writes how "Visitors can place themselves in the writer's space, facing the figures that witnessed his writing. Antiquities are messengers of other ages and cultures. Their obscure messages call out to be interpreted like a dream. We sense their formal beauty, we provide the associations that bring the figures into our life" ("Freud's Sculpture: A View from the Desk").

4   For those familiar with the work of the French-Cuban American diarist Anaïs Nin, Milner's analysis with Winnicott and her championing of diary keeping for its therapeutic potential might seem reminiscent of Nin's involvement with the Austrian psychoanalyst and close colleague of Freud's Otto Rank in the 1930s. Rank's involvement with Nin blurred the lines of the professional and personal much further than that of Winnicott and Milner, however. Rank was simultaneously Nin's analyst and lover for some years. Nin would maintain that the analysis was helpful, but the experience seems to be overshadowed by her practice of diary keeping as a therapeutic tool. Suzette Henke describes how Nin persuaded Rank of its usefulness: "Although Otto Rank initially feared that Nin's compulsive journal-writing might be tantamount to an addictive behaviour, Anaïs convinced him artfully that her diary functioned as a different kind of therapeutic tool. Logorrhoea, free association, and diary-writing all complemented one another by exposing layers of the unconscious that could facilitate abreaction and the reconstruction of a fragmented analytic subject" (143). For Nin, diary keeping allowed her to move from "neurosis to objectivity, expansion and fulfilment" (Rainer 26).

References

Anderson, J.W. "Winnicott's Constant Search for the Life that Feels Real." *The Winnicott Tradition: Lines of Development-Evolution of Theory and Practice over the Decades*, edited by Margaret Boyle Spelman, Routledge, 2018, pp. 19–38. http://dx.doi.org/10.4324/9780429483769

Boyle Spelman, Margaret. *The Evolution of Winnicott's Thinking: Examining the Growth of Psychoanalytic thought over Three Generations*. Routledge, 2018. http://dx.doi.org/10.4324/9780429483769

Caldwell, Lesley, editor. *Art, Creativity, Living*. Karnac Books, 2000. http://dx.doi.org/10.4324/9780429471971

Henke, Suzette A. *Shattered Subjects: Trauma and Testimony in Women's Life-Writing*. Palgrave Macmillan US, 2000.

Hopkins, Linda. "Red Shoes, Untapped Madness, and Winnicott on the Cross: An Interview with Marion Milner." *Annual of Psychoanalysis*, vol. 32, 2004, pp. 233–243.

Letley, Emma. *Marion Milner: The Life*. Routledge, 2014. http://dx.doi.org/10.4324/9780203767122

Meakins, Elizabeth. *What Will You Do with My Story?* Routledge, 2018. http://dx.doi.org/10.4324/9780429484902

Milner, Marion. *A Life of One's Own*. Routledge, 1934/2011. http://dx.doi.org/10.4324/9780203817193

Milner, Marion. *An Experiment in Leisure*. Routledge, 1937/2011. http://dx.doi.org/10.4324/9780203816769

Milner, Marion. *Bothered by Alligators*. Routledge, 2013. http://dx.doi.org/10.4324/9780203140147

Milner, Marion. "Miscellaneous Notes". *P01-E-E-15. Marion Milner Collection*. Archives of the British Psychoanalytical Society, 1990–1996/2020.

Milner, Marion. *The Hands of the Living God: An Account of a Psycho-analytic Treatment.* Routledge, 1969/2010. http://dx.doi.org/10.4324/9780203833643

Milner, Marion. *The Supressed Madness of Sane Men: Forty-Four Years of Exploring Psychoanalysis.* Routledge, 1987.

Phillips, Adam. "Introduction." *The Hands of the Living God: An Account of a Psychoanalytic Treatment*, edited by Marion Milner. Routledge, 2010. http://dx.doi.org/10.4324/9780203833643

Rainer, Tristine. *The New Diary: How to Use a Journal for Self-guidance and Expanded Creativity.* Tarcher/Putnam US, 1978.

Thomson, Martina. "Marion Milner Remembered." *International Journal of Art Therapy*, vol. 3, no. 2, 2001, p. 83.

Walters, Margaret. "New Introduction." *Bothered by Alligators*, edited by Marion Milner. Routledge, 2013. http://dx.doi.org/10.4324/9780203140147

Winnicott, D.W. "Clinical Varieties of Transference." *Through Paediatrics to Psycho-analysis.* Basic Books, 1955/1975, pp. 295–299.

Winnicott, D.W. "Foreword." *The Hands of the Living God: An Account of a Psychoanalytic Treatment.* Routledge, 1969/2010. http://dx.doi.org/10.4324/9780203833643

Winnicott, D.W. *Letter to Clifford Scott. Box 10, PP/DWW/B/A/27. Winnicott Papers.* Welcome Collection Archives, 2020.

Winnicott, D.W. "Living Creatively." *Home is Where We Start from: Essays by a Psychoanalyst*, edited by D.W. Winnicott, and Clare Winnicott. Penguin, 1970/1986.

Winnicott, D.W. "Mind and Its Relation to the Psyche-Soma." *British Journal of Medical Psychology*, vol. 27, no. 4, 1954, pp. 201–209. http://dx.doi.org/10.1111/j.2044-8341.1954.tb00864.x

Winnicott, D.W. *Playing and Reality.* Tavistock Publications, 1971. http://dx.doi.org/10.4324/9780203441022

Winnicott, D.W. "The Use of an Object." *International Journal of Psycho-Analysis*, vol. 50, 1969, pp. 711–716.

Wood, Jon. "Freud's Sculpture: A View from the Desk." *Freud Museum London.* www.freud.org.uk/exhibitions/freuds-sculpture/. Accessed 7 May 2021.

Part 2

The Milner tradition

Chapter 4

Tracing Milner's influence in the twentieth century

This chapter moves beyond an analysis of Milner's books themselves to considering their influence on her readers in the wake of their publication. *A Life of One's Own*, *An Experiment in Leisure*, *On Not Being Able to Paint*, *Eternity's Sunrise*, and *Bothered by Alligators* are all essentially books written and published with a reader in mind, public records of private projects of self-cure. I want to trace through Milner's fan letters, appreciations, and books written in the late twentieth century about autobiographical writing and therapy, how Milner's autobiographical cure leaves a vibrant legacy in its wake.

The question of influence—of what kind of influence Milner's ideas and methods had on her readers—is therefore a key concern of this chapter. Might we understand the influence of her autobiographical books as constituting a kind of Milnerian tradition? If so, what kind of readers do Milner's books create, and in what kind of tradition do they partake? Similar questions have been levelled at various other psychoanalytic thinkers to understand the evolution of their theory and practice over time. The Routledge *Lines of Development* series includes editions on *The Anna Freud Tradition* (2011), *Fairbairn and the Object Relations Tradition* (2014), *The Winnicott Tradition* (2014), and *The Klein Tradition* (2018). As I mentioned in the Introduction, the latest addition to the series will be the forthcoming *The Marion Milner Tradition*, edited by Margaret Boyle Spelman and Joan Raphael-Leff. Whilst in the meantime I can only speculate as to what this book's understanding of a Milnerian tradition comprises, my understanding of a Milnerian tradition will relate specifically to the tradition of the autobiographical cure this study has identified and explored in relation to Milner's work.

The first autobiographical book considered to have inculcated the theories and practices of psychoanalysis is Freud's dream-book. In his piece "Dream Readers," John Forrester following Derrida argues that Freud's *The Interpretation of Dreams* played a fundamental role in creating a Freudian following, launching the practice, professionalisation, and institutions of psychoanalysis. According to Forrester, Freud's readers are required to become Freudian through certain manoeuvres he makes in the text:

DOI: 10.4324/9781003296720-7

the reader of Freud's text is invited to make Freud's interests his own . . .
the roles of desirer and censor are apportioned out between the author and
reader, as they easily exchange roles . . . the reader is expected, on the model
of all Freud's interlocutors, to repudiate forcefully Freud's theories and in
consequence to be drawn ever more tightly into the embrace of his theory, of
an identification with him.

(102)

This "is autobiography not for its own sake," writes Forrester, "but for the pedagogical and analytic purpose of making readers into Freudians" (102–03).

If Freud's psychoanalytic cure employs various textual conversion tactics, Milner's autobiographical cure involves a quieter kind of influence. Her books do
not provide a method or body of theory that the reader must ascribe to in order to
reap their specific therapeutic benefits. Instead, their main function seems to be to
inspire a capacity for one's own self-directed self-realisation and transformation,
which necessarily requires a sense of ownership over the techniques and methods
one chooses to get there with. As we shall see, Milner's work sparks in her readers the desire and confidence to embark on their own journey towards finding the
autobiographical and creative mark-making techniques for curing themselves. In
this sense, to call these readers Milnerians might be in some ways a contradiction
of terms. As Rachel Bowlby articulates in her new introduction to *A Life of One's
Own*, Milner "invites her reader (the singular reader, responsive to intimate form
of address) to discover the kinds of idiosyncratic 'facts' of her own life that Milner
found for herself" (xxxi). *A Life of One's Own, An Experiment in Leisure, On Not
Being Able to Paint,* and *Eternity's Sunrise* in particular, fashion themselves as
self-help handbooks that might allow the reader to embark on her own voyage of
creative self-discovery.

To best understand the nature of Milner's influence on her readers, requires,
I think, an understanding of Milner's own relationship to influence, a relationship that is often charged and conflicted. Her own stance towards being influenced by other thinkers in turn shapes her work and its consequent effects on
her readers. Accordingly, it is to Milner's complicated affair with influence that
we will first turn.

Milner's relationship to influence

At the beginning of *A Life of One's Own* Milner states in no ambiguous terms her
guiding methodology for her enterprise: "trying to manage my life, not according
to tradition, or authority, or rational theory, but by experiment" (9). Her desire to
create a method for lay self-analysis derived solely from her own experimental
methods, and not from the science and psychology books, involves a rejection
of one kind of textual otherness. In her article "Transferred debts: Marion Milner's *A Life of One's Own* and the limits of analysis," Vanessa Smith centres her
engagement with the book on Milner's indebtedness to Freud's psychoanalytic

method. Smith contends that Milner does this in order to emancipate her version of lay analysis in the book "from the realm of expertise altogether, rendering it wholly the property of an individual self" ("Transferred debts: Marion Milner's *A Life of One's Own* and the limits of analysis" 101). The transference and countertransference that arises in relationship to the analyst is necessarily omitted in a self-analysis, thus "Listener and speaker, dream and analysis, candid confession and symbolic elucidation are all encompassed within the territory of 'one's own'" (102). Smith praises the "radicalism of Milner's version of lay analysis" (102) in its rejection of an interlocutor, arguing that *A Life* has the ultimate "aim of fostering a radical, because equally accessible, individualism" (98).

For Smith, Milner's rejection of other textual presences in her work is something to be celebrated. In another article she writes how "There is something about Milner's appeal to the possibility of experiencing something of 'one's own' that invites one to reject any sense of indebtedness to the forgotten source, to feel directly addressed" (Smith, "B-Sides: Marion Milner's 'A Life of One's Own'"). But Smith does acknowledge how Milner's project of individualism involves a complicated relationship to other textual influences in her work. She identifies in Milner's letters the sense of a "perceived exclusion, both literary and intellectual" from the Bloomsbury group and Cambridge set, with whom she had loose connections (Smith 104). In one letter Milner writes "they will jeer at me for taking myself seriously" in relation to her own writing (qtd. in Smith 104). With both the modernists and psychoanalysts Milner seems to feel the need to fight for her own work, feeling keenly a perceived exclusion and disapproval coupled with a fear that their authority might undermine her own originality.

Tapping into this preoccupation with originality, most critics of *A Life of One's Own* have picked up on Milner's unacknowledged reference to Virginia Woolf's *A Room of One's Own*. Lyndsey Stonebridge refers to the book's "obvious allusion to Woolf's essay" (131) and Rachel Bowlby sees Woolf's text as "the unacknowledged precursor of hers, and its unspoken interlocutor" (xxviii). And in her new introduction to *An Experiment in Leisure* Maud Ellmann writes of this book's "reluctance to acknowledge predecessors, most conspicuously Freud's *Totem and Taboo* (1913)" in relation to Milner's preoccupation with images of a sacrificial goat. Freud's thinking "which traces the ceremony of the dying god back to the putative murder of the primal father by his sons" seems to be silently recapitulated in Milner's writing (Ellmann, "New Introduction" xviii). "By ignoring such pioneers," Ellmann writes, "Milner sometimes gives the impression of re-inventing the wheel" (xviii–xix). In observing what Milner's works choose to remember and what they choose to forget, we find in Milner a desire to reinvent the self without reference to others. If these others have the capacity to diminish one's identity, then they must be to some extent forgotten, ignored, or rejected.

Julia Kristeva's concept of intertextuality is helpful here in how it makes the direct link between textual relationships and intersubjectivity. Kristeva's definition in her essay "Word, Dialogue and Novel" understands intertextuality as "a mosaic of quotations; any text is the absorption and transformation of another. The notion of intertextuality replaces that of intersubjectivity, and poetic language is read as at least double" (66). Milner's textual relations reflect her own personal anxieties around absorption and transformation in the hands of another. María Jesús Martínez Alfaro traces the origins and concept of intertextuality back to Montaigne, the philosopher whose essays Milner *does* acknowledge as influencing *A Life of One's Own*. She writes that for Montaigne, he

> believed that the "self" is to be found in a distancing of the reading and writing subject from the anterior "other" (a view much in consonance with the Bloomian concept of "anxiety of influence") and defends a sort of boastful forgetfulness as the best means of escaping the tyranny of past masters.
>
> (Worton and Still qtd. in Martínez Alfaro 270)

Like Kristeva, Harold Bloom's "anxiety of influence" also situates intertextuality within the realm of the intersubjective, understanding "intra-poetic relationships as parallels of family romance" (8). But Bloom presents a paternal, oedipal model for his anxiety of influence, one that exists between male poets and their male forebearers, sons and fathers. Milner's anxieties around intersubjectivity derive primarily from pre-oedipal maternal relations—these tyrannical past masters are not only from the realm of childhood and adulthood, but they are also the relations with others that we have seen dominate much earlier in life, back into the time of infancy where the development of the self is at its most nascent. This other that threatens to overwhelm and annihilate, as Kristeva testifies in *Tales of Love*, is an earlier and more powerful force, since as Donna Stanton summarises, "Before the paternal law is in place, the infant is subject to maternal regulation" (Stanton 161). The lack of distinction between infant self and mother at this early pre-oedipal stage offers a different flavour to the anxiety of influence—influence which does not only make one feel inferior and rivalrous as it does in Bloom's model, but that also threatens to wipe out the sense of oneself as a separate being from another.

It is perhaps significant then that it is Montaigne, who believed "the greatest thing in the world is to know how to belong to oneself," that Milner does acknowledge being influenced by (178). Even more so than Montaigne, there is one influence that is not obscured or evaded, but unabashedly championed in Milner's work. As psychoanalysts have often attached themselves to particular artists or works—Freud to Leonardo, Ella Sharpe to *King Lear*, Ernest Jones to *Hamlet* to name but a few—Milner attached herself to William Blake (Letley 154). An enduring presence in her work, almost all of Milner's books contain references to Blake's poetry and art, his poem "Eternity" even providing inspiration for the title of her book *Eternity's Sunrise: A Way of Keeping a Diary* (1987).[1] Numerous lines from the illuminated books bubble up like mantras in her writing. Blake reminds Milner on many occasions that "Without contraries there is no progression" (*ONBAP* 87), or he prompts her not to forget the existence of "each man's poetic genius" (*SMSM* 214). Two of her theoretical papers are dedicated to an analysis of

Blake's composite art, "The Sense in Nonsense (Freud and Blake's *Job*)" (1956a) and "Psychoanalysis and art" (1956b). In both papers, Milner's insights into the unconscious processes that enable the capacity for creativity hinge upon Blake's *Illustrations of the Book of Job* (1826). Such was Blake's significance to Milner that she even created a mixed-media collage entitled "Ode to Blake," which she showed in an exhibition of her work in Shinjo, Japan in 1992.

Gilbert Rose understands Milner's attachment as stemming from Blake's being "unafraid of mysticism" (qtd. in Letley 152), whereas Emma Letley suspects it was Milner's affinity for the image that attracted her to his art (154). In my view, it is in Blake that Milner finds a mind who is similarly preoccupied with possessing what Milner calls a "creative subjectivity," and whose ability do to so is rendered spectacularly in his consummate poetry and visual art (*SMSM* 169). For Blake, living is creating, conforming is death, and "the imagination is not a state: it is the Human Existence itself" (*Milton*). In the creation of his own mythological universe, Blake was a radical proponent for the creation of his own independent visionary system. As Blake's Los cries out in *Jerusalem: The Emanation of the Giant Albion*: "I must Create a System, or be enslav'd by another Man's;/I will not Reason and Compare: my business is to Create," it is in Blake that I think Milner finds inspiration for her own creative and independent thinking (10).

Milner writes about the "creative subjectivity" in "Psychoanalysis and Art" (1956), a term which she borrows from philosopher Jacques Maritain. Through a reading of William Blake's *Illustrations of the Book of Job*, Milner explores Job's struggles at the mercy of God. She reads the visual and poetic narrative as a parable of the problem of losing touch with one's creative capacities, writing how "I have come to look on Blake's *Job* as the story of what goes on in all of us, when we become sterile and doubt our creative capacities, doubt our powers to love and to work" (Milner, *SMSM* 169). It is Blake who enables her to explore the struggles around achieving a creative subjectivity, but who also aids her in her own personal journey of doing so. Blake's images, as we shall see, seem to facilitate Milner's development of her own system and methods for autobiographical self-cure. For in this paper Milner begins by attending to various thinkers' theoretical propositions about the capacity for creativity, including those of Freud, Melanie Klein, Hanna Segal, Jacques Maritain, and the art theorist Anton Ehrenzweig. But in a startling change of gear three quarters of the way into the paper, Milner interrupts these theoretical investigations and turns her attentions to Blake's images. The reader is presented with charcoal copies of two pictures from Blake's *Illustrations of the Book of Job*, and they amount to a very different way of engaging with questions around creativity (212).[2] Created in 1944, these copies involve a play around outline and its absence, an experimentation with form for insight into the psyche that we have seen is later taken up in *On Not Being Able to Paint*. Milner tells us how these two illustrations, one of which she calls the "Christ Blessing Job and his wife" picture and the other "The God of Eliphaz" picture create in her "a blind urge to get past the richness of the ideas and poetic thought portrayed in them, and to see more clearly the purely graphic formal qualities of feeling" (212). Of the "Christ Blessing Job and his wife" picture Milner chooses in her copy to use "only the pattern of darks and lights . . . leaving out all the linear detail" of the original (see Figures 4.1 and 4.2). Milner's copies are not facsimile-like versions of Blake's work, but almost shadow-like versions of Blake's illustrations. To achieve the quality of insight she is desiring, Blake's outline is done away with, his linear engraving style turned on its head, producing a less defined image of spectral forms.

Interestingly, this is not the first instance of Milner's copying Blake's image in a published work: the second edition of *A Life of One's Own* (published by Chatto & Windus in 1935) includes a full-page reproduction of Blake's "The Ancient of Days" from *Europe*, 1827. Inserted in the next page is a sheet of tracing paper with Milner's copy of the image which traces in thick black pen Blake's Urizen wielding his master compass. Almost twenty years later, however, the need to undo Blake's line, and indeed her own, is given expression in "Psychoanalysis and Art." Undoing Blake's line in her copy of the "Christ Blessing Job and his wife" picture provokes a powerful reaction. Milner tells us of the "intensely disturbing quality of the masses on the right, which seem to be breaking away from the circular forms surrounding the figure of Christ" and "the terror of the Christ figure shown by Job's friends" (212). She understands her reaction to the image as linked with the "fears roused in the logical argumentative mind by the impact of the creative depths" and she could see that "the anxiety is not something to be retreated from, but that it is inherent in the creative process itself" (212). Milner's struggle with anxieties aroused by getting in touch with her creative depths here parallels the Job story and her interpretation of it. Just as Job must acknowledge and accept the shadow of unconscious destructiveness in himself in order to have a creative relationship to the world, not simply following the letter of the law, Milner must also attend to the shadows of anxiety in herself; doing away with the lines that represent her logical thinking in order to access the "depth mind" (215). If the Christ picture deals with the fears involved with giving in to the creative depths, Milner's copy of "The God of Eliphaz" picture puts her in touch with the rewards that can be reaped by taking the plunge. She comes to realise that "if this feeling of emptiness, of something 'without form and void', can be deliberately accepted, not denied, then the sequel can be an intense richness and fulness of perception, a sense of the world newborn" (212–13).

Blake's illustrations thus enable Milner to engage with her own visual methods for exploring and transforming the psyche in such a way that her other theoretical interlocutors in the text do not. Indeed, in another paper from the same year, "The Sense in Nonsense (Freud and Blake's *Job*)," Milner deliberately places Freud and Blake side by side for a comparative analysis of what each thinker can tell us about the human psyche and creativity. Milner's experimentation with Blake's images allows her to explore novel dimensions of psychic experience that she claims furthers psychoanalytic thinking. She tells us how "what Blake is saying in visual and

Figure 4.1 Marion Milner's copy of "Christ Blessing Job and his wife."

Source: By permission of The Marsh Agency Ltd., on behalf of The Estate of Marion Milner.

poetic symbols could be restated, both in terms of current Freudian theory and also in terms of what Freudian theory may be developing towards" (138). What exactly Blake can offer to the Freudian is not fully developed here, apart from perhaps the notion of a creative unconscious, an unconscious that functions also as inspiration. But Blake's creative work is held up as a model for novel thinking, an influence that fosters Milner's own independent creative and curative methods.

This need of Milner's to possess a sense of independent creativity is likely why she found an affinity with Winnicott and the Independent Group of thinkers, which as its namesake suggests, encouraged independence in personal and professional expression. Discussing the idea of a Winnicottian tradition, Margaret Boyle Spelman maintains that Winnicott "found the very idea of discipleship deeply suspect and limiting and he dissuaded those who wished to directly follow him, providing for them instead encouragement in a way of thinking that fostered independence" (Boyle Spelman, *The Winnicott Tradition* xxiii–xxiv). Accordingly, to speak of a Winnicott tradition is "problematic . . . a contradiction in terms," since "a quality of Winnicott's thinking is that it facilitates independent thinking and its own subsequent evolution in

Figure 4.2 Marion Milner's copy of the "The God of Eliphaz."

Source: By permission of The Marsh Agency Ltd., on behalf of The Estate of Marion Milner.

the thinking of others" (Boyle Spelman, *The Evolution of Winnicott's Thinking* xx). Adam Phillips understands Milner and Winnicott's affinity as bound together by a preoccupation with compliance:

> That's what she [Milner] was interested in, in singularity. . . . I think it meant that in terms of her own work, she determinedly went her own way. And of course, Winnicott was the person who put compliance on the map, so to speak, on the psychoanalytic map. And she was very, very non-compliant, not rebellious at all. She was non-compliant.
>
> (Singh 12)

As I have suggested, Milner's works also seem to inspire an independent, non-compliant engagement with creative and autobiographical methods for self-cure that complicates the notion of a Milnerian tradition. As the development of Milner's own autobiographical cure thrived when in relation to such creative free-thinkers as Blake, we shall see how Milner's readers seem to partake in a shared idiom inspired, but not dictated by, her autobiographical work and ideas.

Fan letters and appreciations

Milner's acknowledgements in *Eternity's Sunrise* address "the few friends, not themselves psychoanalysts, who have actually read the manuscript," and her Dedication to the book makes another statement as to whom her readers may or may not be (viii). The book is dedicated "To my grandsons Giles and Quentin, although maybe they will never read it" (vii). Although she betrays a lack of faith in her grandsons' and psychoanalysts' interest in this work, the volume of fan letters and correspondence from loyal readers received in relation to *Eternity's Sunrise* and her other books is not insubstantial. The bulk of these letters, which can be found in Milner's personal papers at the archives of the British Psychoanalytical Society, are written by young women, with many expressing an identification with Milner, her personality, and her troubles as presented in her books. Several writers also include their own creative responses to Milner's work in the form of poetry, short stories, and drawings. Moreover, a number of letter writers share with Milner their own techniques and methods for self-cure at the site of writing and drawing. Significantly, most of the letters are written by laywomen, leading lives and careers untouched by psychoanalysis or psychotherapy. It should be noted that these letters and appreciations held in Milner's archives consist of her own personal collection. This collection cannot give voice to the letters she may have received and subsequently relinquished that may have been of less interest to her, or critical of her and her work.

One woman writing to Milner in March 1976 teaches English at the Sorbonne whilst completing her doctoral thesis on "Melancholy in Victorian Poetry." She tells Milner that she came across *On Not Being Able to Paint* and *The Hands of the Living God* during her doctoral studies, books that have gone on to have much personal significance: "the interest and pleasure I found in them goes beyond mere academic research. If I may say so, your work which is always so humane and so close to the experience of life, strikes deeper chords into one, particularly when one has been a rather perturbed person, which is my case . . ." ("Fan mail"). In a letter from September 1985, another writer simply opens her correspondence with a poem titled "To Marion Milner," which she writes was "Inspired by Chapter 3 of *On Not Being Able to Paint*" ("Fan mail"). With imagery alluding to the chapter "Outline and the Solid Earth," the poem picks up on the themes of colour, the relationship between self and other, and ego-boundaries:

To Marion Milner

Inspired by Chapter 3 of *On Not Being Able to Paint*
Without when
On this journey through seas
how do I know the where?
Where lines between
    are only illusions?
Spaces defined by colors
    shadow dark, stabs of light
    splashes of color.
Even my own body when observed
    appears a texture
of greens, lights, blacks, yellows, purples
(shadows of the not me).
Even my own body when felt
    seems awash
Rocked and swirled, merely marking
    The rhythm of the sea.
and if I move
    I am equally moved.
There is no me and not me.
    only Response.

                                       ("Fan mail")

This poem was clearly well received by Milner—her red pen underlines particular words of interest and rhythmic breaks, and a note on the top of the page states "FOR KEEP." Whilst it remains unclear as to why she chose to underline words such as "colors," "splashes," "texture," and "swirled," the suffixes and prefixes of some words, and the spaces between words in other instances, Milner's close reading of the poem does suggest a keen engagement with creative responses to her work.

Another letter, addressed to Milner in February 1987, relates how she came upon *A Life of One's Own* at

> a second-hand bookstall *years* ago . . . it has been one of the most important books of my life but I have been frustrated in my constant efforts to find further books of yours, and to discover the real Joanna Field. Perhaps, as your first book came to my hand when I most needed it, your subsequent books have yet again become available to me at this turning point in my life.
>
> ("Fan mail")

Writing in 1987, the letter writer is presumably referring to the recent publication of *Eternity's Sunrise*. She is inspired by this book to take pen to paper and write something of her own. She tells Milner

> I enclose (please forgive me if too many people do this to you, and tire and bore you) a piece of writing I have just completed . . . I hope it may please you to know that you helped me make the first vital move in my journey. You must have a huge mail, and I shall not expect acknowledgement of this or reply. But because I feel you to be such an old and dear friend I venture to send you warm and loving good wishes with my thanks.
>
> ("Fan mail")

A meandering work of remembrances and impressions, this piece of writing propels this woman on her own journeying into herself and her life, just as *A Life of One's Own* launched Milner on her own voyage of internal discovery.

In a letter one year later from June 1988, a writer thanks Milner for *A Life of One's Own* which she read "with great great pleasure, but most of all with growing astonishment as to the striking resemblance with my own experiences and problems" ("Fan mail"). Emphasising the connections between reader and author even further, she adds how in embarking on her own crusade of self-discovery "I start this search too at the age of 26, and I study psychology and have got the same (non-experience) kind of disappointments with science as you did" ("Fan mail").

Another female fan writing in November 1987 tells Milner about the effectiveness of her own therapeutic techniques, which were inspired by Milner's: "I discovered through things this autumn . . . writing and drawing which are of such value to me that I wonder if they could be evaluated on a wider basis, if other people might be interested in them too and if you could help" ("Fan mail"). Referring to Milner's concept of bead memories in *Eternity's Sunrise*, she writes how "These beads of yours enchanted me. They are what actually happened underneath what you thought was happening. . . . I was beginning to find, and now find every day "beads" of my own. I call them messages or print-outs. They always surprise me" ("Fan mail"). The writer closes her letter by thanking Milner, writing how "You have helped me immeasurably by publishing your books. . . . If in return I could help in any way with mounting or things like that, do let me know. I used to be a picture framer, and have all the tools" ("Fan mail"). This strikes me as a perfect image of Milner's helping to provide her reader with her own tools for finding an inner frame, accompanying her fan's literal skills for framing pictures in the external world.

A number of these fan letters convey the similar feeling that Milner's books provide them with a frame, a setting, for where they might engage with exploring and transforming themselves. For some letter writers, Milner's techniques and concepts resonate with their own, providing a kind of affirmation of their own home-grown methods. One woman writing in July 1988 tells Milner how *A Life of One's Own* "is a solution to many of my problems, I think I can use a lot of your techniques because I already sort of thought of them myself, only they were still lingering ideas" ("Fan mail").

Another fan's letter from May 1998 thanks Milner for how much her books have helped her in

> my "voyage" thus far and have helped to nudge me back onto the course that I have to recognize as the true one. I shall always be grateful to you for those affirmative reminders and for the encouragement your words have provided and, I'm sure, will continue to provide.
>
> ("Fan mail")

She likens Milner's bead memories to her own term, her "poppies":

> I discovered E's.S [*Eternity's Sunrise*] in a bookstore in Cambridge and was intrigued by the term "bead moments" that was mentioned in the back cover blurb. I wondered if these "beads" might be another name for what I had come to call my "poppies" and was therefore excited by the prospect of an entire book built around a theme that has been so much in the forefront of my thoughts. The term "poppy" stems(!) from a moment in the Agora at Athens.
>
> ("Fan mail")

Milner's book seems to affirm for this woman her own term for her inner experience, stimulating her to engage more fully with the creation of her poppies, and Milner's writing providing a model she can emulate in her explorations. She continues:

> what I'd like to do is to first describe a few of my "poppies" and then go on to some of the miscellaneous observations that arose during my reading of E's. S [*Eternity's Sunrise*]. I'd like to use the same open and ruminative format, spiced with journal entries, that you have employed so effectively in your books. . . . The plan is to follow up the above . . . with some thoughts about the significance of the Poppy Moment.
>
> ("Fan mail")

The impression we get from this letter, and others like it, is that Milner's search for an autobiographical cure and the concepts and techniques she develops for it meets organically with her readers' own searching and technique for cure.

One postcard from September 1987 from a younger man (now a Professor of Psychoanalysis at a London university) congratulates Milner on the publication of *Eternity's Sunrise*, writing how the book "is quite beautiful; and your collected papers are worth more to me than all my years of university training" ("Fan mail"). He wonders if he might see her at the upcoming Squiggle Foundation course which he intends to register for. Various published tributes to Milner by "fans" from within the worlds of psychoanalysis and art therapy also give an insight into her autobiographical books' reception and influence. The psychoanalyst Frances Tustin's piece, "A personal reminiscence" (1988) published in the special edition "Celebration of the Life and Work of Marion Milner" in *Winnicott Studies: The Journal of the Squiggle Foundation*, echoes many of the sentiments expressed in her fan letters. Tustin remembers how in her early twenties she was browsing a bookshop with a friend of hers when she came across *An Experiment in Leisure* for the first time:

> The masterful friend who was with me who enjoyed "putting me down", looked at the book contemptuously and said, "Oh you're surely not buying that mental spewing". For the first time in our relationship I stood up to her and said, "I think this is a very good book." Somehow, buying that book and standing up to my masterful friend, was a landmark in my finding myself. Reading it continued the process of self realisation which was thrusting to begin but which lacked direction.
>
> (57)

In Milner's books, by contrast to her "masterful" companion, Tustin felt "I met a friend who would never 'put me down', and who would be alongside me as, tremblingly, I met myself. I'm sure that I'm not alone in this, and that it has served this purpose for many other readers; some much more sophisticated than I was at that time" (57–58). Reading Milner's books was a formative experience for Tustin, *An Experiment* a book that "radically re-oriented my approach to life. It led me in the direction of self acceptance and understanding" (58).

The art therapist David Edwards' reflective piece "On Re-Reading Marion Milner" (2001) sensitively reflects on the powerful emotional effect reading Milner's books had on him. Edwards comes to write his piece as a way of making sense of the profound yet puzzling sense of loss he felt after Milner's death in 1998:

> I was filled with an acute sense of personal loss. This sense of loss was both unexpected and difficult to comprehend. Marion Milner was not a close friend or relative, indeed I had never met or had any personal communication with her. While recognising that the losses we experience in life unavoidably

remind us of previous losses, albeit often unconsciously, I was nevertheless perplexed by my emotional response. In an attempt to understand better why I felt the way I did, I began re-reading a number of Milner's books.

(2)

Upon this re-reading, Edwards is struck by how much Milner's words put him in touch with a "calming wisdom" (11). "It seems to me now," he adds "that the writing of this article has in many ways been concerned with an unconscious attempt to recreate a lost, loved and possibly idealised object" (11). The act of reading these autobiographical books provides a cure in itself—in Milner's terms we might say these books provide Edwards with an experience of something like the answering activity, or a relation with the ideal object of the pliable medium.

Edwards also suggests something similar is at play in another art therapist's account of reading *On Not Being Able to Paint*. Tessa Rawcliffe's 1987 article "A few of my own experiences of painting in relation to Marion Milner's book" is understood in the following way:

> What Rawcliffe clearly discovered through her retrospective reading of *On Not Being Able to Paint* was the validation of her own experiences. Milner was able to articulate, and in so doing help make sense of, the very kinds of experiences Rawcliffe had endured. The experiences described in Milner's book appear to have provided Rawcliffe with a sense of containment. Moreover, and while the point is not made explicit, what I believe Rawcliffe's article suggests is that an art therapist's function is in many ways very similar. That is to say, our task is to both affirm the client's experience and help make sense of it.
>
> (Edwards 8)

On Not Being Able to Paint is thus felt to provide the reader with an equivalent experience of containment that the art therapist provides for their client. As well as providing the reader with the autobiographical and creative methods Milner devises, the books themselves provide for these readers a containing—or more aptly a framing—experience whereby the therapeutic provisions of the clinical relationship are also to be found in a textual relationship to Milner's books.

The art therapist and artist Rita Simon's contribution to the special edition "Celebration of the Life and Work of Marion Milner" in *Winnicott Studies* recounts how reading *On Not Being Able to Paint* "awakened my interests in psychoanalytic investigations into creativity and art: the work had, and still continues to have, a powerful effect upon me as an artist. I found it also gave me some important clues to a deeper understanding of the therapeutic importance of creative art" (48). Elsewhere, Simon relates how reading *On Not Being Able to Paint* was a turning point in her thinking about art therapy, describing the book as illustrating "our capacity to create visible symbols of things we comprehend unconsciously" and leading her later in her career to become interested in both object relations theory and Kleinian theory (qtd. in Hogan 207). In her book *The Symbolism of Style: Art as Therapy* (1992) she understands "Art as therapy . . . [as] a mirror that the patient makes to find his own self reflected," a statement echoing Milner's work with Susan and the pliable medium of drawing (Simon 9).

"Art and Environment" Open University Course, 1972–76

It is not only through her autobiographical books that Milner's ideas find an audience. One woman's fan letter dated from June 1988 describes how she came into contact with Milner's ideas

> via an Open University programme in which you described your work with drawing in psychotherapy . . . I was up at 7am watching Open University programmes because I couldn't sleep. For a number of months I had been troubled by anxiety and depression to the point where I was fortunate if I could rest for any time during the night.
>
> ("Fan mail")

The letter writer is here referring to Chris Crickmay's interview with Milner entitled "Me and not Me" that was broadcast via the Open University. The letter writer finds the discussion of Milner's work in the course interview "arresting," writing how it

> captured my attention in two ways—first, the substance of the problems (coming to express and to know) felt like mine at the time, and second I was struck by the weight of practical experience, both personal and professional, that sat behind what you said. I got the strong impression that you had learnt something important about living, that you were wise in a way that combined intellectual and practical understanding. And I was drawn to that combination.
>
> ("Fan mail")

This interview was recorded as part of the course materials for the Open University "Art and Environment" module, a practical arts course for home study led by Crickmay which ran between 1972–76.[3] As well as interviewing Milner, Crickmay employed her as a programme consultant, and her influence on the course is clear to see. Crickmay describes the basic objectives of the course as the following: "that, on completing the course, each student will have: 1. Increased their sensory perception and awareness of the world." "2. Stimulated and developed their own potential and capacity for creativity activity," and "3. Increased their 'literacy' in a variety of media, in particular in media other than words and numbers" (5). The course, he writes, may be "seen in the context of a steadily increasing demand for greater public participation in change; a recognition that environments could be shaped by everyone, not just by a few professional planners and politicians" and the "new interest in education for personal growth, rather than factual knowledge" (6). Through these techniques students are invited to engage with personal development aims such as to "challenge stasis in self" (10).

In the section of the course booklet that provides a theoretical background to the course, Crickmay brings together both Milner and Winnicott's ideas around play, creativity, and environment. Drawing on their ideas of the relationship between inner and outer experience, Crickmay writes how important it is "to stress how much we participate in and are part of our environments: we are in them, but also they are in us" (7). Milner's project in *On Not Being Able to Paint* is referenced as illustrative of how the creative process is "something one participates in, of which one cannot be independent, in changing some part of the world one also changes oneself" (7). Winnicott's ideas around play in his paper "The Location of Cultural Experience" (1967) is referred to for the importance of seeing play and artistic creation as located in both the "inner" and "outer" worlds (7). Crickmay quotes Winnicott's statement that "The place where cultural experience is located is in the potential space between the individual and environment," adding in reference to the idea of the transitional object, that one "of the first objects that we ever relate to may be a 'security blanket.' . . . This object is both real and imaginary" (7).

Milner's influence however goes beyond providing the module with its theoretical foundations. As the course booklet states, the "course is not to be found in the course materials . . . but in your own activities whilst doing the projects," and it is tasks like free drawing and free writing that the student is asked to engage with (2). The course booklet includes a number of images and prompts spliced across the page with the aim to help the student creatively engage with the world around them: "If you find you are spending time in a place and it is not stimulating your imagination" it suggests, "try deliberately setting your imagination to work . . . find the slightest glimmering interest. Pursue that aspect with as much intensity as you can, make drawings, comparing similar instances elsewhere etc" (16). As Milner tells Crickmay about her frame in her interview: "The artist needs a studio. . . . Where it's safe to be absent-minded and where you can let go of common sense practicality" ("Me and Not Me"). Crickmay's course is invested in providing the student with a frame through which they can imaginatively and creatively engage with the world around them.

Milner's influence is particularly explicit in Unit 13 of the course, "Boundary Shifting," where in one exercise, "Liberating Objects From Their Outlines," students are asked to experiment with the use of outline in their drawings. As Milner tasked herself with drawing objects without imposing a false boundary around them in *On Not Being to Paint*, students are asked to "draw some groups of objects that happen to be lying around. Avoid the convention of putting a line round each one. Try and draw only what you can actually see. Make several quick drawings" (Crickmay 11). And as she forced herself to attend to the shadow world created by mixing colours and in the undoing of line in her copies of Blake's illustrations, the student is provided with the following prompts to think more deeply around their drawing without outline: "Do things join up with each other? Do they merge with their own shadows? Do the spaces between things become as important as the things themselves? Try drawing only the spaces between, or treating the shadows as if they were as solid as the objects (11).

In the same way Milner found her experiments with line and shadow capable both of providing insight into her psyche and transforming it, the course booklet similarly proposes the psychological and emotional effects of losing outline when drawing. Passages in the booklet are clearly informed by the play with outline and its absence in *On Not Being Able to Paint*:

> The above exercise can be taken simply as a way of learning to draw. However, it might be helpful to think about the idea that one can explore subjective aspects of oneself whilst seeming to make objective observations about the world. Think back to how you felt. Did you have difficulty forgetting outlines? . . . It is possible that in removing the outlines of objects one is upsetting one's hold on reality, which may depend upon keeping things separate? Perhaps, by association we are dealing here, not only with object boundaries, but with personal boundaries.
>
> (Crickmay 12)

Accompanying these Milnerian preoccupations about the self and boundaries, however, is a more general interest in how liberating objects from their outline might also be tied to a liberatory social and political agenda. We are presented with the term "Boundary Shifting," a term presumably coined by Crickmay and which likely developed out of his consultation with Milner and her ideas in writing the course booklet. "'Boundary shifting'" writes Crickmay, implies

> a change in one's sense of self, a change of a society, a change in the way things are classified, a discovery or invention (that pushes back the boundaries of what is known, or what can be done). . . . Boundary changes that are of particular interest are those involving a *transformation* of the way something is structured whether this be a society, a personality, a set of ideas, a way of doing something, a language, a style and so on. The importance, excitement and possible threat of boundary shifting derives from the fact that it challenges our hold upon reality in so far as we treat reality as being the status quo.
>
> (2)

Crickmay incorporates Milner's thinking and methods to inspire his students' own creative approach to everyday life, asking them to "confront the question: how are we personally to grow and change rather than remain within a fixed boundary?" (10). However, he also rejects the notion that this focus on personal boundary shifting is therapeutic or curative. Although

"Huge tracts of psychological and psychiatric literature are relevant" to this task of boundary shifting, nonetheless students and tutors "shall discuss how far we can explore facts about *ourselves* through the medium of art. The section should be considered, not in terms of therapy, but in terms of personal boundary breaking and adventure. I hope you will be drawn into gloomy introspection as a result of it!" (10). Crickmay's uses and application of the methods and theories of Milner's autobiographical cure are distanced from their psychoanalytic aims and instead are applied to the broader aim of encouraging personal growth through a critical engagement of the student's relationship to themselves and society. This course booklet reveals another avenue for where Milner's autobiographical cure is taught and disseminated, as well as where it is adapted and applied with slightly different aims in mind. As we shall see in Chapter 5, some forty years after Crickmay, Milner's methods deeply inform the artist, author, and professor Lynda Barry's university classes on "interdisciplinary creativity" at the University of Wisconsin-Madison.

Self-help and self-improvement books from the 1970s-2000s

Another female correspondent of Milner's during the 1970s (though there is no trace of her letters in Milner's archives) was Tristine Rainer, who wrote the 1978 bestseller *The New Diary: How to Use a Journal for Self-Guidance and Expanded Creativity*. Rainer coins the term "New Diary" to describe what she presents as a novel way of keeping a diary, one that is an "effective, life-long tool for self-therapy and self-guidance" (*The New Diary* 288). She acknowledges Milner's influence on her conception of the New Diary—Milner is the first person mentioned in her acknowledgements in the book, writing: "I am grateful for: Marion Milner's responses to my letters" (8). As "a personal book in which creativity, play, and self-therapy interweave, foster, and complement each other," the nature of the New Diary resonates closely with Milner's understanding of diary keeping (17).

Milner is amongst one of four pioneers of modern journal writing that Rainer identifies in her study, who also include Carl Jung, the Jungian psychotherapist Ira Progoff, and the diarist Anaïs Nin. *The New Diary* emerges from these twentieth-century thinkers' insights into the unconscious and free experimentation in art and writing. For Rainer, Milner's "work in the diary" led to "important philosophical and psychological insights" (23). Reflecting this book's tracing of Milner's work in developing an autobiographical cure alongside her work as a psychoanalyst, Rainer writes how:

> The New Diary and psychotherapy have developed independently though along parallel paths throughout the twentieth century. Quietly and creatively

diary writers have absorbed and applied psychological theories and methods, and recently some psychologists have incorporated autobiographical journal writing into their programs for personal growth.

(284)

Rainer recognises on many occasions the importance of Milner's work to her study, but she also emphasises the "quiet" quality of Milner's influence, writing how

> *A Life of One's Own* was too far ahead of its time to gain popular recognition. And Milner's quiet, personal style and her ideas were easily quelled amidst the other psychological theories then being established. . . . *An Experiment in Leisure* . . . was blitzed out of print by World War II . . . Today she works quietly as a psychoanalyst in England.
>
> (23)

By contrast, Rainer's publishers are more audible in their claims that *The New Diary* "popularized contemporary journal writing and created its lexicon. Never out of print in the States, *The New Diary* has been translated into many European languages and published in Korea (2011) and China (2012)" ("Interview: Tristine Rainer"). But Rainer does stipulate that "The New Diary is not a system of rules on journal writing; it is an expanding new field of knowledge to be shared" (*The New Diary* 13). Certainly, Rainer's book operates within the shared idiom Milner's work engenders.

   Like Milner, Rainer guides the reader on how they might engage with writing and drawing in their diaries to achieve certain therapeutic effects: "In using the diary device suggested for self guidance, you will simultaneously be practicing a full range of creative techniques" (26). These include free-intuitive writing exercises and drawing that involves the creation of "maps of consciousness" that we might note are strikingly similar to the "pictorial maps" Milner describes making in *A Life of One's Own* and *An Experiment in Leisure*.[4] By practicing these mark-making techniques, Rainer comes to strikingly similar conclusions to Milner as to what the diary, writing, and drawing can do for one emotionally. *The New Diary* is:

> a practical psychological tool that enables you to express feelings without inhibition, recognize and alter self-defeating habits of mind, and come to know and accept that self which is you. . . . It is a sanctuary where all the disparate elements of a life . . . can merge to give you a sense of wholeness and coherence . . . a nonthreatening place to work out relations with others and to develop your capacity for intimacy . . . a means of achieving self-identity.
>
> (Rainer, *The New Diary* 18–19)

Whether influenced directly by Milner's concept of the Answering Activity or not, we don't know, but Rainer presents her reader with her own term for an internal guide comparable to that of the answering activity. She describes the "Silver-Lining Voice" as follows:

> *Reflection* as a mode of expression in the New Diary is an observation of the process of one's life and writing. . . . Sometimes reflection takes the form of speaking directly to the self, of giving advice, encouragement, or bits of philosophical wisdom. I call this self-helping, healing, guiding voice the Silver-Lining Voice of the diary, since it often appears in times of stress as a voice of hope. . . . As it is allowed to be heard and to develop, it can expand into the most important guide in your life—your voice of inner wisdom.
>
> (68–69)

Like the trustworthy answering activity that gives the self a sense of guidance and organisation, the Silver-Lining Voice also resembles a good internalized object that can be communed with through these acts of writing.

Rainer also links the capacities of diary writing to that of a mirror in its therapeutic function. She tells us how an alternative term she would sometimes use for talking about her "diary" was "The Mirror Book" (262). Though she does not refer to Winnicott's notion of mirroring, Rainer writes how "The Mirror Book . . . by acting as a mirror to the self . . . encourages personal transformation" (303–04). And she assures the potential follower of her method that as "you write in your own way you, too, will be creating the New Diary. More importantly, you will be re-creating yourself" (27). The potential for this kind of autobiographical writing to transform and disrupt one's sense of identity strongly echoes that of Milner's statements almost forty-five years earlier in *A Life of One's Own*.

As Milner presents her autobiographical cure as at times a rival to psychoanalysis, an accompaniment to it, or a substitute for it, Rainer also compares her methods for the New Diary to that of psychotherapy. She writes how: "For a great many people who cannot afford therapy or who feel they have all the necessary resources within to act as their own counsellors, the diary can substitute for psychotherapy" (288). She also recommends journal keeping be carried out in conjunction with psychotherapy as "a means of accelerating or concluding psychotherapy," the diarists' recording of the therapist's comments a helpful way of reflecting on the session after it is over (285–86). In contrast to Winnicott's estimation of his female diary keeping patient's detailed recording of the analysis in his paper "Mind and Its Relation to the Psyche-Soma," Rainer suggests that "With a personal record of the therapeutic process the diarist can accelerate her growth" (286). Rainer takes up the mantle of Milner's project, expanding its reach to a wider, international audience.

Almost seventy years after *A Life of One's Own* was published in 1934, the turn of the twentieth century saw a noticeable proliferation in the number of book-length studies and handbooks about the therapeutics of autobiographical mark-making, informed, in part, by Milner's autobiographical books. These include Marlene Schiwy's *Voice of Her Own: Women and the Journal Writing Journey* (1996), Gillie Bolton's *The Therapeutic Potential of Creative Writing: Writing Myself* (1999), and Celia Hunt's *Therapeutic Dimensions of Autobiography in Creative Writing* (2000).

With echoes of Woolf's *A Room of One's Own* and Milner's *A Life of One's Own* in her book's title, Marlene Schiwy's *Voice of Her Own* turns to passages from published and unpublished journals and diaries, inviting the reader to "share the journeys other women have made toward selfhood and encourages them to begin a journey of their own" (i). Along with other famous female diary keepers, Schiwy briefly mentions Milner's *A Life of One's Own* and *Eternity's Sunrise* as part of her desire to show her readers how "journal writing is the ideal way to find one's individual voice, an opportunity for women to explore feelings, intuitions, perceptions, and ideas often suppressed in our society, and to record the truths of their own experience" (i).

Gillie Bolton's *The Therapeutic Potential of Creative Writing: Writing Myself* (1999) explores the therapeutic potential of different forms of creative writing within the context of the classroom and in one's own time. Bolton discloses that her "own vital therapeutic journey has been through writing," a journey set into motion after reading Milner's books (12). She adds how Milner "decided not to use psychoanalytic techniques to help her understand her writing but to rely on her own intuitions. These were the books which started me writing, particularly *On Not Being Able to Paint* (which title I read as: *On Not Being Able to Write*)" (33). As Milner's books helped her in her journey of written self-discovery, Bolton seeks to provide her own readers with various writing exercises that might stimulate their own therapeutic ventures. For Bolton, echoing Milner, "the cornerstone of diary and therapeutic writing" is "free-intuitive writing" which provides the opportunity to embark on a "voyage of discovery" (35). And again, this kind of writing is felt to provide a transformation of self, promoting "the discovery, the ordering and making sense, the creation, the re-experiencing, the reaffirmation of the self," to give "a sense of continuity and selfhood and a sense of wholeness" (30).

Like Rainer, Bolton does not explicitly make any reference to Milner's concepts like the answering activity, pliable medium, frame, or bead memory, but there is a shared language that is employed for describing the therapeutic capacities of such autobiographical acts. Therapeutic writing for Bolton allows one to make "contact with the trustworthy, strong, wise, healing self" and she proposes that a "poem, story or drama offers relatively secure boundaries to the writer, who can explore and express their inner self, just as a visual artist is contained by the picture frame" (16, 207). The kind of writing Bolton wants to encourage her readers to take up is "Reflective . . . This is the kind of writing that can tell you what you think. If you can allow yourself to put your ideas on a particular subject down on the page, you will discover a great deal" (43). Evoking something similar to the qualities of the answering activity, Bolton assures us the "diary is a friend, the best friend you will ever find yourself. It is always there, always receptive and it is the only time you can talk openly and be certain that you will not be questioned and that what you say will not be repeated to anyone else. 'Through diary writing we can create our own identities in this private space'" (29). Along with free-intuitive diary writing, Milner also inspires Bolton's advocation of something akin to free drawing. She tells us how "writing might come out attended by scribbly drawings, called *taking a line for a walk* by Marion Milner (1971). Allow these to come too, as they will express as much as the writing. You will be able to read them later in the same way" (40).

Bolton describes a writing exercise she employs in a workshop with a group of writers who "were interested in my writing therapy projects and wanted to experience some of this writing" (49). Here she asked her writers to handle some buttons she had brought with her, since "Objects can be facilitative when they are handled and then the experience written up" (49–50). Like Milner's bead memories inspired by various souvenirs and trophies she picks up on her travels, Bolton's buttons inspire in her writers "poetic memory journeys," "satisfying products" of "such personal delvings" (51). One participant of the workshop wrote in poetic form how "[t]he cascade of buttons returned us/to girlhood; fastening images/of mothers and maiden aunts," a description of how memories and experience are brought to life and given form on the page, much like Milner's notion of bead memories do. Bolton emphasises the emotional and psychological power of partaking in such an exercise. She warns that "The message is clear to the facilitator: opening up images for others may be the 'Box of Delights' for some, but 'Pandora's Box' for others. The kind of exercises suggested for writers to undertake with image-making material must be planned with care . . . someone who had an unhappy childhood might have very different memories, thoughts and feelings brought up by the buttons" (53). Like Milner, Bolton is also duly aware of the powers of these techniques for releasing the unsettling and/or liberatory powers of the unconscious.

In comparison to psychotherapy, Bolton assures her reader that a "piece of paper and pencil is nearly always available, unlike the doctor or counsellor, like having a private therapist day and night" (23). These methods can also provide on demand help without the risk of relationship. One member of a therapeutic writing group Bolton leads testifies that whilst it "helps to talk . . . I find that writing is much better, it's between me and the paper. If I talk, how can I trust the others, and also it is said 'walls got ears'. Writing is ideal, frustration goes on the paper. I don't want to hassle anyone, if the tension goes up I can press harder with my pencil" (23). The pliable medium of pencil on paper seems to absorb and tolerate some of the tensions that another person is not trusted to bear. "One day there *may* be specialists with the label 'Writing Therapist'," speculates Bolton, but she is "not certain this is the very best thing. Psychoanalytic art therapy and counselling often have interpretative agendas. . . . But writing does not necessarily need an outsider to enable the writer to make sense of their work" (27). For Bolton and others, an autobiographical cure provides an attractive alternative to a therapy dependent upon a relationship to someone else.

Almost reaching back through a Milnerian line of tradition, Bolton writes how

> Tristine Rainer (1978) (drawing on Milner) describes an exercise for dis-
> covering joy in ordinary moments, ordinary things, which uses, perhaps,
> an opposite skill to my thumbnail sketches. She calls it "the here and now
> exercise". You write down exactly what you perceive (remembering all your
> senses) about where you are at a particular time.
>
> (40)

The term "here and now" has long been used in psychoanalytic literature, beginning with Otto Rank in his book *Will Therapy* (1929), to describe in analysis the
patient's interpersonal issues that will eventually emerge in the here and now of
the relationship between analyst and analysand. Milner, it seems, inspires a different kind of understanding of the "here and now," one which takes place within
a relationship to pen and paper. In Rainer and Bolton's uses of Milner's work, it
is the project of her autobiographical books that is taken up, rather than her more
directly clinical and theoretical psychoanalytic work, which, despite their distinctiveness, are psychoanalytically informed at the very least.

We find another comparable project with very similar claims for the therapeutic
potential of writing in Celia Hunt's *Therapeutic Dimensions of Autobiography
in Creative Writing* (2000), which explores more specifically the writing of what
Hunt calls fictional autobiography. Echoing her forerunners, Hunt writes how her
study has persuaded her that autobiographical writing, including "freewriting,"
provides "beneficial psychological change, which might include increased inner
freedom, greater psychic flexibility, a clearer or stronger sense of personal identity, and an increased freedom to engage with other people as well as in creative
pursuits" (12–13). And for Hunt too, engaging with a "life map exercise continues
the work of 'objectifying the self' . . . an essential part of the process of finding a
writing voice" (35).

Hunt's study is situated more rigorously than Rainer, Schiwy, and Bolton's
in psychoanalytic theory, particularly that of Karen Horney, Christopher Bol-
las, Winnicott, and Milner. Referring to Winnicott's concept of mirroring,
Hunt suggests that autobiographical writing might perform a similar function in providing a sense of self-identity in adulthood (146). It is Horney's
theories and her understanding of the development of the "ideal self" and
"real self" that Hunt turns to most extensively for thinking about how writing
might help put us in touch with our "real self" (64). But whilst Hunt adopts a
Horneyan framework through which to understand the nature of selfhood and
its development, it is her interest in finding creative, autobiographical writing
techniques for enacting psychological transformation that we see her working
within a Milnerian idiom.

It is worth noting that Rainer, Schiwy, Bolton, and Hunt were working not as psychoanalysts or psychotherapists, but out of women's studies and creative writing
departments across a range of universities and colleges (Schiwy across institutions in
the UK, USA, and Canada; Rainer at UCLA; and Bolton and Hunt at the University of

Sussex). Schiwy and Rainer in particular emphasise the importance of their autobiographical cures to the constitution of a female subjectivity. Rainer tells the reader how

> as a woman I feel that my power to describe my life is a gesture against
> powerlessness. I defy the "official" version of reality with my own version.
> As a result of my power to describe my experiences in the diary, I feel there
> is nothing that can really overwhelm me. . . . As long as I have the power of
> words to describe my experience, I have a bastion of personal control. The
> diary is not just a friend, a mother, a psychiatrist, and a home—it is also a
> weapon.
>
> (*The New Diary* 61)

Rainer's linking here of the powerful feminist potential of engaging with diary
writing brings out a more latent preoccupation within Milner's work around the
specifics of her method and her identity as a woman. In the Preface to *A Life of
One's Own* Milner challenges her contemporaries' prevailing belief that "the only
desirable way to live was a male way" (xxxvi). She explains how:

> Most of the people I knew (both men and women) had made a cult of the
> "male" intellect, that is, of objective reasoning as against subjective intui-
> tion. I had apparently been submissive towards this fashion and accepted its
> assumption that logical symbols were "real", and anything else only "wish-
> fulfilment". So I had for years struggled to talk an intellectual language which
> for me was barren, struggled to force the feelings of my relation to the uni-
> verse into terms that would not fit.
>
> (xxxvii)

By rejecting the reduction of what she calls subjective intuition to "wish-
fulfilment," Milner seems to be implicating a Freudian understanding of the self
as part of this cult of the male intellect, a cult that speaks a language that prevents
access to real self-understanding. For she comes to realize that

> I had tried to live a male life of objective understanding and achievement.
> Always, however, I had felt that this was not what really mattered to me, and
> as soon as I tried to question my experience I began to discover impulses
> towards a different attitude, impulses which eventually led me to find out
> something of the meaning of psychic femininity.
>
> (xxxvi)

Through her explorations into her own psyche, she realizes how she "had not
understood at all that a feminine attitude to the universe was really just as legitimate, intellectually and biologically, as a masculine one; only, because it had
never yet been properly understood, and had certainly not understood itself" (xxxvii). One year before the publication of *A Life*, Freud published in 1933 his New

Introductory Lectures with a chapter on "Femininity." In this work Freud claimed to explore the "the riddle of femininity"—though presumably, Freud's psychoanalytic theories about femininity and the differences between the genders came up short for Milner ("Lecture XXXIII Femininity" 116). In this way, as Maud Ellmann contends in her introduction to *An Experiment*, Milner's work tackles Freud's question that he himself cannot answer: "Was will das Weib?" or What does a woman want? "What is revolutionary about these works," writes Ellmann of *A Life* and *An Experiment*, "is that the author makes herself the subject rather than the object of Freud's notoriously chauvinistic question" (Ellmann, "New Introduction" xiiv). Psychoanalytic "chauvinism," we might say, forgets its own insights into the unconscious, undermining the subject's knowledge of him- or herself.

This woman, as Milner's project declares, wants to develop her own methods for understanding herself and her subjectivity, her unconscious and inner life. But throughout her body of work Milner claims a universality for her method. From the beginning, *A Life* declares its ubiquitous efficacy, and Milner states that the "reason for publishing the book is that although what I found is probably peculiar to my own temperament and circumstances, I think the method by which I found it may be useful to others, even to those whose discoveries about themselves may be the opposite of my own" (xxxiii–xxxv). Whatever the reader's gender identity, it is her objective to awaken her reader to their inner life, helping them to see themselves as a subject with a psyche and subjectivity worthy of exploration.

If Freud is understood as the father of psychoanalysis, educating and disciplining his progeny on the rules and laws of psychoanalysis, Milner's influence might be understood more appropriately as a maternal model of textual influence. Milner's books, her accounts of her personal struggles and the methods she turns to for self-cure provide her predominantly female interlocutors with the very maternal functions Milner is in search of herself. In turn, many of her readers seek to do the same for their own readers. They might be understood then, as partaking in a shared project of reproduction, reproducing what was first birthed into being by Milner's books.

Through a Freudian lens Milner's books might also be understood as encouraging the uptake and generation of a "wild analysis" in her readers, that well-known term of Freud's, first outlined in his article, "'Wild' Psycho-Analysis" in 1910. Published in the same year as the International Psycho-Analytic Association was founded, Jean Laplanche and Jean-Bertrand Pontalis summarise Freud's definition as "the procedure of amateur or inexperienced 'analysts' who attempt to interpret symptoms, dreams, utterances, actions, etc., on the basis of psycho-analytic notions which they have as often as not misunderstood" (Laplanche and Pontalis 480). As Milner's books seek to invent new therapeutic methods and terms, her wild methods enabling encounters with the "wild beasts" of her inner world, her readers similarly take on the project of developing for themselves new creative analytic methods (*LOO* 122). Milner's books encourage a wildness however that is disassociated from the connotations of a primitivism or unruliness that must be mastered, colonised, or tamed (as we see Freud's archaeological metaphor does). Instead, her methods seem to inspire a creative and freeing flourishing of each man and woman's creative subjectivity, much in the same way that Blake fulfilled for Milner, in her repeating like a mantra the existence of "each man's poetic genius" (*SMSM* 214).

A quick browse through the current most popular titles of the ever-expanding self-help market reveals the extent to which books encouraging the take up of journal writing and creative activity attract a sizeable readership. Liz Dean's *My Creativity Journal: Rediscover Your Creativity and Live the Life You Truly Want* (2018) promises a revelatory and healing journey of self-discovery, as does Lee Crutchley's *How to Be Happy (Or at Least Less Sad): A Creative Workbook* (2015) and Caroline Kelso Zook's *Your Brightest Life Journal: A Creative Guide to Becoming Your Best Self* (2018). Meera Lee Patel's *Made Out of Stars: A Journal for Self-Realization* (2018) presents the reader with a technique for journaling "for anyone looking to better understand themselves so they can clear out the 'noise' and be who they are" (8). Her other book, *My Friend Fear: Finding Magic in the Unknown* (2017) is described by Lee Patel as "a book that asks you to look in the mirror without flinching. You won't always like what you see. That's okay. Look anyway" (2).

Perhaps this popularity of the self-help genre reflects something about our current juncture in history, where state funding for mental health services has been chronically depleted and longer-term talking therapy increasingly hard to access. Notwithstanding, creative techniques for self-cure have existed long before Milner first began her study of living and diary writing in 1926, and they will no doubt continue long after it. But Milner's psychoanalytically inflected autobiographical project provides us with the terms, theories, and emotional register through which to think more deeply about these forms of creative self-remedy. And fundamental to the popularity of these methods and guides is, I think, an encouragement of a self-cure that is autogenerated, not dependent on the mind or couch of another, but harnessed in the powers of one's own creative and mark-making capacities.

Notes

1   The title is taken from a line from Blake's short poem, "Eternity":

He who binds to himself a joy
Does the winged life destroy;
But he who kisses the joy as it flies
Lives in Eternity's sunrise.

2   It should be noted that, oddly, in the edition of "Psychoanalysis and Art" as published in *The Suppressed Madness of Sane Men* the pictures that are called Milner's copies are in actuality exact reproductions of the Blake originals, just with the marginalia and text cropped out. The copies that are reproduced in this book are Milner's actual copies as they appear in the first publication of the paper in John Sutherland's *Psycho-Analysis and Contemporary Thought* (1958).

3   Draft versions and the final version of the course booklet along with other course materials can be found in the series "Art and Environment" P01-D-F-01 at the Marion Milner collection, Archives of the British Psychoanalytical Society, London.

4   In *A Life of One's Own* Milner briefly mentions making what she calls a "map of my life" (122). She describes it in the following passage: "One day I thought it would be amusing to draw a map of my life, to show in pictures what I felt had been the most important things in it. I let my mental eye roam over all the happenings, places and situations of my upbringing, and if any had a peculiar quality of emotional significance I tried to represent it in a diagrammatic drawing" (122–23). This map is mentioned again at the start of *An Experiment in Leisure* where it is described as "a sort of pictorial map of my life-experience" (19).

References

Blake, William. *Jerusalem: The Emanation of the Giant Albion*. Princeton University Press, 1820/1991.

Bloom, Harold. *The Anxiety of Influence: A Theory of Poetry*. Oxford University Press, 1997.

Bolton, Gillie. *The Therapeutic Potential of Creative Writing: Writing Myself*. Jessica Kingsley, 1999.

Bowlby, Rachel. "New Introduction." *A Life of One's Own*, edited by Marion Milner. Routledge, 2011. http://dx.doi.org/10.4324/9780203817193

Boyle Spelman, Margaret, and Frances Thomson-Salo, editors. *The Winnicott Tradition: Lines of Development-Evolution of Theory and Practice over the Decades*. Routledge, 2018. http://dx.doi.org/10.4324/9780429483769

Boyle Spelman, Margaret. *The Evolution of Winnicott's Thinking: Examining the Growth of Psychoanalytic thought over Three Generations*. Routledge, 2018. http://dx.doi.org/10.4324/9780429481697

Crickmay, Chris. "Art and Environment Course Materials." *P01-B-B. Marion Milner Collection*. Archives of the British Psychoanalytical Society, 1972–1976/2020.

de Montaigne, Michel. *Complete Essays*. Stanford University Press, 1958.

Edwards, David. "On Re-Reading Marion Milner." *Inscape*, vol. 6, no. 1, 2001, pp. 2–12. http://dx.doi.org/10.1080/17454830108414024

Ellmann, Maud. "New Introduction." *An Experiment in Leisure*, edited by Marion Milner. Routledge, 2011. http://dx.doi.org/10.4324/9780203816769

Forrester, John. "Dream Readers." *Sigmund Freud's the Interpretation of Dreams: New Interdisciplinary Essays*, edited by Laura Marcus. Manchester University Press, 1999, pp. 83–122.

Freud, Sigmund. "Lecture XXXIII Femininity." *New Introductory Lectures on Psychoanalysis*, translation by James Strachey. Pelican Books, 1933/1973.

Hogan, Susan. *Healing Arts: The History of Art Therapy*. Jessica Kingsley, 2001.

Hunt, Celia. *Therapeutic Dimensions of Autobiography in Creative Writing*. Jessica Kingsley, 1999.

Kristeva, Julia. "Word, Dialogue, and Novel." *Desire in Language: A Semiotic Approach to Literature and Art*, edited by Leon S. Roudiez, translated by Thomas Gora et al. Columbia University Press, 1977/1980.

Laplanche, Jean, and Jean-Bertrand Pontalis. *The Language of Psychoanalysis*. Routledge, 2018.

Lee Patel, Meera. *Made Out of Stars: A Journal for Self-Realization*. Tarcher Perigee, 2018.

Lee Patel, Meera. *My Friend Fear: Finding Magic in the Unknown*. Tarcher Perigee, 2018.

Letley, Emma. *Marion Milner: The Life*. Routledge, 2014. http://dx.doi.org/10.4324/9780203767122

Martínez Alfaro, María Jesús. "Intertextuality: Origins and Development of the Concept." *Atlantis*, vol. 18, no. 1–2, 1996, pp. 268–285.

Milner, Marion. *An Experiment in Leisure*. 1937. Routledge, 2011. http://dx.doi.org/10.4324/9780203816769

Milner, Marion. *A Life of One's Own*. Routledge, 1934/2011. http://dx.doi.org/10.4324/9780203817193

Milner, Marion. *Eternity's Sunrise: A Way of Keeping a Diary*. Routledge, 1987/2011. http://dx.doi.org/10.4324/9780203720677

Milner, Marion. "Me and Not Me." *Interview with Chris Crickmay, Typed Transcript of the Interview. P01-B-B-05. Marion Milner Collection*. Archives of the British Psychoanalytical Society, 1975/2020.

Milner, Marion. *On Not Being Able to Paint*. Routledge, 1950/2010. http://dx.doi.org/10.4324/9780203833650

Milner, Marion. *P01-D-F-01. Marion Milner Collection*. Archives of the British Psychoanalytical Society, 1950–1998/2020.

Milner, Marion. *The Supressed Madness of Sane Men: Forty-Four Years of Exploring Psychoanalysis*. Routledge, 1987.

Rainer, Tristine. "Interview: Tristine Rainer." *Spirit of Story*. www.spiritofstory.com/blog/interview-tristine-rainer. Accessed 7 May 2021.

Rainer, Tristine. *The New Diary: How to Use a Journal for Self-guidance and Expanded Creativity*. Tarcher/Putnam US, 1978.

Schiwy, Marlene. *Voice of Her Own: Women and the Journal Writing Journey*. Touchstone, 1996.

Simon, Rita. "Marion Milner and the Psychotherapy of Art." *A Celebration of the Life and Work of Marion Milner, Special Issue of Winnicott Studies: The Journal of the Squiggle Foundation*, vol. 3, 1988, pp. 48–53.

Singh, Akshi. "The Unconscious was Another Word for Inspiration': Adam Phillips on Marion Milner" in "Special Issue: Marion Milner: Modernism, Politics, Psychoanalysis." *Critical Quarterly*, vol. 63, no. 4, 2021, pp. 6–19.

Smith, Vanessa. "B-Sides: Marion Milner's "A Life of One's Own"." *Public Books*, 2018. www.publicbooks.org/b-sides-marion-milners-a-life-of-ones-own/. Accessed 7 May 2021.

Smith, Vanessa. "Transferred Debts: Marion Milner's A Life of One's Own and the Limits of Analysis." *Feminist Modernist Studies*, vol. 1, no. 1–2, 2018, pp. 96–111. http://dx.doi.org/10.1080/24692921.2017.1371929

Stanton, Donna C. "Difference on Trial: A Critique of the Maternal Metaphor in Cixous, Irigaray, and Kristeva." *The Poetics of Gender*, edited by Nancy K. Miller. Columbia University Press, 1986, pp. 157–182.

Stonebridge, Lyndsey. "Taking Care of Ourselves and Looking after the Subject: Marion Milner's Autobiographical Acts." *Paragraph*, vol. 17, no. 2, 1994, pp. 120–133.

Tustin, Frances. "A Personal Reminiscence." *A Celebration of the Life and Work of Marion Milner, Special Issue of Winnicott Studies: The Journal of the Squiggle Foundation*, vol. 3, 1988, pp. 57–59.

Chapter 5

Milner in the comic frame

Lynda Barry and Alison Bechdel's autobiographical cures

This image is a close up from one of the richly illustrated pages of Lynda Barry's hybrid work of autobiography and creativity handbook, *What It Is* (2009) (Figure 5.1). In this watercolour and ink self-portrait, Barry pictures herself reading Marion Milner's *On Not Being Able to Paint*, accompanied by a bird perched on her shoulder watching her read, and a smiling spider peering next to her. This bird features throughout *What It Is*, representing a creative vitality, alive and flying around the pages of the book when Barry is in the throes of creation, juxtaposed with images and drawings of dead birds when she is suffering from creative blockage (149). The spider, with its classical associations to female creativity and the myth of Arachne, also brings to the frame the sense that Milner's book guides Barry to an experience of an alive creative subjectivity. Indeed, across Barry's body of work, Milner's books are acknowledged as playing an important part in her ability to be creative.

The frame that contains the image of Barry reading *On Not Being Able to Paint* resembles a box with a ribbon around it, like a gift or a present. This box is also a recurring motif in Barry's narrative, symbolising Pandora's box, a box Barry refers to as containing something potentially dangerous: "I'd turn back if I were you!" "Caution! Contents under extreme pressure" "S.S. Pandora" (131). Long considered a metaphor for the unconscious, Barry's pandora's box seems to become inhabitable with *On Not Being Able to Paint* as her companion, a frame for where something curative can take place.

As traced in Chapter 4, Milner provides many of her readers with a guiding therapeutic presence. For Barry, Milner seems to fulfil a similar role: the frame in which she depicts herself reading *On Not Being Able to Paint* we might understand as the framing, containing capacity of Milner's book. It is worth noting that on the next page after Barry depicts herself reading *On Not Being Able to Paint*, the same box or frame comes to depict a drawing of a baby monkey sleeping in the arms of what appears to be a large cephalopod creature. This illustration depicts a maternal creature holding or framing the baby who is peacefully asleep, suggestive of the emotional receptivity Milner's words and images put Barry in touch with.

DOI: 10.4324/9781003296720-8

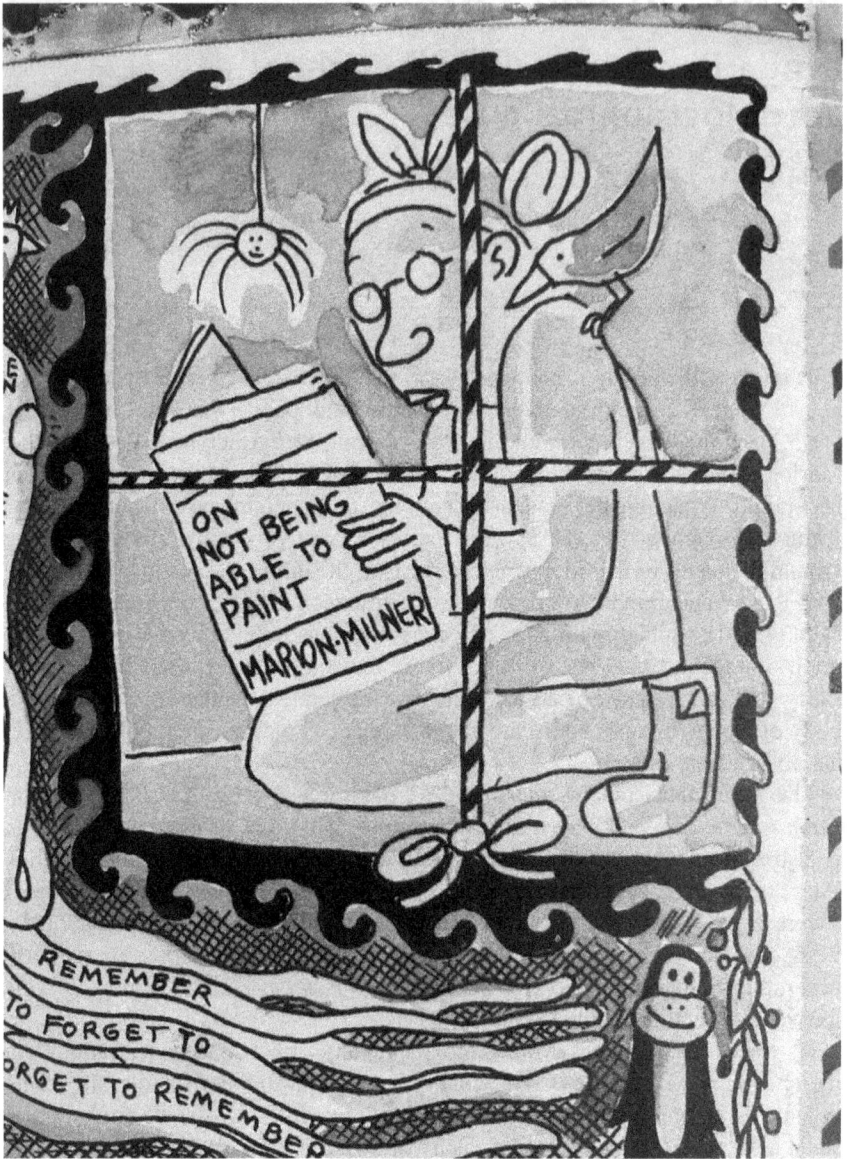

Figure 5.1 Lynda Barry's *What It Is* (Drawn & Quarterly, 2008).
Source: By permission of Drawn & Quarterly.

This chapter will explore twenty-first century engagements with Milner's autobiographical cure in Barry's work, as well as in the work of another American cartoonist and graphic memoirist, Alison Bechdel. Barry and Bechdel's mark-making, which includes diary keeping, drawing, collaging, and their reflection on the emotional and therapeutic potential of such activities echoes Milner's earlier project. Both Barry and Bechdel understand themselves, their relationships, and their creative identities within the context of object relations psychoanalysis. Along with Milner, Barry draws upon Winnicott's ideas and thinking throughout her books. For Bechdel, Winnicott is a figure of particular significance in her graphic memoir *Are You My Mother* (2012). As shall be examined, Bechdel uses Winnicott's psychoanalytic theories to understand her relationship with her mother from early infancy, and to shed light on how it has shaped who she is now. Whilst Milner is not amongst the various psychoanalytic and literary figures on whom Bechdel draws in her memoir, it is Bechdel's approach to psychoanalysis, creative self-expression, and diary keeping, however, that I argue aligns with Milner's autobiographical cure. Milner might be seen as a hidden interlocutor in the background of the memoir, particularly in Bechdel's engagement with Winnicott's diary keeping patient in his paper "Mind and Its Relation to the Psyche-Soma" (1954). It is through the work of these two contemporary authors that we can come to observe contemporary forms of engagement with Milner's autobiographical cure.

Lynda Barry's *What It Is* (2009)

As a celebrated cartoonist, graphic memoirist, and teacher, Barry's distinctive works have helped to consolidate the genre of the graphic memoir as a respected cultural form in the twenty-first century. Barry creates mixed media, visual-verbal compositions to produce richly original autobiographical works (she is responsible for coining the term "autobiofictionagraphy" to describe a genre that melds autobiography, fiction, and graphic art). Many of her books are hybrid works of autobiography and self-help handbook, and they include: *One Hundred Demons* (2002), *What It Is* (2009), *Picture This: The Near-Sighted Monkey Book* (2010) and *Syllabus: Notes from an Accidental Professor* (2014). Despite the time, place, and cultures that separate Barry from Milner (Barry is a first generation Filipino-American cartoonist creating in the twenty-first century), their work engages with similar therapeutic objectives. Like Milner, Barry's autobiographical books present us with home-grown techniques for remediating a wounded subjectivity with pen and paper, compelling the reader to follow in her footsteps.

Barry acknowledges in various instances the importance of Winnicott and Milner's thinking to her work. She writes in *What It Is* how along with Milner and M.P. Follett (the writer on painting whose work Milner also draws upon and quotes in *On Not Being Able to Paint*) she "owe(s) a debt to the work" of D.W. Winnicott (210). In an interview given to *Vice Magazine* in 2008, Barry selects her "desert island books" which include "a complete anthology of Dr. Seuss" and "D.W. Winnicott's *Playing and Reality*" (Kellner, "The Talking Issue: Lynda Barry"). And we find various allusions to some of Winnicott's thinking in Barry's texts. A description in *One Hundred Demons* of a yellow blanket and its importance to her in her childhood is highly reminiscent of Winnicott's transitional object: Barry recalls this blanket possessing "a particular sort of aliveness. . . . The spirit of the Blankie is located in the difference between" (150–99). Like Winnicott's linking transitional space with that of the cultural field, Barry describes "A book, a blanket, a cloth rabbit. A place on our bed post we liked to touch as we fell asleep. Each with a magic lantern inside capable of conjuring worlds" (156). She evokes Winnicott's thinking in "The Use of an Object" (1969) when she writes of how important it was that with the blankie, she and her brothers "could abuse it (and we often did!) and it wouldn't bite back. It seemed to have an enormous capacity for understanding" (151). This attachment to an object was one that Barry's own mother couldn't sympathetically grasp: "Some adults are made nervous by such passionate attachment in a child. They give reasons for stopping it that sound sensible at least to themselves" (152). Barry accompanies this passage with a cartoon illustration of her mother shouting "That thing was a rag! It was filthy! I was ashamed for you! You were too old!" (152). But in this scene we also begin to see a commitment to a relationship provided by creative play with an object that is more Milnerian than it is Winnicottian. "There is something brought back alive during play," Barry writes, reminiscent of the primitive reciprocity provided by the pliable medium, "and this something, when played with, seems to play back" (Kellner, "The Talking Issue: Lynda Barry").

One Hundred Demons is also centred around a technique for visual expression akin to Milner's free drawing, albeit stemming from a different cultural practice, that of Japanese brush painting and the Buddhist notion that each person must overcome 100 demons in a lifetime. Through Japanese brush painting Barry finds a therapeutic method for coming to awareness of her "demons," which she proceeds to explore in twenty autobiographical comic strip stories. As Milner comes to discover her "monsters within" through free drawing in *On Not Being Able to Paint*, Barry's technique for brush painting is similarly transformative, her inner world and unconscious coming to life when it felt previously hidden and unknown (*One Hundred Demons* 41). Barry tells us how "Discovering the paint brush, ink stone, ink-stick and resulting demons has been the most important thing to happen to me in years," imploring the reader to "Try it! You will dig it!" (100). A section at the end of her autobiographical book is dedicated to encouraging the reader to take up this technique of painting, with Barry recommending brands of brushes and paint that might best bring these inner demons into inky existence.

Barry's books are all made up of richly illustrated compositions of collage, comic strips, and handwritten text and drawing scrawled across the page. But if *One Hundred Demons* is preoccupied with the autobiographical therapeutics of free drawing, then in *What It Is* (2009) Barry turns loosely to acts of writing, asking on the front cover, "Do you wish you could write?" This is followed by a return to visual art making in *Picture This* (the reader now asked on the book's cover, "Do you wish you could draw?"). This loose distinction in these books between an interest in the therapeutics of writing and drawing is reminiscent of Milner's—*A Life of One's Own, An Experiment in Leisure,* and *Eternity's Sunrise* as we know all focusing on the technique of free writing and diary keeping, with *On Not Being Able to Paint* engaged more deeply with the activity of free drawing.

We first meet Barry as a reader of Milner's work in *What It Is*. In one scene, Barry includes drawings of various book titles that she turned to during a difficult time suffering from creative blockage. Her bibliography ranges from literature, children's books, psychoanalysis, and Chinese philosophy (*What It Is* 132). But out of all these texts, it is *On Not Being Able to Paint* that seems to take pride of place in her bookshelf for helping her overcome her block. Her subsequent books, *Picture This* and *Syllabus* also contain direct and indirect references to *On Not Being Able to Paint*. Extracts from pages of the book are photocopied, cut, and pasted into her work, including an extract printed in *On Not Being Able to Paint* from lines of the metaphysical poet Thomas Traherne's poetry about infantile experience (Barry, *Syllabus* 167). Barry writes in the acknowledgements page to *Syllabus* how "*On Not Being Able to Paint* by Marion Milner has been a big help to me when I get stuck" (225). She also directly quotes from *On Not Being Able to Paint* when she transcribes the following words of Milner's onto the pages of one of her course syllabuses: "How does the capacity to make a whole picture in which every part is related connect with the capacity to be a whole person?" (Milner qtd. in Barry, *Syllabus* 172). Through reading Barry as a reader of Milner, we start to see their shared preoccupations around the relationship between being creative and being a person. And like Milner, Barry also builds a picture for her reader of a childhood that was haunted by traumatising familial relations.

For Barry, it is difficult relationships with both her parents in childhood, but particularly to her mother, that is the source of what she calls a "deadness" inside of her (*What It Is* 134). In *What It Is* she paints the following portrait of her parents: "My parents were not reading people. They worked, shouted, drank, spalled, belted and were broke. They had affairs and secret lives my two brothers and I had no part in, and if they could have turned back time to the days before we were born, I believe they would have. But there we were" (26). The belief that her parents would have preferred her not having been born is painfully clear here, suggestive also of an experience of never having really felt alive in the minds of her mother and father. We learn that Barry's father leaves the family for good when she was a child, leaving her in the sole care of her mother who was a terrifying and abusive presence. This abusive relationship is portrayed in cartoon illustrations of her mother who would say things to Barry like, " 'Look at me when I talk to you! Hah?' SLAP! 'Why are you looking at me? Hah? You want another one? You see how mad you make it? You see what you do?' " (66). Barry associates these demands around looking and the menacing gaze of her mother with the monstrous figure of Medusa. She tells us that as a child the character of Medusa, a Gorgon, was the monster she was most afraid of. "I hated the thought of her," she writes,

> but she was often on my mind. I made plans for how to defend myself from her, I'd scare myself with the thought of seeing her behind me in the mirror— of accidentally looking at her face. She paralyzes you. You have to cut off her

head without looking at her face. Sometimes I managed—and other times she got to me. I'd practice being paralyzed, and turning into stone. . . . Sometimes I did this in front of my mother to see if she would notice. Sometimes I turned to stone in the front yard.

(63–64)

Barry's "very Gorgon-like mother" makes her feel like she must turn to stone in order to survive, a feeling of deadness as a defence against this "furious woman with terrifying eyes" (it is, perhaps, also an apt description of "stonewalling," in modern psychological terms) (66). Periodic feelings of paralysis and deadness continue to haunt her in adulthood, making her feel personally and creatively stuck.

Barry's description in this passage of the emotional effects of this kind of relationship is not dissimilar from that of *An Experiment in Leisure*, where we even find the figure of Medusa making an appearance in Milner's text. In one passage Milner describes the painful emotional state she would find herself sporadically taken over by, becoming

obsessed by memories and forebodings, "the dark backward and abyss of time", [that] can become a looming presence overshadowing and threatening your own existence. It can make you feel you are as nothing, nothing to say, nothing to feel, nothing to be . . . your attention is not there to attend to ordinary things, it is held by the Medusa vision of disaster.

(*EIL* 145)

Barry and Milner's description of a Medusa vision evoke the failures of maternal mirroring, Medusa's annihilating vision an apt myth or metaphor for the gaze of the mother that Winnicott describes fails the baby.[1]

Like Milner in *A Life of One's Own*, Barry expresses a need to find ways of making her inner world and subjectivity alive and explorable to counter the annihilatory Medusa vision. As Barry relates, "When your inner life is a place you have to stay out of, having an identity is impossible" (*One Hundred Demons* 70). *What It Is* also opens with a recognition of a mind feeling unknown to itself: "There is a song called, 'My minds got a mind of its own'" Barry tells us, "It's a good way to put it. . . . The thing I call my mind seems to be kind of like a landlord that doesn't really know its tenants. . . . Where do sudden troublesome thoughts come from?" (*What It Is* 5–6). Like *A Life of One's Own*, Barry's desire to understand herself better and get a tighter grip on her identity is the catalyst for the exploration of her inner life through various autobiographical mark-making techniques, which the reader comes to witness over the next two hundred and more pages of the book.

Barry seems to describe something akin to the therapeutic functions of the answering activity and pliable medium when she writes the following about the effects of drawing on her: "Something happens to my thinking when I start to draw . . . it becomes more like listening than formulating . . . while I move my pen, I hear sentences, like this one for example. Spoken internally from one part of me to another. Spoken and listened to—heard and recorded" (157). She finds how making marks on paper puts her in "a state of mind which is not accessible by thinking. It seems to require a participation with something. Something physical we move like a pen like a pencil. Something which is in motion" (106). In *What It Is* the words "I.C.U.2" and "Hello" feature repeatedly, free-floating, over many of the pages and drawings in the book. Hilary Chute reads this as "images [that] signal that they are both looked at and themselves looking" (*Graphic Women* 127). These drawings "are seeing us, addressing us; they are undead" (127–28). Barry seems to create for herself an alive image world that looks back at her in recognition, the opposite of her mother's annihilating gaze. In *Picture This*, drawing is appreciated explicitly as a therapeutic activity: "What if drawing was a way to get to a certain state of mind that was very good for us? And what if this certain state of mind was more important than the drawing itself? . . . Drawing is one of the oldest ways of working things out" (223).

The feeling of aliveness that Barry's creative acts provides her with is contrasted to deadness she feels when stuck watching endless hours of television, both as a child and as an adult. The frame of the television also seems to force her into a stone-like state: "What else could stop my experience of being alive so completely?", she asks (Barry, *What It Is* 93). Television can bring on a deadening withdrawal from life, but it is a numbing agent against a harsh reality, for "If your kingdom has gone dark inside," writes Barry, "and there is a light which flickers and speaks in a way that makes you forget these things—you will go to it. You will go to it and willingly turn to stone. What else can you do?" (93).[2] Passively watching TV images, however, can never provide the reflective looking back that creating images affords: "The television eased the problem by presenting channels to an ever-lively WORLD I COULD WATCH. Though it couldn't watch me back, not that it would see much if it could. A girl made of stone facing a flickering light, 45 years later a woman made of stone doing the same thing" (53). The frame of the television is in contrast to the lively reflective capacities of the framing creative and autobiographical work of journal keeping, collaging, writing, and drawing.

As Milner describes in *Eternity's Sunrise* being influenced by the image of Ruskin recovering from illness on his travels after drawing a tree, a similar image of resuscitation through a solitary creative act is to be found in *What It Is*. In Barry's image she depicts herself as a child, drawing alone in front of the television (105). She tells us how she loved to draw

> comics at night in front of the TV. I liked ballpoint pens on notebook paper and a show on I didn't care about. Sometimes I drew with the radio on. It was a form of transportation. I did it because it helped me to stay by giving me

somewhere else to go. Drawing can help us stand to be there. That, alone, is something.

(105)

To stand to be there is not only to be able to tolerate an intolerable situation, but like Ruskin, it is also about standing to be alive and oneself. The frame of creative activity helps Barry to do this standing in a way that the pseudo-frame of the television cannot.

This struggle to stand to be oneself is described in *What It Is* when Barry recalls how in her younger years her identity was for a long time tied to copying other's identities on and off the page:

> I was copying other people's lives and personalities, hair, clothes, table manners, conversation-style, way of laughing, way of anything that was part of the future I wanted to be in. I copied old illustrations and ads and then photographs. I copied poems and song lyrics. Copied thoughts of others and tried to change my situation by copying my way into another world.
>
> (115)

But like Milner, who in *An Experiment* laments her inability to know what she wants for herself and is too quick to adapt to other's needs, Barry finds that this copying of others only serves her for so long. Under the guidance of her college tutor, Marilyn Frasca, she is encouraged to ask a number of questions about images: "What is an image? Where is it located? What form can it take? How does it move through time? What is it made of? How is it used?" (116). These were startling inquiries, since "Copying was all I had done for so long, the image question baffled me" (116). The image is aligned for Barry with aliveness, a vibrant subjectivity, the act of copying by contrast erasing her subjectivity. This act of copying that effaces the self recalls Milner's tracing over of Susan's E.C.T drawing, in marked contrast to her creative inversions of Blake's illustrations.

What It Is is also very much preoccupied with how autobiographical and creative acts can provide Barry with a subjectivity that acquires a sense of form, shape, and being when externalized on the page. "What do drawing singing dancing music making handwriting playing story writing acting remembering and even dreaming all have in common???" Barry asks, and then proceeds to answer: "They come about when a certain person in a certain place in a certain time arranges certain uncertainties into a certain form" (81). Hilary Chute's chapter on Barry, "Materializing Memory: Lynda Barry's One Hundred Demons" in her book *Graphic Women* (2010) understands Barry's work as part of a deliberate drive to materialise her memories through capturing them in drawing, writing, and collage. In this way, Barry strikes us as sharing the same desire to imbue memory and subjective experience with a tangibility and materiality as Milner does through her creation and collection of bead memories and her desire for "crystallization" (*EIL* 129). The ways in which both Milner and Barry speak of their memories, imagination, and thoughts is as if their inner worlds are made up of the properties of the material world. On the pages of *What It Is*, Barry asks a number of questions about the physical qualities of internal phenomena. As if adhering to Newtonian laws of physics, she asks "Do memories have mass? Do they have motion? Do they have inertia?" (Barry, *What It Is* 36). Other questions include: "What are thoughts made of? . . . What is an idea made out of? . . . What is movement? Do thoughts move? Do images have motion??" (70–83). In asking these questions, Barry compels the reader to imagine an inner life obeying the laws of the physical world, and in doing so, she imbues her subjectivity with an alive sense of being—a continuity of being—the opposite of a deadness that diminishes the self.

Like Milner, Barry recognises the importance of the provision of a space and time in which to engage with creative pursuits. In *One Hundred Demons* she remembers gratefully how one of her childhood schoolteachers allowed her to come to class "early and stay late. There was a special art table at the back of the room. I spent a lot of time there. She gave me something *no one* could take away" (177). Milner's concept of the frame for describing the therapeutic settings of the artist's studio and psychoanalyst's consulting room fits with Barry's thinking here as well as the comic frames which Barry employs in her autobiographical narratives. In the final section of *What It Is*, Barry presents her reader with an activity book containing a variety of writing and drawing exercises designed to encourage adults who have stopped writing or drawing. Michael Chaney emphasises the importance of the teacher–student dynamic in the book, writing how *What It Is* is "Part activity book, part lesson plan, part autobiography (recounting Barry's path towards art), and full of shimmering watercolor and meticulous collages, *What It Is* is a dizzying, exhilarating, sometimes even maddening *performance* of teaching" (312).

Syllabus is more exclusively about Barry's work as a teacher, as "assistant professor of interdisciplinary creativity" in the Art Department at the University of Wisconsin–Madison (1). The book comprises a collection of Barry's richly decorated course syllabi, many of which closely resemble the pages of her own books. The syllabi are from courses that include: "Writing the Unthinkable," and another, which shares the same title as her book, "What It Is."

In one syllabus Barry tells us how significant keeping a journal and diary has been for her throughout her adult life, an activity that she also asks her students to take up:

> I wasn't quite 20 years old when I started my first notebook. I had no idea that nearly 40 years later, I would not only still be using it as the most reliable route to the thing I've come to call my work, but I'd also be showing others how to use it too, as a place to practice a physical activity—in this case writing and drawing by hand—with a certain state of mind.

(4)

Students are guided on how to practice a "way of writing and keeping a working notebook using image-based, spontaneous exercises" using "autobiography and fiction techniques to write a lot" (36). She impels her students to practice these techniques with some degree of intensity: in a handout for students provided towards the end of the course, Barry reminds her class how they have "kept a diary for 21 days and written 14 stories and colored 8 pictures and made almost 56 little drawings" (115). Milner, I think, would approve.

Milner's influence is palpable in one passage in particular where Barry makes a case to her students of the value of keeping a notebook to provide insight into one's interior life. Like Milner's desire to "catch" her "back-of-my-mind thoughts" through free writing in her diary in *A Life of One's Own*, Barry tells her students in her course notes to (110):

> [t]hink of your composition notebook as a catch-all that collects samples from all the elements if your day-to-day life. . . . Patterns start to emerge that can be very helpful in trying to understand what this thing I call "the back of the mind" is up to. I think of the comp book as a place for the back of the mind to come forward. If you keep up with your comp book all semester, when it comes time to decide what your final project should be about, your composition notebook will already contain the answer.
>
> (Syllabus 62)

"This practice," Barry writes, "can result in what I've come to consider a wonderful side effect: a visual or written image we can call 'a work of art,' although a work of art is not what I'm after when I'm practicing this activity. What am I after? I'm after . . . being present and seeing what's there" (4). Barry's classes, like her books, encourage thinking about what writing and drawing can do for one emotionally. One week's homework is outlined in the following passage:

> Homework: Think of the most difficult time of your childhood—what happened? What helped you get through it? How alive is this time in your mind? How long will it stay with you? What forms does it take in the here and now? Your homework is to think about these questions. And wonder about your own way of using images in times of trouble.
>
> (173)

In taking her course and practicing the advised autobiographical and creative exercises, the students will enjoy a personal development that reaches beyond the confines of the classroom, echoing Chris Crickmay when she assures that, "A new way of seeing comes about," and "a new approach to problem-solving and working that extends beyond the limits of our class time into other aspects of daily life" (59).

Importantly, Barry's pedagogical techniques encourage an independent, solitary creativity in her students. In one syllabus, Barry lays down the following classroom etiquette for the semester: "When classmates read aloud [their writing], we do not look at them. Instead, we draw tight spirals slowly. We don't chat. Instead, we get to know each other through the images in our work" (55). It is the creative work that fosters relationships, and not the other way around. In *What It Is* she asks "How do images move and transfer? Something inside one person takes external form—contained by a poem, story, picture, melody, play, etc—and through a certain kind of engagement, is transferred to the inside of someone else. Art as a transit system for images" (9). Here we find Barry proposing a different kind of intersubjective relations, via the sharing and transmission of images between one person and another.

Like Milner (and her other readers Rainer, Bolton, and Hunt), Barry champions her methods as doing something comparable to psychoanalysis. In an interview about her book *What It Is* with Michael Dean for *The Comics Journal*, we find the following exchange:

> Michael Dean: At one point in *What It Is*, you make the observations that sometimes the best way to remember something you're having trouble remembering is to forget about it for a while and let it come back to you on its own and that sometimes the best way to forget something that is troubling you is to fully remember it. Although I don't think you directly mention Freud or his theories anywhere in the book, I can picture him nodding approvingly at this, which sounds very like the strategy of traditional psychoanalysis. How do you feel about psychoanalysis and Freud, who is not so much in favour these days?
>
> Lynda Barry: Actually, when people say this way of working with images is like psychoanalysis, I always say, no, psychoanalysis is like this way of working with images. And this way of working with images is very very old. It existed long before the word subconscious existed, and even when it was unnamed it was fully functional. Telling stories and remembering and forgetting and associative aspects of memory are things which have been with humans all along. Playing has always been with us. All of the things we call art or psychology or even the skeletal system were there before they were named. They come with the package of being human. So Freud noticed something, but he didn't invent it.
>
> (3)

Barry's statement here invokes Freud's famous admission that "The poets and philosophers before me discovered the unconscious. . . . What I discovered was the scientific method by which the unconscious can be studied" (qtd. in Trilling 34).

In the vein of Milner's decidedly unscientific research and therapeutic endeavour, I understand Barry to be another inheritor and propagator of Milner's autobiographical cure. We might situate Barry, like Milner, in the "bastard line" of poets that Sabine Prokhoris understands Freud as partially disavowing in the development of his psychoanalytic thinking and treatment (6). Barry might also be understood as working under the sign of a more Blakean influence in her richly illustrated word-image compositions. Her compositions have been likened to Blake's composite art by "taking the reader into a world and vision all of her own" (Dean 3). One journalist describes Barry's collages as "densely visionary compositions, as if William Blake had clipped out his cosmology from old magazines" (Randle, "Interview: Lynda Barry: 'What is an image? That question has directed my entire life'"). Indeed, Blake's "radical form of mixed art" has been understood as a precursor to today's literary comics (Mitchell 3). Barry has herself considered the connections between her work and Blake's, writing how "If William Blake were alive and producing his work in 2013, how would we categorize it? Would we think of it as alt comics? A graphic novel? Why? What did they call it in his day?" (*The Near-Sighted Monkey*). We might characterise Milner and Barry's uses of visual and verbal expression as a composite, creative, and curative method. For both authors, the act of creating the book held by the reader is crucial to the process of working towards psychic health. The act of creation puts them in touch with an inner sense of aliveness and goodness, providing a vital vision of their subjectivities in all their messy, vibrant, complicated glory.

Alison Bechdel's *Are You My Mother?* (2012)

I now want to turn to the work of another celebrated American comic artist, Alison Bechdel and her 2012 graphic memoir *Are You My Mother? A Comic Drama*. Following on from her first graphic memoir *Fun Home: A Family Tragicomic* (2006) which explores her relationship with her late father, in *Are You My Mother?* Bechdel turns her attentions to her relationship with her mother in a complex, multi-layered and psychoanalytically informed work of comic image-text. Bechdel is deeply invested in understanding herself as a psychoanalytic subject, specifically as understood through the prism of an object relations understandings of the development of the self in preverbal, pre-oedipal life. "What I really want to write about is self and other," states Bechdel in an interview about the book, "which seems like a very vexing problem. Inevitably, if you're talking about relationship you've got to talk about your mother because that's who your first relationship is with" (qtd. in Rüggemeier 2016, 255).

It is the figure of Winnicott and his psychoanalytic ideas that feature most prominently in these investigations into herself and her relationship with her mother. The memoir is formed of seven chapters, many of its titles alluding to Winnicottian concepts: Chapter 1 is titled "The Ordinary Devoted Mother," Chapter 2 "Transitional Objects," and Chapter 6 "Mirror."[3] Bechdel's narrative begins with her coming to read Winnicott for the first time, taking us with her on her journey of trying to understand his ideas and using them to help her make sense of her own emotional development.[4] Since Winnicott is the main psychoanalytic presence in the book, it follows that *Are You My Mother?* has been written about and understood by scholars through the lens of Winnicottian theory, namely through the concept of the transitional object. This concept is unquestionably important to the book—the book's last chapter, "The Use of an Object," contains a reproduction of the diagram Winnicott includes in his paper "Transitional Objects and Transitional Phenomena" to represent the place of the transitional object residing between mother and infant. Further, Bechdel reflects at length on the significance of transitional objects in her own experiences, including her childhood attachment to her toy bear, Beezum. In her review of *Are You My Mother*, Heather Love wonders whether "One might understand this book itself as an attempt to mimic the look and feel of the transitional object" ("The Mom Problem"). Winnicott's concept lends itself to thinking about the role of the memoir as a way of helping Bechdel to make sense of herself and her relationship with her mother, facilitating an emotional transition from dependence to independence and to a more separate sense of selfhood and individuality.

In her article "Graphic Analysis: Transitional Phenomena in Alison Bechdel's *Are You My Mother?*", Lisa Diedrich makes a similar argument, writing how "Bechdel creates transitional phenomena through both the form and content of her graphic narrative" (184). Diedrich understands Bechdel's interest in Winnicott as thanks to her concern with

> the process, as much as the product, of making . . . this explains for me what has drawn her to psychoanalytic theory and practice in general and Winnicott's theories and practices in particular. The turn to psychoanalysis in *Are You My Mother?* makes more explicit graphic work as healing work—or perhaps we should say, graphic play as healing play.
>
> (185–89)

Winnicott's ideas and practices are able to accommodate and inspire what Diedrich calls Bechdel's "graphic analysis—a long and difficult therapeutic and creative process of doing and undoing the self in words and images" (183). In this way, Diedrich suggests, Bechdel's therapeutic creative work provides her with a "what Winnicott would call a holding environment" (185).

It is likely that Winnicott's interest in creativity and psychic health is a large part of why Bechdel finds Winnicott such a generative thinker for her memoir. But, as I want to argue, it is worth considering Milner as a less conspicuous, yet nonetheless significant foremother of Bechdel's. Bechdel's approach to psychoanalysis, creative self-expression, and diary keeping arguably aligns most closely with Milner's thinking and practices. Milner's thinking about the potential for autobiographical mark-making for therapeutic transformation provides an important framework, I think, through which to understand Bechdel's work. Though no reference is made to Milner or any of her ideas in *Are You My Mother?*, it is through Bechdel's engagement with Winnicott's diary keeping patient in his paper "Mind and Its Relation to the Psyche-Soma," that some kind of Milnerian presence comes into view.

About two-thirds of the way into *Are You My Mother?* Bechdel includes an excerpt from Winnicott's case study. She tells the reader how in this paper Winnicott "gives an illustration of his work with a forty-seven-year-old woman who 'felt completely dissatisfied, as if always aiming to find herself and never succeeding'" (Bechdel, *Are You My Mother?* 151). The patient's use of a diary and Winnicott's interpretations of her diary keeping capture Bechdel's attentions and an identification is swiftly set up between Bechdel and this female patient, with excerpts from Winnicott's case study interwoven with scenes depicting Bechdel in her own therapy sessions, struggling with similar interpretations about her diary writing from her own therapist. As was speculated in Chapter 3, this female patient may very well have been Milner, and in this way *Are You My Mother?* might be read as staging, unknowingly, some of this possible encounter between Winnicott and Milner. Bechdel nonetheless does knowingly stage a dialogue between the talking cure and a diary keeping cure, and their respective ability to provide therapeutic resolution.

The question running through Bechdel's narrative revolves around whether diary keeping is a form of relating, or a disruption of it. We learn through Bechdel's comic narrative that she kept a diary throughout her childhood. Bechdel's therapist, Carol, suggests that diary keeping was a way to distance herself from other people and from her family's troubled emotional life. According to Carol, Bechdel's mother's encouragement of her diary writing "makes her complicit" in Bechdel's withdrawal from these relationships (151). Carol tells Bechdel that she relates to her mind as if it were an object, "like it's an internalized parent or lover.... Being attached to your work, your mind, the way you would be to another person—that cuts you off from the world" (152). This is an interpretation that resounds with Winnicott's evaluation of the diary as a symptom of his patient's withdrawn reliance on her own psyche, out of not feeling she can depend on the mind of another.

Part of "Carol's diagnosis" is the sense that Bechdel's mother was "complicit" in her daughter's emotional withdrawal into diary writing as a child (151). Bechdel however presents us with a more ambivalent take on her mother's role. As Love puts it, "it is clear that Bechdel's mother was both an enabling and a blocking figure in Alison's psychic, sexual, and artistic development" ("The Mom Problem"). Bechdel recounts how as a child she suffered from bouts of OCD, which would entail obscuring her diary entries with "repetitive markings" (*Are You My Mother?* 49). These were "an attempt to ward off evil from the people I was writing about. By far the most heavily obliterated word is 'I.'" (49). As her OCD was at its worst after her twelfth birthday, she remembers her mother helping her with her diary keeping, writing down what Bechdel would tell her, an arrangement that continued for six weeks. Love observes how Bechdel's illustrations of this collaborative act of diary keeping between mother and daughter are not dissimilar to the scenes of therapy in the book:

> Alison cozy in her pajamas and her mother seated next to her, absorbed in her task, her posture expressive of care but also of a sustaining neutrality. . . . That neutral posture is familiar as that of the psychoanalyst. Bechdel juxtaposes past and present, interspersing these childhood images with scenes of herself as an adult, lying on the couch, talking while her therapist silently takes notes.
>
> ("The Mom Problem")

In these parallel scenes, healing is found both in the frame of the analyst's couch and in a collaborative autobiographical act.

Bechdel struggles with both "Carol's diagnosis" and Winnicott's judgements of his patient's diary keeping. For both Winnicott and Carol, the diary writing expresses and promotes a faulty sense of self—faulty in its being cut off from relations with others. And yet, Bechdel is pictured in a frame on her own, in a sense resisting this interpretation, exclaiming: "But . . . My diary saved me!" (Bechdel, *Are You My Mother?* 151). We learn that Bechdel continues to keep diaries as an adult (without her mother's assistance), creating *Are You My Mother?* seemingly providing her with something equally resuscitative: "The irony of the fact that I'm writing a book about all this is not lost on me. Yet I don't seem to have a choice" (152). Like Winnicott's diary keeping patient, Bechdel is highly invested, as Milner is, with how autobiographical mark-making can do something reparative.

It is also significant that on the same page that Bechdel tackles Carol and Winnicott's diagnoses, in the following frame we are transported to the pages of another woman's diary, that of Virginia Woolf's. Bechdel transcribes part of a passage from Woolf's diary dated from 1928, in which she describes how writing *To the Lighthouse* (1927) enabled her to lay to rest her unhealthy obsessions with both her parents (152). We are then shown Bechdel talking to Carol from the couch, bemoaning her inability to finish the memoir that is *Are You My Mother?* Her mother's critical editorial voice haunts her: "I can't write this book until I get her out of my head. . . . But the only way to get her out of my head is by writing the book! It's a paradox" (23). In the frame below, Bechdel writes how she envies Woolf's comparative lack of writer's block, but she is also envious of the therapeutic resolution Woolf finds when completing the novel. She copies out another passage from Woolf's diary, where she writes how on completing *To the Lighthouse*: "I ceased to be obsessed by my mother. I no longer hear her voice; I do not see her. I suppose I did for myself what psycho-analysts do for their patients. I expressed some very long felt and deeply felt emotion. And in expressing it I explained it and then laid it to rest" (qtd. in *Are You My Mother?* 18).

In an earlier part of the memoir, Bechdel imagines a near encounter between a young Winnicott and an older Woolf passing one another on the streets of Bloomsbury in London where Woolf lived, and where some decades later, Winnicott would work (24–25). I understand this scene as representative of Bechdel's staging an encounter between the two tools in her arsenal for understanding and healing her-self—the writer/diarist and the psychoanalyst, and the similar but differing tech-niques both offer, and both of which Bechdel makes use of. What psychoanalysis can do, and whether this always happens, or can only happen on the couch, is a large part of what Bechdel's memoir grapples with: "I'm trying to figure out—from both sides of the couch—just what it is that psychoanalysts do for their patients" (21). From both sides of the couch suggests being both patient and one's own analyst, taking on the role of both. Towards the end of the memoir Bechdel states in more unequivocal terms: "What I really want is to cure myself. To be my own analyst" (149).

In her article "Beyond Psychoanalysis: Resistance and Reparative Reading in Alison Bechdel's *Are You My Mother?*", Tammy Clewell argues that Bech-del interrogates the idea of the classic psychoanalytic cure. Bechdel's memoir "articulates the effectiveness—and limits—of psychoanalysis as a therapeutic tool . . . [it] requires us to reconsider the frequently maligned idea that literature can serve therapeutic aims" (Clewell 53). For Bechdel, like Milner, creating thera-peutic forms for themselves is a form of self-reparation, a compensation for the disappointments of early care.

The effects of this first relationship on Bechdel's adult relationship with her mother, with herself, and with others is carefully observed. She asks: "At some point most of us wonder. How much of me is me?" (Bechdel, *Are You My Mother?* 140). Similar to Milner, and indeed Winnicott in his poem "The Tree," Bechdel comes to realise how "I have, in fact, been trying to heal my mother for as long as I can remember" (83). She describes "the strangely inverted relationship I'd always felt I had with my mother . . . the sense that I was her mother. . . . This had been a problem for me all my life" (53). She often feels her mother takes no inter-est in her life: "I always call her, she never calls me. . . . I listen to her go on and on about people I don't know, I support her, encourage her, but she doesn't want to hear about my life" (62).

In *Are You My Mother?*, it is a photographic image that sparks an insight into the author's relationship with her mother and the origins of their relationship in Bechdel's infancy. Early on in the memoir she tells the reader how she had "always been fascinated" by a photograph of herself as a baby in her mother's arms (31). Bechdel's reproduction of the photograph in drawing features herself making happy faces with her mother, a scene depicting an untroubled attune-ment between mother and baby. With the help of her mother, Bechdel tracks down a sequence of photos from which this image was taken. Though she can only guess the correct chronological order of these photos, in her arrangement of them "the rapport between Mom and me builds until I shriek with joy" (31). But this happy moment of reciprocity is followed by a photograph depicting her baby-self looking suspiciously at the camera: "Then the moment is shattered as I notice the man with the camera. . . . At three months, I had seen enough of my father's rages to be wary of him" (33). There is a particular emotional quality to the paternal third/interruption Bechdel depicts here—she does not just "notice" him: he says something painful and dismissive that cuts across the joy, a com-petitiveness accompanying her father's interruption.

Although in this sequence it is Bechdel's father who seems to interrupt the provision of care and understanding, *Are You My Mother?* is primarily concerned with exploring the quality of maternal care she received. "I don't want to suggest that my own highly capable mother was not 'good-enough'" she tells us, but some babies can, quoting Winnicott "'tolerate the results of frustration' sooner than others" (61). Like Milner, Bechdel sensitively explores the difficulties her own mother faced in her life and its impact on her ability to care for her baby.

It is in the creative act of assembling and drawing these photos in this particular chronology that Bechdel creates a narrative in which the state of relations between mother, infant, and father are brought to consciousness. The self-knowledge generated by creating this sequence of images is integrated into her understanding of herself and relationship to her mother, leading her to make more sense of why events like her mother abruptly stopping kissing her goodnight at the age of seven "felt almost as if she'd slapped me" (137). The double page in which Bechdel reproduces these photos is littered with the paraphernalia of artistic creation—a fountain pen, brush, rubber, and ruler arrange themselves on the page amongst the photos portraying the mother–infant dyad and its interruption by the paternal third. This, I think, depicts the kind of analytic tools Bechdel brings to her task: there is the frame that contains Winnicott's words and Bechdel's paraphrasing of them, but Bechdel's drawn images take centre stage as a site for analytic work.

Bechdel compares her own autobiographical acts to that of her mother's. Bechdel's diary provides a repository where she can express the details of her life, internal and external. "Like my mother," Bechdel tells us, "I keep a log of the events of daily, external life. But unlike her, I also record a great deal of information about my internal life. Although I'm often confused about precisely where the demarcation lies" (17). The function of diary writing for Bechdel couldn't be more different to what Bechdel calls her "mother's insistence that her own journal is little more than a completed to-do list [and] that she never re-reads it" (17). Whereas her autobiographical writing involves a search for and exploration of the self on the page, Bechdel reports her mother telling her plainly: "The self has no good place in writing" (200).

Importantly, it is Bechdel's commitment to finding the self in writing, and providing self-reparation through diary keeping and drawing that introduces a competing therapeutic approach to the work of psychotherapy. Bechdel's therapists throughout her adulthood, Carol and Joyce, though helpful in many regards seem unable able to live up to the most important psychoanalytic presence in the book, which is Winnicott, imagined and engaged with in the memoir through his writings. In one scene, Bechdel describes Winnicott's case study, "The Piggle" (1980) which charts Winnicott's analysis with a girl named Gabrielle from the ages of X to five. In contrast to when she began the analysis, at thirteen Gabrielle is now "unself-conscious . . . spontaneous . . . very much part of a group . . . at school" (Winnicott qtd. in *Are You My Mother?* 156). Bechdel, who calculates she is one year older than Gabrielle, compares their lives by writing how, "At thirteen, I was so paralyzed with self-consciousness that sometimes I'd get home from school and realize I hadn't spoken out loud all day" (156). Gabrielle is presented here as Bechdel's healthier double—how life might have been different, Bechdel seems to suggest, had Winnicott been her therapist. In another scene, Bechdel recounts an early period of therapy soon after she had discovered Winnicott's work. She tells her therapist that she had wished Winnicott had been her mother. Her therapist asks her why, to which she replies: "I dunno. . . . But I know that if he had been my mother, I wouldn't be suffering over this book. . . . I'd be doing something useful" (23). Her phantasy of what kind of mother Winnicott might have been is perhaps the kind of mother that successfully cares for her baby, mirroring and holding so sufficiently fulfilled that in later life the substitutive care of the analyst would be unnecessary. Most significantly, she would not have felt compelled to write the memoir she finds herself painfully struggling over now.

This I think draws into sharper focus the motivations behind Bechdel's need to engage with her own autobiographical cures. Winnicott's writings provide her with an intellectual and emotional framework and support through which to think about her own relationship with her mother, his theory perhaps doing a kind of "holding work" for her as a writer. Bechdel writes and draws into existence a Winnicott that she encounters through her reading about him. We might even understand *Are You My Mother?* as in some way playing a squiggle game with Winnicott, a game played not in the frame of the consulting room, but within the margins of the page. In Bechdel's text, Winnicott is above all a textual and visual presence, and not the flesh and blood analyst with reactions and emotions that Milner encountered. Crucially, Winnicott as textual analyst bypasses the countertransference of the conventional analytic encounter. In comparison with Milner's analyst substitutes in *Bothered by Alligators*, however, for Bechdel talking therapy is felt more straightforwardly to be an aid alongside, rather than as a potential substitution for a "couch analysis." Indeed, Bechdel acknowledges the profound help she received from her analysis with Jocelyn, telling us how "With Jocelyn, I began to feel more real" (146).

Bechdel practically demonstrates through her work how writing and drawing autobiographically has helped her, and like Milner, she expands the notion of a therapeutic relationship to that of a relationship to a medium. She describes how as a child how important it was to have the experience of "getting away from the press of others' needs. . . . I would build myself an "office." I would barricade myself off in the back of a closet or a corner of the drawing room and work there at my drawings. The sensation of being invisible, inviolable, was a kind of ecstasy" (130).[5] As an adult she describes a frame-like experience during "a period of intense creative ferment. I was not only working on the dad book, and my comic strip . . . but I was also spending long hours writing down my dreams and reading about psychoanalysis. I felt a piercing lucidity, as if the hood on my life had been lifted and I could see its inner workings" (253). The frames of the consulting room, drawing room, and comic frame provide the space and time through which it is possible to engage with oneself without the impingements of another. Operating more closely within a Milnerian tradition than a Winnicottian one, this is a psychoanalytic work done in relation to a self-created object rather than in the relation to an analyst.

Readers of this book will, I hope, agree that through a greater familiarity with Milner's terms, concepts, and methods, our understanding of these other authors' multifarious therapeutic projects is deepened and enriched. Milner's notion of the frame and the framed gap (1952) seems particularly relevant for thinking about the comic frame, and provides a different perspective on its uses and effects. As Scott McCloud points out, "what's between the panels is the only element of comics that is not duplicated in any other medium" (McCloud 13). Composed via a series of frames and white spaces that are called gutters, comic frames have been typically understood as "boxes of time" that present a narrative that is "threaded through with absence," which makes it particularly adept at "mimic[king] the procedure of memory" (Chute, *Graphic Women* 6, 4). With Milner's understanding of the frame, we can see the function of the comic frame in authors like Barry and Bechdel's work as providing the space on the page through which a particular kind of creative engagement with self and world can take place and be safely contained.

Bechdel's graphic memoir engages deeply with the visual qualities of Winnicott's thinking, and thereby, indirectly, with Milner's work. Included in *Are You My Mother?* is a reproduction of Winnicott's drawing of what Bechdel names his "diagram of relation" from "Transitional Objects and Transitional Phenomena" in *Playing and Reality*. Drawn to depict the "territory between the objective and the subjective" between mother and baby, we are reminded of Milner's *Two Jugs* picture and its influence on Winnicott (Winnicott qtd. in Bechdel, *Are You My Mother?* 258). Following this, Bechdel reproduces a diagram Woolf made to depict the form of *To the Lighthouse*, as "two blocks joined by a corridor" (255). Lisa Diedrich reads this as Bechdel "calling attention to the advantages of her own medium by pointing to what she sees as a potential limitation of Woolf's," yet she grants "Woolf something of the status of a comics artist: Bechdel represents her as a spatial thinker, if not an actual cartoonist" (64). Since *To the Lighthouse* is a novel about "subject and object and the nature of reality," Bechdel seems to be drawing parallels between Winnicott and Woolf's shared preoccupations around the self and its relation to the other, and the pictorial form these concerns best find expression in (Woolf qtd. in Bechdel, *Are You My Mother?* 255).[6] This might help to explain why Bechdel initially began the memoir as a piece of written prose, but that soon she "started hitting a dead end with that" and had to turn to the conflation of image and text to be able to express what she wanted to (Bechdel qtd. in Chute, "An Interview with Alison Bechdel" 163–64). It is perhaps apt that it is the work of the graphic memoir, narrating the self across the mediums of writing and drawing, that has most recently taken up Milner's composite, visual-verbal autobiographical cure.

Hilary Chute has written how thanks to the medium's "spatial conventions, comics is [sic] able to map a life, not only figuratively but literally. It can diagram a life on a page" (109). Bechdel also emphasises the cartographic capacities of comics, saying how: "Cartoons are like maps to me," and that her earlier graphic memoir about her father, *Fun Home*, "is a fairly accurate map of my life" (Bechdel qtd. in "An Interview with Alison Bechdel" 109). As we know, Milner also makes use of mapping in her autobiographical work, mentioning making "a sort of pictorial map of my life-experience" during the time of writing *A Life of One's Own* and *An Experiment in Leisure* (*EIL* 151). I read Winnicott's diagrams and doodles of the mother–infant relation and the space between them as also performing a kind of mapping—of the self in its location and relation to the other, the contours of mother and infant in space. We might understand Milner, Bechdel, and Barry's visual-verbal autobiographical acts as doing this also. In trying to find and understand the location of the self in relation to the (m)other, they stake out a claim for a place and space for the self through a relationship with the medium of pen and paper, and in doing so, redraw their map of relations.

On the final page of *Are You My Mother?*, Bechdel depicts the following scene: we see Bechdel as a young girl playing a ritualised game with her mother, in which she pretends she is a crippled child and her mother must help her stand up. Reflecting upon this scene, Bechdel tells us how: "I always thought of the crippled child game as the moment my mother taught me how to write" (*Are You My Mother?* 288). This leads her to the conclusion, and perhaps resolution, that "There was a certain thing I did not get from my mother. . . . There is a lack, a gap, a void. . . . But in its place, she has given me something else. . . . Something I would argue, that is far more valuable. . . . 'I think I can get up now.' . . . She has given me the way out" (288–89). I read this "way out" as Bechdel's ability to provide herself with the self-curative techniques of creativity and autobiographical mark-making, to alleviate some of the haunting disillusionments of early care. This appreciation of a creative "way out" is the autobiographical cure, one that Bechdel, Milner, and Barry all share in providing for themselves, their students, and as Milner suggests in *Bothered by Alligators*, her own son, John.

* * *

In the winter of 2010, the portrait artist Riva Lehrer began a collaborative artwork with Alison Bechdel. A short film directed by Charissa King-O'Brien called *The Paper Mirror* (2012) captures moments from this project (Figure 5.2). Lehrer first drew a black and white portrait of Bechdel looking in a mirror, with Bechdel then asked to contribute to the work in any way she liked. Over the top of Lehrer's figure of her, Bechdel painted in blue an illustration of her mother in her characteristic comic style.

The final painting was completed during the time in which Bechdel was working on *Are You My Mother?*, and its themes are continuous with the memoir's. Like the memoir, the symbol of the mirror is central to the composition and meaning of the painting. In Bechdel's self-reflection is a mother who does not meet her daughter's gaze but is instead preoccupied by a book. Self-reflexive autobiographical work—a "paper mirror" as the film's title aptly calls it—supplies a medium through which she can find a mirror to reflect herself.

The different sorts of therapeutic work that Bechdel and Barry's methods comprise—drawing, collage, diary writing, and the visual-verbal medium of the graphic memoir all share with psychoanalysis the fundamental desire to better

Figure 5.2 Alison Bechdel.
Source: Riva Lehrer, 2011.

understand the basic relationship of the self with the other. Whether via the talk-ing cure or through a drawing or writing cure, these are methods for repairing and redrawing intersubjective relations. But these autobiographical cures in the wake of Milner are, fundamentally, accessible to anyone. The cures afforded by diary keeping, doodling, free writing, and collage making demand neither artistic nor lit-erary talent, nor the resources required for an analysis. Perhaps it makes sense then that it is Barry and Bechdel, women working with the medium of comics who we might understand as Milner's successors in the twenty-first century. As the diary was once snubbed as a minor domestic, feminine form, comics were long dismissed as products of low and popular culture. One critic describes Barry's oeuvre as fusing "Blakean high-art traces with the domesticated, female tradition of scrapbooking," and indeed, the autobiographical cure is one that aims towards a democratisation of the resources of both the artist and psychoanalyst (Michael 1). In her championing of the *New Diary*, Tristine Rainer writes how "The diary is now shedding its old skin of guilt, shame, and unnecessary isolation to become a free and open means of achieving deep intimacy with the self and with others" (Rainer 304). Barry and Bechdel's work might also be understood as doing the same for the genre of the graphic memoir, elevating the medium to the heights of therapeutic apparatus.

For these authors, the act of writing the book we are holding is an essential part of the process of working through and achieving psychic health. Whilst neither therapy nor diary writing can fully alleviate the void felt when a motherly touch or gaze might have been lost, they can gesture towards its absence, and in doing so, provide another kind of presence. Future readers of Milner's will, I think, continue to adapt different genres of self-expression for these curative purposes, finding in Milner a spark that sets into motion their own therapeutic journeys.

Notes

1   In archetypal terms, the Medusa myth symbolises the most negative, dreadful aspects of the feminine principle, but she also symbolises protection (Bjorklund 91). Medusa also appears elsewhere in Greek mythology as a protective talisman on weapons and shields (91). Athena affixed Medusa's head to her breastplate and Perseus kept her image emblazoned on his shield, using her decapitated head to disarm his enemies. The double-sided nature of Medusa, her terror but also her protectiveness, suggests a particular kind of maternal force that is lifesaving but also life threatening. It also suggests the kind of a terrible power imbued only to women, and mothers, in the cultural imagination. In the Greek myth there are no reported instances of Medusa turning a woman to stone, only men. Milner and Barry's rewriting of the myth then describes a particular kind of mother–daughter relation.
2   For further discussion on the television as understood as a type of companion, see Roger Silverstone's work on *Television and Everyday Life* (1994).
3   The cover of the 2013 edition of the book features a mirror made from a shiny, reflective paper, the book reflecting the reader's own face back to them.
4   Bechdel also provided the illustrations to Brett Kahr's 2016 *Tea With Winnicott*, a "posthumous interview" in which Kahr imagines himself in discussion with Winnicott.
5   In relation to this desire to be alone and inviolable, see Winnicott's paper "The capacity to be alone" (1958). In this article Winnicott outlines the importance of developing from infancy a capacity to be alone when in the presence of someone else as well as when physically isolated.
6   Bechdel understands Lily Briscoe's act of painting as her "trying to work out the relation of shapes in her painting, but she's also trying to understand the relation between Mr. and Mrs. Ramsay" (*Are You My Mother?* 256). The potential for painting as a way of revealing and working out intersubjective relations is reminiscent of Milner's experimentations with form, colour, and outline in *On Not Being Able to Paint*.

References

Barry, Lynda. *One Hundred Demons*. Drawn & Quarterly, 2002

Barry, Lynda. *Picture This: The Near-Sighted Monkey Book*. Drawn & Quarterly, 2010.

Barry, Lynda. *Syllabus: Notes from an Accidental Professor*. Drawn & Quarterly, 2014.

Barry, Lynda. *The Near-Sighted Monkey*, 2013. thenearsightedmonkey.tumblr.com/post/41411859798/if-william-blake-were-alive-and-producing-his-work. Accessed 7 March 2021.

Barry, Lynda. *What It Is*. Drawn & Quarterly, 2008.

Bechdel, Alison. *Are You My Mother? A Comic Drama*. Mariner Books, 2012.

Bjorklund, Patricia. "Medusa Appears: A Case Study of a Narcissistic Disturbance." *Perspectives in Psychiatric Care*, vol. 36, no. 3, 2000, pp. 86–94. http://dx.doi.org/10.1111/j.1744-6163.2000.tb00698.x

Chaney, Michael, editor. *Graphic Subjects: Critical Essays on Autobiography and Graphic Novels*. Wisconsin University Press, 2011.

Chute, Hilary. "An Interview with Alison Bechdel." *MFS Modern Fiction Studies*, vol. 52, no. 4, 2006, pp. 1004–1013. http://dx.doi.org/10.1353/mfs.2007.0003

Chute, Hilary. *Graphic Women: Life Narrative and Contemporary Comics*. Columbia University Press, 2010.

Clewell, Tammy. "Beyond Psychoanalysis: Resistance and Reparative Reading in Alison *Bechdel's are You My Mother?*" *PMLA*, vol. 132, no. 1, 2017, pp. 51–70. http://dx.doi.org/10.1632/pmla.2017.132.1.51

Dean, Michael. "The Lynda Barry Interview." *The Comics Journal*, no. 296, 2010, pp. 1–3.

Diedrich, Lisa. "Graphic Analysis: Transitional Phenomena in Alison Bechdel's Are You My Mother?" *Configurations*, vol. 22, no. 2, 2014, pp. 183–203. http://dx.doi.org/10.1353/con.2014.0014

Kellner, Amy. "The Talking Issue: Lynda Barry." *Vice*, 2008. www.vice.com/en_uk/article/avjdxa/lynda-barry-162-v15n10. Accessed 7 May 2021.

Love, Heather. "The Mom Problem." *Public Books*, 2012. www.publicbooks.org/the-mom-problem/. Accessed 7 May 2021.

Lowy, Jill. "Looking Inside Pandora's Box." *The Mystica*. www.themystica.com/mystica/articles/l/looking_inside_pandora's_box.html. Accessed 7 May 2021.

Michael, Olga. "Scrapbooking Caravaggio's Medusa, Reconfiguring Blake: What It Is, One! Hundred! Demons! and Lynda Barry's Feminist Intervention in the (Male) Artistic Canon." *Image Text*, vol. 9, no. 2, 2017, pp. 1–33.

Milner, Marion. *A Life of One's Own*. 1934. Routledge, 2011. http://dx.doi.org/10.4324/9780203817193

Milner, Marion. *An Experiment in Leisure*. Routledge, 1937/2011. http://dx.doi.org/10.4324/9780203816769

Rainer, Tristine. *The New Diary: How to Use a Journal for Self-guidance and Expanded Creativity*. Tarcher/Putnam US, 1978.

Randle, Chris. "Interview: Lynda Barry: 'What is an Image? That Question Has Directed My Entire Life.'" *The Guardian*, 2015. www.theguardian.com/books/2015/may/14/lynda-barry-art-comic-books. Accessed 7 May 2021.

Rüggemeier, Anne. "Posing for All the Characters in the Book': The Multimodal Processes of Production in Alison Bechdel's Relational Autobiography Are You My Mother?" *Journal of Graphic Novels and Comics*, vol. 7, no. 3, 2016, pp. 254–267. http://dx.doi.org/10.1080/21504857.2016.1199466

Trilling, Lionel. *The Liberal Imagination* (3rd edition). New York Review of Books, 2012.

Winnicott, D.W. "Mind and Its Relation to the Psyche-Soma." *British Journal of Medical Psychology*, vol. 27, no. 4, 1954, pp. 201–209. http://dx.doi.org/10.1093/med:psych/9780190271350.003.0047

Conclusion

In search of legibility?

Milner's handwriting acquired something of a reputation amongst her friends and colleagues. Mathew Hale, Milner's assistant who helped transcribe her handwritten notes for the manuscript for *Bothered by Alligators* was "thought by his friends to be something of a genius for being able to decipher" her scrawling pen (Letley 168). Hale found her writing to be "a curious mixture of the spidery and the emphatic, often in red or black felt pen. Her sentences would meander across a page and then frequently explode into capital letters as she reached her point" (Hale qtd. in Letley 168).

Interestingly, Milner herself seemed to have developed an inability to read her own handwriting in later life. She describes her relationship to her writing in *Bothered by Alligators*:

> Suddenly I could see a new aspect of my Satanic rebellious self, shown in an extreme inhibition of my ability to read my own handwriting, though I could still read typescript. More and more I could feel myself behave as if I were saying, "Why should a letter be that shape not a different one?" (you, who said, cheerfully, mockingly, "You want to create your own alphabet").
>
> (251)

Perhaps this inhibition stemmed from reading through her old diaries (such as the diary she kept of John's early years which she attends to in *Bothered by Alligators*), a resistance with encountering a younger version of herself. Or perhaps this discomfort emanated from reading through her own handwritten notes for *Bothered by Alligators*, which we know was in parts painful to write. The details of this readerly inhibition are not elaborated further in the book, but a resistance around her writing and its discernability can also be traced to much earlier in her life. In a notebook she kept during her training analysis, Milner wrote "I don't wish it to be legible," and as Emma Letley testifies upon reading the document, "her handwriting bears this out" (x). This is evidence, Letley writes, for a commitment to illegibility that "turned a full circle from its presence in her thirties as her wish to be illegible until her nineties" (185).

DOI: 10.4324/9781003296720-9

Milner's resistance to legibility at these different points in her life seem at odds with the aims of her published autobiographical books and their desire to make herself and her inner world legible and alive to herself and her readers, a project of self-constitution and self-definition that this book has traced. But it is perhaps less surprising given Milner's own ambivalence towards being understood, read, and interpreted in her analyses and relationships with others. Milner's autobiographical cure is self-administered and self-directed: the other, and the reader, is always necessarily outside of it, a witness and not a participant in her efforts to give herself legibility.

As a visitor to Milner's archives, I can attest first-hand to Milner's often hard to read handwritten notes, notebooks, diaries, and annotated documents. In my probably less patient attempts to decipher her handwriting, I haven't always been able to enjoy the level of comprehension that Mathew Hale was capable of. And I have found, more generally, in my experience of researching and writing this book, that I have come up against an intractability, a resistance to legibility, that extends beyond Milner's handwriting. The difficulties I have found in teasing out, understanding, and organising Milner's ideas and her work at the site of autobiography, have, I think, been closely tied to my attempts at giving Milner and her ideas a legibility and coherence that she herself in many ways resists.

Unlike the psychoanalytic cure that, depending on the group or school of thinking to which you ascribe comes with a more or less defined (though not necessarily tidy) set of psychological theories and therapeutic techniques, Milner's autobiographical cure does not present itself as a clear nor defined metapsychology. What I have understood as the concepts and methods that make up Milner's autobiographical cure are an attempt on the part of this study to give her work and her thinking a comprehensibility that Milner herself often does not do. As Letley puts it, "her approach is a long way from any aspirations towards seeing psychoanalysis as a science" (166). I am sure that in trying to do the work of elucidation and organisation, something invariably gets lost in the process, in the translation, you might say, from spidery handwriting to the clarity of the book typescript. As a reader of Milner's work, I think there is probably a degree of having to resign oneself to accepting that her writing cannot be neatly subsumed into psychological theory or framework, and nor should it. As Paul Watsky puts it, "because she is hard to categorize she is hard to own" (457). In the same way that she claims a life of her own, through her own methods, Milner's project ultimately belongs only to herself. It is a project perhaps best understood as a lifelong experiment of working through, at the site of written and visual mark-making.

Nevertheless, this book has, I hope, engaged with Milner's work in such a way as to bring her ideas and unique contribution to life, rather than, in Wordsworth's terms, murdering to dissect. As Hale found with Milner's handwriting, that "once you got the hang of it," you would begin to see "her thinking happening across the page," this study has sought to bring into view Milner's thinking across the pages of her autobiographical books (qtd. in Letley 168). We have seen how from the first autobiographical book, *A Life of One's Own*, Milner is invested in exploring different ways of reflecting for herself a sense of self; the "answering activity" a useful term to describe the reflective functions of free writing and diary keeping; the term "bead memory" to describe the giving of form and being to experience through a way of diary writing. In my analysis of *On Not Being Able to Paint*, I have explored how Milner's experiments with painting and free drawing also generate insights into how this form of mark-making can be therapeutic, her concepts of the "pliable medium" and "frame" arising out of these artistic experiments. In her books *Eternity's Sunrise: A Way of Keeping a Diary* and *Bothered by Alligators*, we see a reinvigoration, in the last decade of life, of her commitment to exploring the therapeutic benefits of her autobiographical cure. Finally, we have traced the quality of influence of Milner's methods and thinking on her readers and on many of their own projects of self-expressive, creative self-cure. Most recently, we have seen how the genre of the graphic memoir has in its own way taken up the mantle of the autobiographical cure. One handwritten document held in Milner's archives I think embodies the fundamentals of Milner's lifelong autobiographical cure: at the centre of what resembles a mind map surrounded by notes of varying legibility, Milner writes in clear capitals "ALL TO DO WITH FINDING WHAT IS SELF" (Figure 6.1). This finding of the self via making marks on the page is what this book has traced, at the core of Milner's personal needs and of her therapeutic methods.

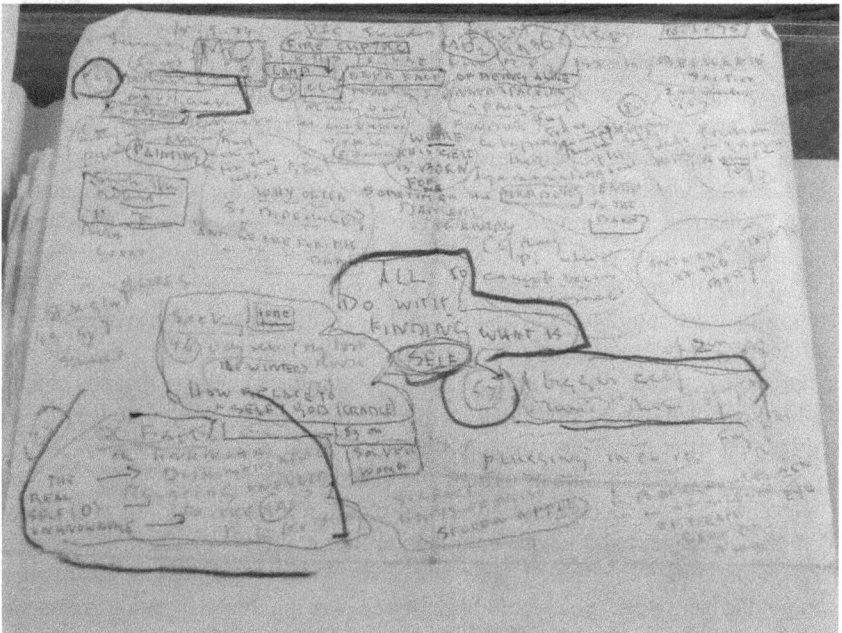

Figure 6.1 Document by Marion Milner. P01-H-A. Marion Milner collection, Archives of the British Psychoanalytical Society, London. January 2020.

Source: By permission of The Marsh Agency Ltd., on behalf of The Estate of Marion Milner.

Some questions of course remain. Does her life-long, restless search for different creative therapeutic methods really get Milner any closer to "finding what is self" in any meaningful, long-lasting way? Do the many mediums she employs—writing, drawing, painting, collage-making, clay sculpture, etc . . . provide substantively different qualities of insight and help, or are they more symptomatic of a doomed search for a cure that is never to be found? Accordingly, is the danger of the autobiographical cure a slide into solipsism or lack of relationality? I do wonder whether emotional difficulties that are borne out of broken relations can be as deeply addressed and helped when outside of the context of therapeutic relationship, when transference and countertransference are unavailable. It may be more fruitful, however, to think of the autobiographical cure as best used in tandem with psychotherapy or psychoanalysis, rather than as something to be used in lieu of it. Ultimately, Milner herself is practitioner and participant of both.

Milner has often been described as a "mystic," a label used rather vaguely I think, to point to that quality in her thinking that resists intelligibility. The same label has been levelled at Wilfred Bion and his thinking in his later years. His book *The Memoir of the Future* has been described by another psychoanalyst as "an allusive work which reworks many of Bion's theoretical ideas in the form of a novel, something he had always wanted to attempt" (Mawson, "Wilfred Bion"). This book's approach to Milner's autobiographical work might open up ways of engaging with work like Bion's and his turn to the novelistic and autobiographical in order to think through or do something psychoanalytic. We might explore Bion's work here, as I have done with Milner's, as an exercise in doing something psychoanalytic away from the clinical setting and in a creative relationship to a literary genre. Certainly, this study has made a claim for how Milner's autobiographical cure might have influenced, but also remained distinct from, the work of that other psychoanalytic thinker of this generation, Winnicott.

It seems fitting then to conclude this book with a poem written by Milner. *Bothered by Alligators* ends with an Appendix that reflects the last pages of the manuscript as left when she died on 29 May 1998, at ninety-eight years old. Here we find an untitled poem written by Milner. The poem also exists in three slightly different versions in Milner's archives, handwritten and in typescript form, all written in 1994.[1] I include the last version from *Bothered by Alligators* as it is the most legible and the most recently revised version before her death. The book's editor, Emma Letley, informs us that this "lovely toy" the poem refers to was "a wire biplane given to Milner by Alexander Newman, Milner's colleague and friend, with whom, I understand, there had been some disagreement" (qtd. in Milner, *BBA* 269).

This poem, I think, expresses in poetic form some of the integral elements of Milner's life-long autobiographical project. With this "lovely toy" gifted to her by Newman, Milner starts dancing on her own "in a totally dark place," the lights of the toy on her fingertips, "leaving a glowing trail in the dark," in much the same way her creative, autobiographical techniques illuminate self and world. The shape of these glowing lights, "like the cocoon a silk worm makes," provides the cocoon or frame where a transformation of self and inner world might come into being. Even out of the ashes of broken and failed relationships, Milner suggests, there is the gift of creative expression so that one might rewrite and redraw oneself. In doing so, "something quite different may emerge."

> When your lovely toy arrived
> I saw it
> As if each of my middle fingers
> Had a light on its tip
> like a glow worm has
> Only I think it has it on its bottom
> And I was dancing in a totally dark place
> With the light on my finger tips leaving a glowing trail
> Like the white trail across the sky that an airoplane sometimes leaves
> And then I saw it was an airoplane you sent
> For months I have not found a word for the shape my weaving lights make
> But this morning, at 6 a.m. I knew it was like the cocoon a silk worm makes
> Out of which something quite different may emerge[2]

(Milner, *BBA* 271)

Notes

1   See series P01-J-07, "Poetry," in the Marion Milner collection, Archives of the British Psychoanalytical Society, London.
2   Reproduced by permission of The Marsh Agency Ltd., on behalf of The Estate of Marion Milner.

References

Letley, Emma. *Marion Milner: The Life*. Routledge, 2014. http://dx.doi.org/10.4324/9780203767122

Mawson, Chris. "Wilfred Bion." *Institute of Psychoanalysis: British Psychoanalytical Society*, 2012. psychoanalysis.org.uk/our-authors-and-theorists/wilfred-bion. Accessed 7 May 2021.

Milner, Marion. *Bothered by Alligators*. Routledge, 2013. http://dx.doi.org/10.4324/9780203140147

Watsky, Paul. "Marion Milner's Pre-Freudian Writings, 1926–1938: The Originality and Origins of Her Creative Model." *Journal of Analytical Psychology*, vol. 37, no. 4, 1992, pp. 455–473. http://dx.doi.org/10.1111/j.1465-5922.1992.00455.x

Index

Anderson, J.W. 116
"Angry Ape, The" 62
"Angry Parrot, The" 62
animals 35, 36; *see also* butterflies;
  horned goat
Answering Activity 15, 18, 26, 52–53,
  176; in *Bothered by Alligators* 49, 99,
  109, 115–116; in *Eternity's Sunrise*
  45–46, 48; in *Experiment in Leisure,*
  An 44–45; influence 142–143, 156; and
  mirroring 46–47
appreciations *see* fan letters
art *see* collages; creativity; free drawing;
  images; painting
art school 72, 78
art therapy 93, 135–136, 144; *see also*
  Edwards, David; Simon, Rita
attunement 15–17, 21, 61, 70; *see also*
  mirroring; mother-infant relationship;
  reciprocity
Auden, W.H. 36, 55n3; *see also* poetry
autobiographical books *see*
  autobiography
autobiographical cure 2, 8–9, 15, 18–19,
  175–177; and Barry and Bechdel
  151, 153, 168–171; and *Bothered by*
  Alligators 94–95, 99, 104–105, 110;
  influence 123–124, 131, 135, 140, 142,
  144; and *Life of One's Own, A* 26, 54;
  Milner's doubts about 116–117; and *On*
  Not Being Able to Paint 58, 79, 85, 88;
  and Winnicott 110, 113
autobiography: and psychoanalysis 6–10;
  theory of 52–54; *see also Bothered by*
  Alligators (BBA); *Eternity's Sunrise:*
  A Way of Keeping a Diary (ES);
  Experiment in Leisure, An (EIL); *Life of*
  One's Own, A (LOO)

Bacon, Francis 91n13
Bakhtin, Mikhail 52
Balint, Michael 5, 67–68
Barry, Lynda 19, 140, 151–152, 156–157,
  160–162; memory 158–159; Milner's
  influence 153–155, 169–172n1;
  Winnicott's influence 153–154
bead memories 15, 18, 52, 54, 176;
  collecting 49–51; influence 133–134,
  143, 144, 158
Bechdel, Alison 19, 151–153, 162–171,
  172n4
Bion, Wilfred 6, 10; autobiographies 9,
  177; *see also* containment
birth 109
Blackett, Arthur (father) 3–4, 12,
  98–100, 116
Blackett, Patrick 3–4
Blake, William: and Barry, Lynda 162,
  171; and Freud 129; illustrations
  127–129, 131, 148n2; outline 139;
  poetry 61–62, 90n5, 126–127, 148n1;
  story of Job 127–129; *see also* poetry
blind thinking 34
Bloom, Harold 126
Bloomsbury group 125
body 46, 48, 64, 80, 132
body ego 64
Bolton, Gillie 143–145, 161
Bothered by Alligators (BBA) 1–2, 9, 12,
  19, 21; *see also* autobiography; couch
  analysis; diaries; Milner, John (son)
boundaries 79, 85, 97, 139–140, 143; in
  art 57, 72, 138; in the mind 64, 132,
  66–78, 132; *see also* fusion
Bowlby, Rachel 3, 27, 34, 124–125
Brande, Dorothea 36
British Psychoanalytic Society 2, 11, 84

"Bursting Seed-Pod" 88–89
butterflies 11, 29, 35–36, 54n1; *see also*
    animals

Cézanne, Paul 65
child analysis 19n4, 61, 87; *see also* Ruth
    (patient); Simon (patient)
clay figures 17, 101
Clyne, Michael *see* Simon (patient)
Coleridge, Samuel Taylor 37; *see also*
    poetry
collages 98–100, 109; Barry's 154,
    158–159, 162, 170; Milner's 2, 17, 94,
    101–102, 127, 177; *see also* creativity;
    "Green Baby, The"; "Woebegone"
colour 62, 64–66, 69–70, 132, 139, 172n6
comics 151, 154, 159, 162, 164, 168–171;
    see also graphic memoir
containment 14–15, 20n8, 26, 45, 85;
    see also Bion, Wilfred
continuity of being 13–15, 27, 46,
    109, 159
Controversial Discussions 5
couch analysis 19, 93–95, 98, 102, 168;
    see also Bothered by Alligators (BBA)
countertransference 83, 98–99, 102, 104,
    168, 177
creative apperception 16, 69
creativity: Milner's theories of 6, 12,
    15–18, 80, 108; *see also* collages; free
    writing; free drawing; *On Not Being
    Able to Paint* (ONBAP); Winnicott,
    Donald
Crickmay, Chris 70, 73, 137–140, 160;
    see also Open University, the
crystallization 29, 50, 158

Defoe, Daniel *see Robinson Crusoe*
Descartes, René 32
diaries 4, 33, 53–55, 145–146, 104;
    see also Bothered by Alligators (BBA);
    *Eternity's Sunrise: A Way of Keeping a
    Diary* (ES); *Experiment in Leisure, An*
    (EIL); *Life of One's Own, A* (LOO)
diary keeping *see* diaries
disillusionment 62, 65, 69, 85, 110,
    117n2; *see also* illusion; mother-infant
    relationship
doodling *see* free drawing
drawing *see* free drawing
"Drawing without a Name" 61
dreams 36, 69, 113, 116, 147, 168

Edwards, David 90n4, 135, 136; *see also*
    art therapy
ego-boundary *see* boundaries
Ellmann, Maud 3, 9, 35, 125, 147
Erikson, Erik 116
*Eternity's Sunrise: A Way of Keeping a
    Diary (ES)* 1–2, 8, 26, 35, 45; *see also*
    Answering Activity; autobiography;
    diaries
Experiment in Leisure, An (EIL) 1–3,
    26–27, 42–44; fan appreciations 135,
    141; *see also* autobiography; diaries;
    Field, Joanna (pen name); free writing

fairy tale writing 43
fan letters 19, 123, 131, 134–135
fantasy 71; *see also* phantasy
feminism 146–147
Field, Joanna (pen name) 3, 19n2, 49,
    113, 133; *see also Experiment in
    Leisure, An* (EIL); *Life of One's Own,
    A* (LOO)
Fielding, John 50
Forrester, John 40, 123–124
frame 15, 19, 68, 71–74, 78–81, 176,
    178; comic 151, 159, 165, 167–169;
    influence of concept 84–85, 138, 143,
    145; picture 57–58, 90n9, 99, 134;
    see also On Not Being Able to Paint
    (ONBAP)
framed gap, the *see* frame
free association 1, 36, 43, 64, 118
free drawing: benefits of 64–65, 69–70,
    74, 76; influence of 138, 144, 15;
    method of 40, 57, 60, 62; *see also*
    creativity; image-finding; *On Not
    Being Able to Paint* (ONBAP);
    painting
free writing 33–36, 60, 113, 138, 160;
    see also creativity; *Experiment in
    Leisure, An* (EIL); *Life of One's Own,
    A* (LOO)
Freud, Anna 5–6, 58–59
Freud, Sigmund 12, 42; diaries 8, 41–42;
    and Milner 2, 4, 7, 8, 127–128
fusion 62, 69, 70, 76, 85, 108–110, 117;
    see also boundaries; mother-infant
    relationship

graphic memoir 19, 152–153, 162,
    169–171, 176; *see also* comics
"Green Baby, The" 99–100

Hale, Matthew (assistant) 174–175
Hands of the Living God, The (HOLG) 6, 7, 58, 73, 90n10, 91n11; *see also* Susan (patient)
Harris Williams, Meg 10, 53
Haughton, Hugh 3, 12, 50
"Hens, The" 5–6
holding 14, 17, 50, 20n8, 151, 168; environment 72, 85, 163; *see also* containment; Winnicott, Donald
Hopkins, Linda 93, 97
horned goat 35–36, 44, 87, 125; *see also* animals; mythology
"Horrified Tadpole" 62–63, 88
Human Problem in Schools, The 4
Hunt, Celia 143, 145, 161

identity 62, 79–80, 104, 108, 116, 125; and autobiography 10, 53, 141–142, 145–147, 156, 158; Milner's sense of 26–29, 31–32, 34, 39, 50, 59
illusion 6, 62, 72, 78, 116, 132; and symbol formation 69, 73; *see also* disillusionment; mother-infant relationship
image-finding 47; *see also* free drawing
images 40, 48, 58–60, 163; *see also* free drawing
Imago Group 6
impressionism *see* Cézanne, Paul
Independent Group 3, 5, 67, 129
infancy: Milner's 13, 27; Susan's 80; *see also* mother-infant relationship
Institute of Psychoanalysis *see* British Psychoanalytic Society
internal objects 35, 52, 62

Jacobus, Mary 11, 80
Job, Book of 127
journal writing *see* diaries

Khan, Masud 13, 67, 93, 116
Klein, Melanie 6, 13, 59; and Milner 16, 27, 45, 61–62, 71–72; *see also* Simon (patient)
knowing 45–46, 64, 99, 109; *see also* not-knowing
knowledge *see* knowing
Kristeva, Julia 125–126

Lawrence, D.H. 12, 91n11; *see also* poetry
Lejeune, Phillipe 10, 53–54

life map 141, 145, 149n4, 169–170, 176
Life of One's Own, A (LOO) 1–4, 18, 19n1, 54, 117, 176; birth of a method 25–27, 30, 37, 41–42; and *Experiment in Leisure, An* 57, 60; readers 116, 123–126, 133–134, 141–143, 156, 160; and Winnicott 11, 36, 105–106, 108, 109; *see also* autobiography; diaries; Field, Joanna; free writing
line *see* boundaries

map of consciousness *see* life map
Maynard, Caroline (mother) 3, 4, 12–13, 100, 106
Medusa 155–156, 172n1
Middle Group *see* Independent Group
Milner, Dennis 4, 96, 104
Milner, Dennis (husband) 4, 96, 104
Milner, Giles and Quentin (grandsons) 5, 101, 131
Milner, John (son) 94–95, 99, 102, 103–105; *see also Bothered by Alligators* (BBA); story-book (John)
Milner, Marion: babyhood 12, 100; childhood 4, 28, 50; education and training 4–5, 40, 54, 113; handwriting 174–175
mirroring 14, 16–17, 26, 46–47, 53, 87–88; influence of concept 142, 145, 156, 168; *see also* attunement; reciprocity; Winnicott, Donald
Miss A *see* Susan (patient)
modern art 68
modernism 11–12, 36, 54n1, 68, 90nn8–9, 125
Montaigne, Michel de 27, 126
mother-infant relationship 14, 59–60; *see also* attunement; disillusionment; fusion; illusion; infancy; preverbal experience; reciprocity
Mr X *see* Winnicott, Donald
mysticism 120, 127, 177
mythology 43–44, 47, 127, 151, 156, 173

New Diary, the *see* Rainer, Tristine
non-differentiation *see* fusion
not-knowing 46, 109; *see also* knowing

object relations theory 1–3, 13–15; Milner's contribution to 45, 47, 50, 58–61, 84–85
O'Casey, Sean 44

oceanic feeling 20n5, 76, 90n6
Oedipus complex 76, 117, 126, 162
omnipotence 14, 77–78, 85, 113, 116;
    Freudian theory 90n6, 71
oneness *see* fusion
On Not Being Able to Paint (*ONBAP*)
    1–2, 6, 13, 18, 26, 35, 176; and analytic
    technique 68–71, 73, 75–78, 105;
    and Barry 151, 153–155; and fan
    letters 131–132; influence of 67, 69,
    118, 123–124, 136–139, 143; and
    psychoanalysis 40, 58–61, 94–95,
    107, 108; and theory 84, 88; and visual
    language 63, 65; *see also* creativity;
    frame; free drawing; painting; pliable
    medium; preverbal experience
Open University, the 137; *see also*
    Crickmay, Chris
outline *see* boundaries

Pailthorpe, Grace and Reuben Mednikoff
    59, 90n3
painting 29, 50, 53, 57–58, 87–88,
    176–177; and Barry 153–154; and
    Bechdel 170, 172n6; collages of old 94,
    99; Milner's 1–2, 5, 6, 19, 90n2; in *On
    Not Being Able to Paint* 57–60, 63–66,
    68–74, 78–80; *see also* free drawing;
    On Not Being Able to Paint (ONBAP)
Pandora's box 151
Parsons, Michael 48
Pelmanism 54n2
phantasy 68, 72, 80, 90n6, 117, 168
Phillips, Adam 3, 9, 83, 93, 110, 131
Picasso, Pablo 68
Pickworth, Farrow E 40
pictures *see* free drawing; images
Playing and Reality 13, 46, 69, 85, 91n12,
    105–106; and Barry and Bechdel 153,
    169; *see also* Winnicott, Donald
pliable medium 95, 101–102, 176; in
    analytic work 73–76, 80, 88; influence
    of concept 136–137, 143–144, 154,
    156; theory of 15, 19, 58, 68–71,
    84–85, 91n13; *see also On Not Being
    Able to Paint* (ONBAP)
pliant medium *see* pliable medium
poetry 3, 37, 111–112, 131, 155, 178;
    see also Auden, W.H.; Blake, William;
    Coleridge, Samuel Taylor; Lawrence,
    D.H.; Wordsworth, William
potential space *see* transitional object

preverbal experience 14, 64, 76; *see also*
    mother-infant relationship; *On Not
    Being Able to Paint* (ONBAP)
primary narcissism 75, 76, 90n6
Prokhoris, Sabine 17–18, 161
Putnam, Dr Irma 4, 37–39, 95

Rainer, Tristine 140–143, 145–146,
    161, 171
reciprocity 61, 69–70, 154, 166; *see also*
    attunement; mirroring; mother-infant
    relationship
Riviere, Joan 5, 116
Robinson Crusoe 25, 42, 52
"Royal Free July 95, At" 113–114
Ruskin, John 52, 58
Ruth (patient) 73, 75–78, 80; *see also*
    child analysis
Rycroft, Charles 9, 53

Sayers, Janet 3, 20n7, 95
Schact, Lore 87
Schiwy, Marlene 143, 145–146, 150
schizophrenia 79, 98
Scott, Clifford: analyst of Milner 5,
    97–98, 117n2, 119; cosmic bliss and
    catastrophic chaos 62, 76, 90n6
Sedgwick, Eve Kosokfy 71
self-analysis 8, 39, 40, 59, 124–125;
    see also autobiographical cure
self-cure *see* autobiographical cure
self-help books 2, 31, 124, 140, 148, 153
self-other relationship *see* boundaries
self-portrait 1, 7, 62, 91n13, 151
Sharpe, Ella 5, 59, 68, 126
Simon, Rita 136–137; *see also* art therapy
Simon (patient) 73–77, 80; *see also* child
    analysis; Klein, Melanie
Smith, Vanessa 11, 124–125
Spelman, Margaret Boyle 3, 112, 123, 129
squiggle game 86–87, 168; *see also*
    Winnicott, Donald
Stonebridge, Lyndsey 10, 72, 125
story-book (John) *see* Milner, John (son)
Suppressed Madness of Sane Men, The
    (*SMSM*) 6, 8, 11, 52, 107, 148n2
surrealism 36, 59, 61
Susan (patient): analysis with Milner 73,
    75, 76, 79, 84, 90n10; drawings 80–82;
    Milner's tracing 83, 137, 158; Post-ECT
    drawing 78, 81; and Winnicott 94, 96–97
symbol formation 73

talking cure *see* psychoanalysis
Thomson, Martina 93–94, 101
transference 14, 58, 74–75, 99, 125, 177
transitional object 50, 72, 84–85, 138, 153, 162–163, 169; *see also* Winnicott, Donald
trauma 66, 106, 109, 155
travel diaries 48
"Tree, The" 110–111, 166; *see also* Winnicott, Donald
Tustin, Frances 135
"Two Jugs" 66–67, 169
Tyson, Helen 11, 36, 54n1

Walters, Margaret 3, 5, 6, 11, 104, 117
wild psychoanalysis 31, 147
Winnicott, Alice 96, 117n2

Winnicott, Donald: analyst of Milner 5, 96–99, 100, 102, 105–106; diary-keeping patient 108–109, 142, 153–154; theories of creativity 16, 106–107; *see also* creativity; holding; mirroring; *Playing and Reality*; squiggle game; transitional object; "Tree, The"
Winning, Jo 11, 90n9
Woolf, Virginia 30, 50, 165, 169; *A Room of One's Own* 125, 153
"Woebegone" 99, 109
Wordsworth, William 37; *see also* poetry
World War II 2, 41, 95, 141

Yeats, W.B 43

Taylor & Francis Group
an **informa** business

Taylor & Francis eBooks

www.taylorfrancis.com

A single destination for eBooks from Taylor & Francis
with increased functionality and an improved user
experience to meet the needs of our customers.

90,000+ eBooks of award-winning academic content in
Humanities, Social Science, Science, Technology, Engineering,
and Medical written by a global network of editors and authors.

TAYLOR & FRANCIS EBOOKS OFFERS:

A streamlined
experience for
our library
customers

A single point
of discovery
for all of our
eBook content

Improved
search and
discovery of
content at both
book and
chapter level

REQUEST A FREE TRIAL
support@taylorfrancis.com

Routledge
Taylor & Francis Group

CRC Press
Taylor & Francis Group

For Product Safety Concerns and Information please contact our EU
representative GPSR@taylorandfrancis.com
Taylor & Francis Verlag GmbH, Kaufingerstraße 24, 80331 München, Germany

www.ingramcontent.com/pod-product-compliance
Lightning Source LLC
Chambersburg PA
CBHW050654280326
41932CB00015B/2905

9 781032 282954